# Critical Curriculum Leadership

"This book brings much-needed balance to scholarship on instructional leadership, which has focused on *how* we lead while neglecting curriculum content—or *what* we lead. In this insightful book, Ylimaki convincingly argues that in our obsession with test scores, we are failing to teach our children and youth how to think rationally and critically about the increasingly complex world they will inherit."

—Gary L. Anderson, Professor of Educational Administration,
New York University

"Ylimaki introduces, explains, and illustrates a sophisticated, critically-informed definition of curriculum leadership that is vital to the future of democratic societies. This well-balanced, clearly argued, and carefully researched book presents an inspired vision for the future of leadership development and artistry in education."

—James Henderson, Professor of Curriculum Studies,
Kent State University

Although traditional curriculum and instructional leadership frameworks have dominated educational administration training for almost thirty years, it has become increasingly clear that even the most recent frameworks have failed today's leaders who struggle with the politics of curriculum decisions on a daily basis. *Critical Curriculum Leadership* is an examination of curriculum leadership in the wake of U.S. testing mandates and school reforms, all of which seem to support a particular set of conservative ideologies. Drawing from her own longitudinal ethnographic study and from existing literature and research in the field, Ylimaki explores the formation of curriculum leadership in relation to broader cultural and political shifts. She shows how traditional leadership frameworks have come up short, and makes the case for an alternative leadership theory at the intersection of educational leadership and curriculum studies. She provides analytical tools that inspire progressive education and offers critical theories, strategies, research examples, problem-posing cases, and research ideas essential for curriculum leadership in the present conservative era. *Critical Curriculum Leadership* will appeal to the many educational leadership scholars and practitioners who are interested in developing effective and socially just curricula in their schools and districts as well as curriculum scholars who are interested in leadership issues.

**Rose M. Ylimaki** is an Associate Professor in the Educational Policy Studies and Practice Department at the University of Arizona.

# Critical Curriculum Leadership

A Framework for Progressive Education

**Rose M. Ylimaki**

Routledge
Taylor & Francis Group

NEW YORK AND LONDON

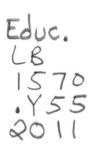
First published 2011
by Routledge
270 Madison Avenue, New York, NY 10016

Simultaneously published in the UK
by Routledge
2 Park Square, Milton Park, Abingdon, Oxon OX14 4RN

*Routledge is an imprint of the Taylor & Francis Group, an informa business*

© 2011 Taylor & Francis

The right of Rose M. Yimaki to be identified as author of this work has been asserted by her in accordance with sections 77 and 78 of the Copyright, Designs and Patents Act 1988.

Typeset in Minion by EvS Communication Networx, Inc.
Printed and bound in the United States of America on acid-free paper by IBT Global

*Library of Congress Cataloging in Publication Data*
Ylimaki, Rose M.
Critical curriculum leadership : a framework for progressive education / Rose M. Ylimaki.
p. cm.
1. Education—Curricula—United States. 2. Educational leadership—United States. I. Title.
LB1570.Y55 2010
375.000973—dc22
2010035967

ISBN 13: 978-0-415-87621-6 (hbk)
ISBN 13: 978-0-415-87622-3 (pbk)
ISBN 13: 978-0-203-83505-0 (ebk)

Dedicated to the late Oiva and Irene Ylimaki

# Contents

# List of Problem-Posing Cases

# Preface

This book examines how curriculum leadership identities, beliefs, and practices have evolved in relation to recent cultural and political shifts that appear to support a particular set of conservative ideologies and professional management roles. More specifically, I examine varying ways in which principals/curriculum leaders interpret and enact their identities and roles in the wake of recent cultural political movements, accountability mandates, and curriculum reforms that influence educational curriculum and pedagogy in today's schools. For present purposes, I define curriculum leadership as individual and collective influence on cultural politics as well as the content and pedagogy of education—what is taught, how it is taught, and to whom. Curriculum leadership identity can be defined as a sense of self in relation to others and the meanings people attach to curriculum-related roles in schools and society (hooks, 1991; Stryker & Burke, 2000; Weis, 1990).

I examine literature from several fields in relation to data from a 4-year longitudinal study of four schools in the U.S. Northeast, that is, literature in educational administration, cultural politics, and curriculum studies, to create case studies that explore the nuances and complexities of contemporary curriculum leadership identity formation and practices. My purpose is to provide current and aspiring educational leaders with theories and analytical tools that move beyond mainstream leadership roles, perspectives, and ideological arguments about curriculum content, instruction, and assessments to help all children realize the promise of a socially just, democratic education. Such an education promotes not only high academic performance but also lifelong growth, compassion, and community transformation. It is created not through ideological debates, but by curriculum leaders with the theoretical understandings and tools to make their communities better places to live.

Whereas many texts on educational administration use "instructional leadership" to describe the principal's role as the top pedagogical decision maker in a school, I purposefully use the term *curriculum leadership* because the meaning of "curriculum" extends beyond teaching practice to the political aspects of educational content decisions: what is taught and to whom. The critical curriculum leadership approach described in this volume can have a transformative influence on the purpose, content, and performance of education in schools and communities. In several places, I use the term *instructional leadership* to illustrate how traditional studies use a term divorced from the politics of educational content decisions.

Like many research projects and books, *Critical Curriculum Leadership: A Framework for Progressive Education* is a personal journey. The idea originated in my growing perplexity about what it meant for me to be a curriculum leader in the early part of this decade, a time of national and community anxiety over the ability of public schools to provide an equitable and excellent education. How could I help teachers and students balance the joy of learning with tested academic standards? How long could I resist pressures to adopt scripted programs that deskill teachers, differentiate curriculum (school knowledge) in ways that reproduce culture and perpetuate social inequities in our community? These questions came out of my practice without theoretical labels or terms. I learned about concepts like cultural reproduction and hegemony in the Curriculum and Instruction Department at the University of Wisconsin-Madison but struggled with how to apply them on the ground as a curriculum leader in schools. These questions brought me to this research project and ultimately to this book.

**Organization of This Book**

In the chapters of this book I examine curriculum leadership identities, meanings, and practices using the literature and examples drawn from my 4-year study conducted from 2002 to 2006 as well as problem-posing cases and reflection activities. *Problem-posing education* is a term coined by Paulo Freire (1970/1993) and refers to a method of teaching that emphasizes critical thinking for the purposes of social change. I use the problem-posing cases as a way to help readers reflect on the material in each chapter and consider common curriculum and leadership practices more fully. Chapters 2 to 6 draw on the literature and my ethnographic research data to offer examples of what I call "new professional" and critical curriculum leadership, examining changes in leadership identity over time, the role of the school culture in leadership identity formation, curriculum development processes, and curriculum leadership influence on school–community relationships that inspire progressive education. Pseudonyms are used for all individuals and locations featured in this book.

Chapters 2 and 3 highlight principals' and other study participants' voices during interviews and observations. For readers who are or will be working on qualitative research projects, these examples may provide useful models. The next three chapters (4, 5, and 6) explore interconnected dimensions of and influences on curriculum leadership identity and practices—political awareness and advocacy skills, critical perspectives and analytical tools, school culture, curriculum, community relationships, political awareness, and advocacy—that can contribute to progressive social and educational movements. In these chapters, I conclude with problem-posing cases for reflection about issues in practice. My argument across these three chapters is that principals'/ curriculum leaders' influence, combined with their commitment to democratic principles, creates an environment in which teachers, students, and parents or community members are able to question the underlying assumptions of circulating discourses about curriculum and to mobilize their own agency and growth as coleaders of progressive educational and social movements. Through theory, empirical examples, and problem-posing cases, I illustrate how principals, faculty leaders, and parents can affirm their own capabilities to develop curricula that are grounded in students' lives and community needs.

### Chapter by Chapter Breakdown

The Introduction provides a description of leadership studies, curriculum theories, and literature on cultural political movements that informed my study. Drawing on theories across leadership, curriculum, and critical education fields, I present a new curriculum leadership model that may inspire progressive educational and social movements. This chapter concludes with a description of the communities featured in my study and this volume.

In chapter 2, I describe two schools in which principals, many teachers, and parents became increasingly supportive of the ideologically based processes of current federal and state policies, shifting their priorities and practices to reflect and enhance their support for the broader political movement. In particular, this chapter describes how curriculum leaders (somewhat unconsciously) can encourage the hegemony of conservative ideology through the language they use to affirm particular standardized teaching programs, testing procedures, and enactments of their professional curriculum leadership identities and roles. These two principals interpreted their "instructional leadership" roles as "data-driven leaders of learning" and "productive leaders." I present observations and excerpts from interviews that illustrate how these two principals and other members of the school community shifted their language and practices over the course of 4 years to align with, encourage, and support the ideological processes of the conservative modernization and new public management (NPM), spending enormous amounts of time on data analysis processes and test preparation, frequently telling teachers and parents about policy requirements, and at several points, asking what they ever did before they had state standards and externally developed curriculum programs. Additional vignettes illustrate how participants seek standardized programs in order to provide instructional consistency and close achievement gaps and gradually begin to see themselves in relation to "Other" laissez-faire educators. As these leaders plunge forward into the realm of conservative curriculum and accountability politics, looking for solutions to achievement gaps, traditional models and tools of "instructional leadership" fall by the wayside, replaced by what I call the new professional model of curriculum leadership.

In chapter 3, I focus on how principals at two other schools in the same community use political awareness and tools to identify and critique conservative discursive practices, circulate counternarratives to them, and lay the groundwork for community-based curriculum and the emergence of progressive educational and social movements. I demonstrate how these two principals identify the elements of good sense in current accountability and curriculum policies as well as elements of concern for democratic education. They look for consensus and fault lines within the conservative alliance, and then leverage these to resist the conservative doctrine. In particular, I demonstrate how curriculum leaders of all kinds can take advantage of discourse as an analytical tool, one that is rarely discussed in mainstream educational administration literature. For example, discourse tools assist in ascertaining tensions and underlying assumptions of current policies and school reforms. It is important to note that the professional and critical curriculum leadership identities are not polar opposites. Chapter 3 illustrates the nuances and complexities involved in critical curriculum leadership that uses the positive points of current policies and politics to improve students' learning and growth.

Chapter 4 examines the influence of teachers and the school culture on curriculum leadership identity formation. In some schools, many teachers encourage the use of more traditionalist teacher-centered practices. They appreciate the specific guidance of state standards and curriculum pacing calendars. At the same time, their fears with regards to testing prompted them into an emphasis on factual content, teacher-centered pedagogy and worksheets, all of which had negative effects on teacher and student morale. Most teacher concerns are underground, however, because the school culture supports norms of collegiality and harmony over open debate. This chapter also presents two cases in which curriculum leaders recognize these negative impacts of conservative curriculum and testing. Conflicts over curriculum choices emerge, and these conflicts lead to more progressive options and democratic ideals in their schools.

Chapter 5 demonstrates how principals/curriculum leaders can use democratic ideals and grassroots, community-based curriculum development processes to meet current mandates, rather than relying primarily on packaged programs and state standards. Using curriculum theory and examples from my case studies, I present curriculum development models in which principals and teachers shape what is important to students' lives in school and later in life.

Although principals/curriculum leaders must be realistic and informed about requirements of current accountability policies, in chapter 6 I argue that it is time to reaffirm Dewey's (1916/2008) argument that the finest outcomes of education are human beings willing and able to engage intelligently and ethically with a changing world. Growth is not simply a personal matter but is of concern for the whole society. When students (adults and children) find strengths within themselves, however small they may initially be, these strengths become the source of agency—and ultimately, of a better community and society. More specifically, I examine how curriculum leaders foster school–community relationships and curriculum processes that inspire progressive social movements.

Chapter 7 offers a wrap-up and lays the groundwork for a new field of curriculum leadership at the intersection of educational administration, curriculum theory, and critical education studies dealing with cultural politics. I suggest that curriculum leadership is engaged in the process of remaking itself in light of current policies and mandates. As they reconstitute themselves on a daily basis, curriculum leaders and broader cultural political movements in particular school and community contexts are in a dialectic and dynamic process of reformation. At the same time, there are critical moments of critique and intellectual resistance when curriculum leaders can offer curricular and political tools that interrupt and shift circulating discourses of the conservative restoration in their schools and communities. Finally, I outline implications for future research on curriculum leadership, policy revision, and curriculum leadership preparation.

The appendices feature a description of the research methods and design used in my ethnographic study of school principals as well as a course activity that challenges rhetorical aspects of new professional curriculum leadership identity. In the "Research and Methods" section (appendix A) I introduce my own researcher identity, share how I gained access to these cases, and provide a description of specific data collection and analysis procedures. Appendix B, "Challenging the Rhetorical Identity of Curriculum Leadership" presents sample course activity.

Across these chapters I fulfill the purpose of this book to provide current and aspiring educational leaders with theories and analytical tools that move beyond mainstream leadership roles, perspectives, and ideological arguments about curriculum content, instruction, and assessments to help all children realize the promise of a socially just, democratic education.

# Acknowledgments

Over the years, my thinking and writing about this project have been influenced and supported by a number of people. I spent nearly 4 years in the field, exploring the curriculum work lives and experiences of those curriculum leaders who live and work in Treelane and Hillside. Although these study participants must remain anonymous, I express my deep gratitude for their time, energy, and insights. This volume should not in any way be taken as a criticism of these individuals. They are part of broader cultural–political movements just as we all are, and my task has been to understand the dialectical relationships among broader movements and today's curriculum leadership.

Many of my colleagues and mentors have contributed to my understandings of curriculum leadership in this project. In particular, I am grateful to Cryss Brunner, Lois Weis, Yoshiko Nozaki, Clif Conrad, Paul Bredeson, Al Phelps, Michael Apple, and Chris Day for their mentoring and support over the years. Kirsteen Anderson provided copy-editing services for this volume, and I thank her for her diligence and skill. Routledge editor Heather Jarrow read early drafts of this manuscript, and her comments helped to make it better. Doctoral students Jingjing Fan and Dave Mandel provided essential support in the development of this project.

My Educational Leadership colleagues at the University of Arizona, Kris Bosworth, John Taylor, Jeff Bennett, Bob Hendricks, and John Pedicone have provided me with a collegial and supportive work community, and I am sincerely grateful for their support and encouragement. Doctoral students, particularly those in the Spring 2010 Curriculum Leadership course, have challenged and enhanced my thinking in important ways. Finally, I would like to acknowledge the contributions of family members and lifelong friends who have encouraged and supported me through this project, including Leslie McClain, Annie Boote, Irene Grage, Rita Vallier, Diane Fillazetti, Dave Nyman, Sue Mattson, Patty Friz, Kimberly Rogers, Mike Ford, Max Ylimaki, and Zach Ylimaki.

# 1
# Introduction

This volume is situated at the intersection of educational leadership and critical curriculum studies. Since the 1980s, I have been greatly influenced by literature from two distinct fields: (1) educational administration studies of "instructional" leadership practices that contribute to improvements in teaching and learning (e.g., Hallinger & Murphy, 1985; Jackson, 2000; Purkey & Smith, 1983); and (2) studies of how curriculum theory and critiques are situated within broader cultural–political movements (e.g., Apple, 1996, 2004). I draw on literature from both fields as well as empirical research on curriculum leaders/principals to suggest that effective curriculum leaders must have the analytical tools to challenge and move beyond (conservative) ideological arguments and cultivate neoprogressive educational and social movements.

## Studies of "Instructional Leadership" from the Field of Educational Administration

Within the field of educational administration, there has been some debate about whether instructional leadership is an individual or collective (distributed) domain, but the more important question is how formal leaders influence curriculum content decisions, other classroom practices, and communities. Educational administration studies typically identify high-achieving schools then attempt to identify the specific leadership qualities and behaviors that foster high academic performance and successful student outcomes. Whether one approaches instructional leadership by analyzing primarily individual administrators (principals), as Phil Hallinger and Joe Murphy (1985) do, or the distributed school leadership (capacity), as Helen Marks (2003) and James Spillane (2003) do, the argument is essentially that leadership has a strong but indirect influence on teaching and learning (student outcomes). Most often, recent "instructional" leadership studies draw on psychology and learning theories to generate a menu of individual or collective (distributive) leadership strategies that improve classroom practice. Although these studies have provided many understandings about effective leadership behaviors, they provide insufficient information relative to curriculum, cultural politics, and lifelong growth in democratic education.

In seeking to identify the direct and indirect instructional leadership tasks and behaviors that "work" because they influence academic achievement, scholars of educational administration too often pose binary questions. In other words, traditional leadership studies are typically grounded in positivistic assumptions and ask either–or questions to measure inputs (instruction-related leadership tasks and functions) against outputs (student achievement scores). Although not all of these studies have been quantitative in nature, their general goal has been to seek the "truth" about which curriculum (or instructional) leadership practices affect student outcomes and how they affect them. They frequently rely on large-scale surveys and therefore promise generalizable findings about which instructional leadership roles and practices are effective in schools. For example, the model developed by Bossert, Dwyer, Rowan, and Lee (1982) hypothesizes that characteristics of the individual principal, the district, and the external environment influence management behaviors, which in turn, affect school climate and instructional organization. School climate and instructional organization then shape teachers' behaviors and students' learning experiences. Heck, Larsen, and Marcoulides (1990) tested this contingency model and found support for its basic hypothesis. Principals indirectly influence student achievement when they: (1) create instructional organizations in their schools; (2) use participative actions for instructional improvement; and (3) build a school climate and culture characterized by clearly communicated goals and high expectations for academic achievement and social behavior.

In empirical literature, the term *instructional leadership* emerged from the literature on "outlier schools"; that is, those that effectively educated children from low socioeconomic backgrounds (e.g., Berman & McLaughlin, 1976; Edmonds, 1979; Hallinger & Murphy, 1985). Such studies (Berman & McLaughlin, 1976; Edmonds, 1979; Hallinger & Murphy, 1985) challenged the Coleman Report (Coleman, 1966), which concluded that out-of-school variables (such as socioeconomic status) were more important to student achievement than in-school variables, which largely had no effect. These studies found instead that a strong, even directive instructional leadership role from the principal was essential for the creation of a positive learning culture and a safe, orderly school that enabled students to succeed regardless of out-of-school characteristics. Other factors frequently identified as important were a clear and focused school mission, high expectations for all students, high student time on task, and positive home–school relations. Gender, race, and political ideology are not mentioned as important influences or aspects of instructional leadership roles.

Following this same tradition, Murphy (1984) conducted a large-scale survey of principals and other educators and identified four leadership tasks or functions that distinguish high-achieving from low-achieving schools. According to Murphy's findings, effective instructional leaders:

a) develop and communicate a clear mission and goals for the schools;
b) promote quality instruction through formal and informal supervision, effective use of instructional time, parent involvement strategies, and regular assessment of academic goals;
c) promote a school culture of learning by maintaining high expectations and standards, being visible in classrooms and the school, rewarding good teachers (e.g., through increased leadership responsibility, recognition) and high-achieving students (e.g., through rewards), and fostering professional development;
d) develop a supportive work environment, characterized by a safe and orderly learning climate, clear and consistent discipline procedures, opportunities for meaningful student involvement (e.g., decision-making councils) and teacher involvement (e.g., decision-making councils, informal leadership roles), staff collaboration and cohesion, the securing of outside resources in support of school goals, and links between the home and the school.

Over time, Murphy's (1984) instructional leadership characteristics and behaviors were corroborated by other empirical research studies (e.g. Hallinger & Murphy, 1985; Purkey & Smith, 1983; Sheppard, 1996). For instance, based on a similar large-scale survey, Hallinger and Murphy (1985) identified several "instructional leadership behaviors" that yielded improved student outcomes: setting high expectations and goals; supervising and evaluating instruction; coordinating the curriculum; and monitoring student progress. Hallinger and Murphy did not, however, find any connections between curriculum decision-making structures or learning culture and student achievement. A decade later, Sheppard (1996) replicated Murphy's (1984) study and identified the additional factors of teacher commitment, professional involvement, and innovativeness as essential influences on classroom practice. For almost 2 decades, educational leadership training programs focused on teaching prospective principals the instructional leadership factors and behaviors identified in these and other similar research studies.

Yet despite the assumption that using quantitative methods would produce findings that could be replicated and generalized, the link between instructional leadership and student outcomes has remained elusive. In other words, the impact of instructional leadership on academic achievement—the dependent variable most often identified in these studies—is inconclusive. Further, the effects of leadership on other outcomes, such as teacher involvement in curriculum decision making, are contradictory because schools vary widely in their organizational structure, commitment to collaborative decision-making processes, professional development, level of teaching experience among the faculty, and underlying curriculum philosophy.

In an attempt to clarify the contradictory results of these early studies, some scholars have examined particular leadership processes (e.g., school organizational structure, underlying curriculum philosophy, professional development) that may mediate between inputs and outputs but be ignored or controlled for in large-scale studies, in order to refine measurements of curriculum leadership. Here the ultimate goal is to find an indirect causal model of curriculum leadership, in which a particular variety of shared or collaborative approach to instructional leadership is necessary but not sufficient for high-quality teaching and learning (e.g., Jackson, 2000; Marks & Printy, 2003).

For example, Marks and Printy (2003) used hierarchical linear modeling (HLM) to analyze survey, observation, and interview data from 24 nationally recognized, restructured schools. Their findings indicated that by *modeling* appropriate instructional leadership behaviors and inviting teachers to share leadership responsibilities, principals build instructional leadership capacity for systemic school change, which in turn, increases student engagement and learning. Marks and Printy concluded, "When teachers perceive principals' instructional leadership behaviors to be appropriate, they grow in commitment, professional involvement, and willingness to innovate" (p. 5). Similarly, Jackson (2000) used a mixed-methods approach to examine schools that consistently performed well on various assessment measures; he found that what he called an "interactive leadership model"—whereby principals invited teachers to lead curriculum improvement efforts and then worked with them in a shared instructional leadership capacity to develop instructional innovations—could improve student learning. Jackson (2000) further identified differences in the particular curriculum philosophy and pedagogy that individual principals advocated; specifically, strong curriculum leaders fostered the use of constructivist and innovative pedagogy rather than drill-and-practice activities in their schools.

As with earlier traditional studies of instructional leadership, however, the link between leadership and student outcomes remains inconclusive. Whereas Marks and Printy (2003) and Jackson (2000) agree that modeling instructional leadership behaviors is important for administrators, they differ as to the specific leadership behaviors that should be modeled. These studies do not provide contextualized understandings (macro or micro) of curriculum leadership. Further, because researchers assume clear-cut, measurable differences in principals' curriculum leadership behaviors, they add and average within-study and between-study anomalies to subsume discrepant behaviors and characteristics. The presence of discrepant cases, however, suggests that the very units of analysis in traditional curriculum leadership studies may be inaccurate: in reality the characteristics that constitute strong versus typical and weak curriculum leadership may not be so easily distinguished as categorical labels suggest or statistical analysis requires, particularly if researchers consider influences of personal identity like gender and race or hegemony and politics.

A second issue is that educational administration studies have provided leaders with clear guidance on *how* to influence teaching and learning in schools, but rarely mention *what* educational content leaders should influence. For example, Spillane and colleagues (2001) define instructional leadership in terms of the various forms of capital that followers' value (e.g., social, cultural, human). Spillane et al.'s definition of human capital encompasses curriculum content knowledge, but human capital is not explicitly grounded in social or curriculum theory. Some curriculum leadership textbooks (e.g., Glatthorn et al., 2004 provide current and aspiring leaders with curriculum development models; however, there is little discussion about educational content and the role of politics in curriculum decisions.

Although it is understandable that traditional instructional leadership frameworks have dominated educational administration training for almost 30 years, during a period when political and academic curriculum trends remained relatively stable, it is becoming increasingly clear that these frameworks fail today's school leaders who struggle daily with the politics of curriculum content decisions. Educational leadership scholars and practitioners frequently talk about leadership theory: how formal and informal leaders influence organizational members toward some direction or reform initiative. Without denying the importance of leadership perspectives to educational change, I argue that *what* we lead (individually or collectively) is just as important as who leads and what strategies are used to achieve educational goals. Further, choices about what we lead are influenced by personal identities, philosophies, and broader cultural politics. Today's educational leaders must have a deep understanding of the curriculum in relation to broader cultural politics that they consciously or unconsciously attempt to influence in their schools.

## Curriculum Theories in the Fields of Curriculum and Critical Education Studies

Kliebard (1992) reminds us that theories have their origins in human problems, thoughts, and curiosity. The problem that gives rise to curriculum theory is that teaching requires making choices about what to teach; hence, curriculum development may be defined as that activity which gives systematic attention to the question of what we should teach. According to Kliebard (1992), the central question of what we should teach gives rise to other problems: (1) Why should we teach one thing rather than another? (2) Who should have access to that knowledge? (3) What rules should govern the teaching of whatever content has been selected? (4) How should the various parts of the curriculum be interrelated in order to create a coherent whole?

Progressive and conservative (traditionalist) educators and scholars have debated these questions for more than a century; however, these debates have rarely made their way into the instructional leadership literature used in educational administration certification programs or into doctoral programs and postcertification professional development, many of which emphasize practical models or strategies. As a result, unless educational leaders have a strong master's or doctoral minor in curriculum studies, they may have to remember back to their undergraduate courses or study curriculum theory development on their own. Several early instructional leadership models (e.g. Heck et al., 1990 Murphy, 1984) and more recent textbooks (e.g., Glatthorn et al., 2004 merely allude to curriculum issues, indirectly advising leaders to use rational, step-by-step curriculum development and management procedures.

## Rational Technical Curriculum Theories

This section begins with a review of the rational curriculum theories suggested in several instructional leadership models from the 1970s and '80s, then moves on to more critical, progressive theories relevant for today's curriculum problems. One of the earliest curriculum theories postulates that children learn content through stern mental discipline such as rote memorization—a theory echoed in the back-to-basics movement that has recently gained some traction as educators are pressured to quickly raise student achievement scores on state-level standardized tests. Ralph Tyler (1949) developed one of the most frequently cited applications of mental discipline theory. Although he presented his publication as a means of viewing, analyzing, and interpreting the program of an educational institution, it has been interpreted as a step-by-step procedure for curriculum construction: (1) designation and alignment of purpose; (2) educational experiences; (3) organization; and (4) assessment. Tyler uses the psychology of learning as a "screen" that enables educators to determine what can actually be learned and what cannot, which goals are practicable for schools, and so on. Essentially, Tyler's commitment is to a highly rationalized, comprehensive *method* for arriving at logical and justifiable curricula of many different kinds. In this way, Tyler's rationale concentrates on the *how* of curriculum making, not the *what* of curriculum itself, and his concentration has influenced generations of instructional leadership research and training programs, as well as popular comprehensive reforms such as Success for All. Schwab (1971) developed a less linear and more flexible model than Tyler's (1949) rationale but still recommends the same steps for curriculum content and instructional decision-making processes. Tyler's (1949) and Schwaub's (1978) models have been the historical sources of many school district curriculum-development processes and scope-and-sequence charts in major textbook series, with management of these processes gradually assumed to be an essential part of what it means to be a "good instructional leader" in schools. More recently, these technical rational processes have been promoted and enhanced by literature on professional leadership approaches to accountability issues (e.g., Maxcy, 2009).

Kliebard criticizes Tyler on several counts, including the wisdom of using an evaluation procedure that merely verifies the attainment of stated objectives and the assumption that learning experiences can be selected and organized. However, these criticisms have not been reflected in the items related to curriculum in state administrator standards and related certification tests. Further, many schools and districts (including two of the schools featured in this book) now require all teachers to use "pacing guides" that specify daily curriculum objectives, alignment to state standards, and assessment procedures. While such practices provide leaders with a practical way to deal with accountability requirements, they can also reinforce professional and managerial roles.

Such prevailing school practices can also deskill teachers and promote rote memorization of fixed subject matter defined in adult terms with little regard for how children think or for broader cultural inequities. The problem posing cases presented in this book will explore these sorts of issues.

## Progressive Curriculum Theories

Three opposing critical curriculum theories address the challenges and possibilities of critical curriculum leadership roles; namely, Apple (2004) and Bourdieu's (2001) theories of education as reproduction of culture, Freire's emancipation approach to curriculum (1970/1993), and Dewey's theory of growth and its relation to the individual and to democratic society (1916/2008). I will now outline these theories.

### Education as Reproduction of Culture

Bourdieu's (2001) and Apple's (1992) theory of curriculum as cultural reproduction offers an alternative, critical curriculum theory that may suit curriculum leaders who seek radical social change in the current political era. This theory sees the primary function of schools as "cultural reproduction"; that is, reproducing in each new generation the social patterns and power relations of the prior one. According to Apple (2004), the United States is governed by the interests of capitalist big business and corporations, which control the media and the production, consumption, and distribution of goods. These dominant interests exercise hegemony on everyone in society through sometimes subtle but very powerful mechanisms of domination in which schools play a major part. Schools preserve the existing power relations of society through the "hidden curriculum"; that is, the school rules that all students know but were never explicitly taught.

Cultural reproduction theory brings into focus dimensions of curriculum that we might not otherwise consider. For example, the metaphor of cultural capital focuses attention on the equal versus unequal distribution of knowledge through the curriculum; it raises the question of whose interests are served by a maldistribution of cultural capital. What and whose knowledge are principals/curriculum leaders influencing in schools and communities? Regardless of whether curriculum leadership is conceptualized primarily as an individual or a collaborative process, scholars and practitioners must consider what and whose knowledge they teach, as well as how inequitable distribution of school knowledge affects current and future generations.

### Education as Emancipation in Community-Based Curriculum

Freire's emancipation approach to education (1970/1993) provides a possible strategy for interrupting cultural reproduction in society. His fundamental concern is with the liberation of poor, powerless, and ignorant people whom the wealthy have subjected to slavelike domination (Walker & Soltis, 2004). According to Freire (1970/1993), the primary purpose of education is to help oppressed people overcome fatalism, self-deprecation, and emotional dependence and replace these with active freedom and human responsibility. As such, Freire's main purpose in curriculum development is to stimulate and sustain *critical consciousness* among oppressed people. This cannot be done by treating them as objects whose behaviors are to be transformed by educators. Rather, they must be treated as active human agents who deserve teachers' help in achieving their own liberation through dialogue. The educator's task is to pose "the problems of men in their relations with the world" (p. XX). Students and teachers thus become collaborators or coinvestigators developing a shared consciousness of reality and images of a possible, better reality. Walker and Soltis (2004) describe Freire's (1970/1993) curriculum development process when they state, "This ability to step back from an unconscious acceptance of things as they are and to perceive the world critically, even in the midst of pervasive, powerful, subtle forces tending to distort and oppress is what Freire means by attaining *critical consciousness*" (p. 39).

In order to develop curriculum, Freire proposes that a team of educators work with the people of a given locality to develop "generative themes" that reflect their view of reality, based on and taken from their local way of life. First, the team members meet with representatives of the people to be educated in order to discuss their plans and secure the permission and cooperation of the prospective students. Members of the team would observe how the people live at home, at work, at church, and at play; the language they use; and their behavior, dress, and relationships. The observers would look for anything and everything that indicates how the people construe reality and their situations, in order later to help them raise their consciousness about these things. Preliminary findings of these observations would be presented in a series of evaluation meetings held in the community. From these discussions would emerge the contradictions that, if clearly perceived, reveal to the people their oppressed state.

The curriculum is implemented through thematic investigations in actual instruction, using curriculum materials related to each theme. Data gathered to assess community needs or issues are presented as problems, not answers. Thus, the people's own lives are reflected back to them in a way that encourages critical awareness of their situation, not passive acceptance of oppression. Their consciousness is raised, and they are encouraged to question the world. Although Freire does not outline a rational and linear curriculum development procedure in the way Tyler does, at some point these procedures lead to goal selection, choices of methods, organization, and evaluation with the ultimate aims of emancipation and growth.

### Education as Growth

Dewey's (1916/2008) *Democracy and Education* set the stage for progressive education in the first half of the 20th century. Dewey frequently described his project as a philosophy of education that would connect the growth of democracy with contemporary forces and trends. Here, Dewey emphasized the idea of *connection* in his educational and democratic outlook, along with its associated concepts of communication and continuity. "The entire philosophy will pivot around the familiar, provocative, still controversial idea of 'growth,' which Dewey describes not as *having* an end or outcome but as [*being*] *itself* the finest end or outcome of education" (Hansen, 2007, p. 54). In other words, education has no greater end than to create the capacity for further education in students. That is, a democratic way of life is not a means to some larger end or outcome. It is in itself the realization of political, social, and educational ends supportive of growth.

In his seminal work, *Democracy and Education*, Dewey also argues that the aim of democracy is democracy itself, just as the aim of growth is further growth. As Dewey (1916/2008) put it, "A democracy is more than a form of government; it is primarily a mode of associated living, of conjoint communicated experience" (p. 93). Hansen (2007) further clarifies that if human beings are understood as entities that do not have predetermined destinies, but rather can influence their very nature through education and social interaction, and then it behooves them to learn to question, to criticize, to converse, and to be modest and fair-minded in their claims. Further, Dewey views students as intentional, independently capable, autonomy-deserving persons deserving of the deepest and most profound consideration in the processes of education (Fenstermacher, 2006).

Dewey does not specifically make curriculum a topic of *Democracy and Education*; however, he threads understandings about curriculum throughout the book. He puts subject matter at the heart of education, and puts curriculum—along with teaching and administration—at the heart of schooling. "As he makes clear, one cannot teach or learn without teaching or learning *something*. That 'something' is subject matter, and the subject matter of the school is the curriculum" (Page, 2006, p. 39). Further, Dewey argues that curriculum is an important means by which societies define and maintain themselves. A democratic society is dependent on a "humanized curriculum" in which knowledge is meaningful to students because it connects with the common interests of humans as humans.

Dewey also identifies several pitfalls of subject matter in formal, humanized education—an argument that provides compelling leverage for curriculum leaders in the current political environment (Page 2006). According to Dewey (1916/2008, p. 189), the chief hazard in school lessons is that "the bonds which connect the subject matter of school study with the habits and ideals of the social group are disguised and covered up." Page (2006, p. 51) adds that when the knowledge acquired in school is disconnected from the needs of society, two deleterious consequences follow. First, and most important, the manifest curriculum in schools becomes the "hiding curriculum." Educators hide the value of knowledge from youth when they present subject matter as "merely academic" knowledge divorced from human purposes, as existing only for its own sake separated into discrete subjects and requiring only "mental" operations and "pure world practical constraints." Students learn in school to see knowledge as merely the school's gambit (e.g., test preparation and performance), not as a resource that they and all people depend on in successfully navigating a precarious world.

Here, Dewey is not talking about the hidden curriculum as described by Apple. Rather, he is talking about the formal, explicit curriculum (e.g., social studies, algebra) in academic content knowledge. Further, Dewey claims that all students—the advantaged along with the disadvantaged and the high-scoring along with the low-scoring—are turned away from education that is merely scholastic rather than humane, because they will not see knowledge as a tangible, material resource that they can rely on and create when they wrestle with particular problems in everyday life. "With Dewey's multilayered method of analyzing subject matter, we gain a variety of contexts or vantage points from which to 'see' what we are about today and reconsider whether our educational ideas and practices are what we intend. Does our curriculum reflect and re-create the democratic 'form of life' we say we prize?" (Page,

2006, p. 59). Leadership is clearly necessary in resolving these issues; however, few curriculum studies focus on leadership.

## The Role of Leadership in Curriculum Studies

Giroux (2001) and Bourdieu (1996) are two of the few scholars who write about leadership when they exemplify the role of public intellectuals in political activism and agency with regards to curriculum. Giroux draws upon Pierre Bourdieu when he argues that educators should become "public intellectuals" who provide opportunities for praxis and critical pedagogy. More specifically, he suggests that educators must be leaders who empower teachers, community members, and students to take an active political stance against prevailing ideologies that are not in the best interests of children in a democratic society. Such a view of educational leadership suggests a key role that the administrator, teacher, or community leader can play in influencing the curriculum in the modern school: the public intellectual leader unveils the politics of educational content decisions, and thereby intervenes in the power relations between groups and classes, perhaps even helping to modify them. This type of curriculum leadership is, at least in part, critical. When one asserts that a critical curriculum leader can potentially modify relations between social classes this amounts to a strong claim for the power of school knowledge in modern stratified societies and for the role of the critical curriculum leader in influencing public policy. In the current debates over back-to-basics versus holistic curriculum practices, standardized programs, and testing mandates, critical curriculum leaders resist the "deskilling" of education practice as well as the standardization and stratification of educational content in schools. This form of critical curriculum leadership was evident in two of the schools described in this book.

In sum, critical progressive curriculum theories deal with complex issues of what and whose cultural capital becomes official knowledge; whose vision of the family, government, and economy are realized in our schools and other institutions and our consciousness; and what resources (economic and analytical) we employ to challenge existing social relations and inequities. Today's educators face unprecedented demands from high-stakes accountability policies and curriculum improvement mandates at all levels of government. As a result, along with knowing how to be effective leaders, principals and other curriculum leaders need deep understandings of curriculum theory and cultural politics in order to make critical decisions about what to teach and to whom. These understandings go well beyond the vague language of "curriculum management" or "professional learning community leader" frequently found in administrative standards and instructional leadership literature. Further, as leaders make curriculum decisions, they must recognize that the language in policies and in the day-to-day practices in a school is shaped by broader cultural politics (Cornbleth, 2008).

## Recent Cultural Political Movements

The years from the early 1980s through the early 21st century have witnessed major shifts in national cultural politics, including a resurgence of conservative policies and agendas. Educational administrators who have been in leadership positions since the 1980s remember how the publication of *A Nation at Risk* (National Commission on Excellence in Education, 1983), of Goals 2000 (Educate America Act, Title III, 1998) in the Bush and Clinton presidencies, and of related state standards changed curriculum dialogue in schools, putting greater emphasis on student outcomes and alignment of local with state standards. These trends were reinforced and codified through the No Child Left Behind Act (2001) and its inherent "test data-driven" priorities and consequences for schools that fail to attain and sustain high academic performance over a series of years. Many administrators in my courses comment that they cannot remember the last time they attended a district or state meeting where someone did not use the phrases "data-driven leadership," "standards alignment," or "leadership for learning." These shifts in the common sense about, language, and priorities of education can be explained by the circulating discourses of the conservative modernization.

### *The Conservative Modernization, Discourses, and Hegemony*

As Apple (1996) explains, "The rightist policies now taking center stage in education and nearly everything else embody a tension between a neoliberal emphasis on 'market values' on the one hand and a neoconservative attachment to 'traditional values' on the other" (p. 6). A strictly neoliberal agenda would suggest that the state must be minimized, preferably by setting private enterprise loose, whereas a strictly neoconservative agenda would posit that the state needs to mandate the teaching of particular knowledge, norms, and values. Both agendas find common ground in a belief that society is falling apart primarily because schools do not achieve either agenda effectively since federal and state governments have yielded too much control over education and do not sufficiently mandate what schools are supposed to teach.

Apple (1996, p. 6) describes the current conservative philosophy or agenda as a new hegemonic alliance with a wide umbrella that creatively encompasses and unites the contradictions and tensions among its various submovements. Gramsci (1971) referred to this hegemony as "the process by which the dominant classes or class factions propagate their values through their privileged access to social institutions (such as the media)" (p. 81). Apple and Jungck

(1990) drew on Gramsci when they argued, "Hegemony acts to saturate our consciousness so that the educational, economic, and social world we see and interact with, and the commonsense interpretations we put on it, becomes the world tout court, the only world" (p. 5). According to Apple (1996), a hegemonic alliance of the current conservative era is a coalition of four major groups: (1) dominant economic and political elites intent on "modernizing" the economy and the institutions connected to it; (2) largely White working-class and middle-class groups who mistrust the state; are concerned with security, the family, and traditional knowledge and values; and who form an increasingly active segment of what might be called authoritarian populists; (3) economic and cultural conservatives (such as American conservative pundit and politician Bill Bennett) who want to return to "high standards," discipline, and social Darwinist competition in schools; and (4) a faction of the new middle class who may not totally agree with these other groups, but whose personal professional interests and advancement depend upon the expanded use of accountability, efficiency, and management procedures that are their own cultural capital. I discuss each group within the conservative restoration alliance in the next several sections.

### Neoliberalism

Neoliberalism is a particular narrative about the relationships among the economy, the social formation, the state and its institutions, and the people that constitute all of these. Because this narrative is enacted by quite powerful groups and individuals, it has tremendous material and discursive effects, both nationally and globally (e.g., Ball, 1994; Whitty, Power, & Halpin, 1998). For neoliberals, a person is most properly understood not as a member of a community or society, but rather as a self-interested individual who, given proper conditions, makes rational choices as a "consumer" within a competitive marketplace.

Conservative discourse is evident in recent neoliberal policies and general arguments asserting that on graduation young people must be able to compete for high-paying jobs in a global market economy. The basis of this discourse is the production of wealth. For example, the federal government provides funding to schools that enact comprehensive reforms which promise to raise achievement of all students regardless of socioeconomic status. Many of these reforms also make overt ties between schooling and (paid) work or the economy. In particular, the rhetoric around these reforms is grounded in a number of economic challenges: at a time of severe international competition, schools are failing to produce the skilled workforce necessary to make the United States competitive in the global economy. Schools need to reform all aspects of the educational system (i.e., organizational structure, curriculum, pedagogy, parent involvement) in order to make substantive improvements in workforce development. Further, schools need leaders who can manage teacher quality and productivity in a professional and efficient manner.

Neoliberal discursive practices over the last 2 decades have fundamentally altered the common understanding of the relationship between the individual and the state, and between the public and private spheres by defining essentially everything that is public as bad, and everything private as good (Apple, 1996, 2001; Ball, 1994). Neoliberals also advocate that "the managerial state" be responsive to consumers of education through competitiveness and attention to "values." In the name of efficiency, administrative structures and responsibilities within schools have been radically transformed through the introduction and dominance of managerialist discourses (Ball, 1994). Anderson (2009) draws on Kumashiro (2008) and Lakoff (2002) when he argues that, "Neoliberalists have understood that the language we use to talk about reality is as important, if not more important, than reality itself. The right has constructed and framed a new neoliberal common sense, while the left, in trying to accommodate to it rather than reframe the issues, has moved to the political right" (p. 143).

### Neoconservativism

In contrast, neoconservative elements of the hegemonic alliance call for a strong state that serves as the agent and guardian of higher standards, both moral and scholastic. These higher standards are achieved through the increased accountability imposed by high-stakes testing, the resuscitation of educational canons and traditional subject matter within a common curriculum, and the teaching via strict discipline and "character education" of those values that, according to neoconservatives, have historically provided the foundation for the nation's educational, moral, and material success (Apple, 1996, 2001; Hirsch, 1996). Like neoliberals, neoconservatives are concerned with decreased U.S. competitiveness in the global marketplace; however, they attribute this decline to a drop in American citizens' moral, intellectual, and vocational competencies. Further, neoliberals assert that this reduction in competencies was caused by a series of misguided, nonscientific curriculum interventions promoted by progressives. Even though as Kliebard and others have demonstrated, successful (widely implemented) progressive reforms are rare in U.S. curriculum history, neoconservative arguments against progressive curriculum and pedagogy have gained traction.

One of the distinguishing features of neoconservativism is its vision of traditional "character." There is a clear preference for rewards over the encouragement of social altruism, although reformers and policymakers often cite altruistic motives for accountability and the use of national curriculum standards. Lakoff (2002) notes that in this context reward and punishment are moral not just for their own sake. They have a further purpose in terms of the Strict Father model: life is a struggle and survival in the world is a matter of competing successfully. To do so, children must learn discipline and develop their character. At the same time, some conservative reformers promote the use of "character education" to increase the work ethic and values of children (primarily inner-city children of color or children of single mothers).

In recent years, the federal government has assumed a more direct role in curriculum decision making in schools through the enactment of various policies. For example, the No Child Left Behind Act (2001) requires schools to meet a goal of 100% of students achieving proficiency on state tests by the year 2014. Further, Reading First (Office of Elementary and Secondary Education, 2002) provides funds for schools to adopt "scientifically based" reading programs that appear to support both a particular set of ideologies and the use of skills-based curricula and instructional programs (Allington, 2002). For schools whose students fail to meet set goals for adequate yearly progress on state tests, current policies impose consequences ranging from conversion to charter school status to staff restructuring and reconstitution. Likewise, in order to receive and retain Reading First funds (Office of Elementary and Secondary Education, 2002), schools must demonstrate improved student performance on state-level tests of academic knowledge.

Some state administrator standards advise leaders to analyze assessment data and select only "research-based" programs and practices that align with state standards and raise student achievement. Further, many states now require aspiring administrators to take exams focused on how to improve teaching and learning. Although these tests are not generally multiple choice, they tend to set up a binary of correct versus incorrect answers, with the correct answers decontextualizing children and individual situations. In fact, test-takers are penalized for critiquing curriculum decisions that are insensitive to issues of social class, race/ethnicity, or gender (Anderson, 2001).

### Authoritarian Populism

Authoritarian populism, which has become increasingly popular in recent years, features a religious base. Although economic problems are important to authoritarian populists, their argument centers on the alleged displacement of religion in favor of secular humanism. Schools are seen as a primary threat to moral, religious family life in that they are a site for the elite and foreign knowledge that contradicts the sound, traditional teachings of the American Christian family. Such conflicts over the spiritual and physical lives of children are evident in recent attacks on curriculum content, the use of literature for reading instruction, and teaching methods in schools. Authoritarian populists have found allies in this hegemonic alliance, particularly among neo-conservatives, because they call for more traditional pedagogy, testing, and standards; yet, there are tensions between the national curriculum agenda and the authoritarian populist calls for local control in schools. This split demonstrates that the conservative modernization is hardly monolithic, as will become evident in the case studies in later chapters.

### The New Middle Class

Within Apple's (1996) framework, the last group within the conservative hegemonic alliance is a particular faction of the new professional and managerial middle class. This faction gains social mobility by virtue of professional expertise it is able to provide for the hegemonic alliance in terms of educational standards, measurement, and management. Neoliberals and neoconservatives can stand under the same ideological umbrella largely because the publication of test scores of various competing schools will supposedly permit consumers to make "informed" choices within the educational marketplace. The members of the new middle class are those who provide the technical, legal, procedural, and bureaucratic expertise to make this system of standardization and comparison possible. These individuals bring to the process of the conservative restoration their competence with "neutral" efficiency, measurement, and management instruments that will enhance the ability of schools to function as stratifying mechanisms. In Apple's view, because this new middle class has fluency in these management areas, they and their children stand to gain from the prevalence of standardization in schools because they will have a competitive edge over their peers, and thus, enhance their social capital. For example, some of my national colleagues in the educational leadership field have developed expertise in data-driven decision-making procedures, efficient curriculum mapping, and professional learning communities (focused primarily on data analysis procedures and professional development aimed at the improvement of student outcomes), and these experts command several thousand dollars per day for their services. While these individuals have had some misgivings about costs related to these trainings, they also recognize that "business consultants earn far more" and that "someone needs to provide these skills to leaders in an accountability environment that is not going away."

According to Apple (1996), these four groups together constitute a hegemonic alliance within the U.S. social order because they are able to sustain leadership and advance a particular agenda largely through winning consent to their social vision among many diverse groups of people who might traditionally have promoted more progressive views. Groups within the hegemonic alliance accomplish this in two ways: (1) by compromising with one another over what the elements of that vision are to be and (2) by (re)shaping the terrain of common sense within the larger culture so that it increasingly, although never totally, resonates with their cultural messages and interpretations (Apple, 1996, p. 15). For example, many U.S. citizens and educators are concerned about declining educational achievement and increasing dropout rates, illiteracy, and violence in schools. Dominant groups within politics and the economy use these concerns and fears to shift the educational debate (and other aspects of society) toward their own agenda of traditionalism, standardization, productivity, and market-driven economic needs. Some Western countries have articulated related movements toward New Public Management (NPM). While NPM has not been as widely discussed in U.S. educational literature, the leadership characteristics and qualities promoted in this literature are evident in many U.S. schools, including two cases described later in this book.

### New Public Management (NPM)

Many elements of professional curriculum leadership may be traced to a phenomenon known as new public management (NPM), which has been most explicitly articulated by Hood (1991). NPM denotes an approach to public reform and an associated set of practices informed by an underlying managerial ideology with regards to efficiency, client-driven services, and productivity. Proponents of NPM called for a "reinvention" of government along more entrepreneurial lines in order to contain costs, improve public support, and enhance performance. Innovation and entrepreneurialism have been fostered in NPM by devolving authority over operational decisions, reconfiguring accountability relations, promoting increased emphasis on targets, and invoking competitive pressures.

Pollitt (1990) examined NPM-type educational reforms in the United States and United Kingdom and noted new trends toward scientific management and efficiency or neo-Taylorism as well as a "professional and managerial ideology" underpinned by five core beliefs: (1) progress defined according to and pursued through economic productivity; (2) faith in information and organizational technology to enhance productivity; (3) dependence on a disciplined workforce pursuing a productivity ideal; (4) the promise of professional management to improve productivity through effective planning, implementation, and monitoring; and (5) a crucial need for managerial discretion to pursue productivity improvement (pp. 2–3). Anderson (2009) further notes that today's education has been reinvented from the top and recultured from within: "Here, by recultured, I mean that the language and ways of thinking are 'managed' to conform to the new paradigm of performance outcomes" (p. 143). Study of curriculum leadership identity formation and practices over time reveal similar professional management intensification expressed in two schools of my study, expressed in language and thinking related to: (1) curriculum mapping formats aligned to efficient literacy and math test score improvement; (2) test data analysis procedures; (3) productivity in professional learning cultures; and (4) school–community relationships aimed at marketing their schools and securing resources for intervention programs.

As a hegemonic alliance, these four groups, along with new public management (NPM) have been successful in imposing a conservative ideology by circulating certain kinds of discourses to create a new "common sense" about curriculum and pedagogy in schools (Apple, 2004; Pedroni, 2007). Discourses specify what can be said and thought, as well as who can speak when, where, and with what authority. As Foucault (1980) put it, we do not speak discourses; they speak us. Discourses dictate that words be ordered and combined in particular ways while other possible combinations are displaced or excluded. Further, discourses are practices that systematically form objects (Foucault, 1980). Discourses are not about objects, they create objects, and in the process of doing so, they conceal their own invention (Ball, 1990). Thus, when school leaders announce that new policies require the use of "skills-based" curricula that raise standards and foster fairness through their consistency, then devote most faculty meetings and curriculum documents to data analysis, they can unwittingly foster rightist agendas and hegemony in their schools. To be clear, I am not suggesting that administrators should avoid conveying policy requirements to staff members. Rather, I am advising that they learn how to recognize and use the elements of good sense in these policies (Apple, 1996) and have the analytical tools and skills to interrupt (when necessary) the circulating discourses that manifest in unjust language and practices. Such curriculum leadership abilities require leaders to assume new, more critical identities in schools and communities.

## Curriculum Leadership Identity

In this volume, identity is defined as the way we see ourselves in relation to others (Stryker & Burke, 2000). According to hooks (1991), identity can be used as a reference to the parts of self that are attached to the roles people play in society, such as mother, African American, or female principal. The roles people play in society are fluid and affected by the ways in which we see ourselves in relation to others as well as by the ways in which other people identify us. For example, teachers may see someone as an African American principal, but her husband identifies her as a wife and mother. Others may identify her as a community organizer or a church member. In other words, we generally ignore the other contexts that create identities beyond the one with which we interact.

From a sociological standpoint (e.g. hooks, 1991; Stryker & Burke, 2000), scholars also suggest that our identity or "who we are" shifts and changes according to the different circumstances in which we find ourselves. For example, a principal sitting in a data analysis meeting with the superintendent may think twice about raising objections to a new intervention program designed to raise student achievement scores. A Latina principal may choose one set of language to explain the Arizona immigration and bilingual education laws at a meeting with school-business partners and another set of language when speaking to her family members in Mexico or a group of Latina leaders. Here identity and related language uses are also connected to hegemony in that hegemony explains how some groups of people are subjugated by other groups of people through circulating discourses about what and who is normal or "good" and what and who is not. If a district superintendent continually tells the principals that he/she values efficiency and productivity above all else—and this message is continually reinforced by many teachers, community members, and professional peers, the principal's notion, language, and practices of "good" leadership begin to emulate efficient and productive models from business and a host of professional leadership workshops. While leadership identity is always in flux and influenced by personal characteristics like gender and race, this principal and others like him or her begin to assume a professional curriculum leadership identity with all efforts geared toward efficient production of student outcomes. We must consider hegemony and hegemonic alliances (e.g. neoliberalism, neoconservativism, authoritarian populism, and the new middle class/new public management) and their relationships to understanding what a good curriculum leader is. We must look beyond traditional "instructional leadership" models and strategies for critical perspectives and analytical tools that help us fully consider hegemonic alliances, recognize the elements of good sense, and seek progressive curriculum theories and strategies that help us sustain democratic, public education in an accountability era and beyond.

## Curriculum Leadership and Progressive Education: A New Model

The model below briefly introduces my conception of curriculum leadership that can inspire progressive educational and social movements. The triangle indicates that curriculum leadership involves three interrelated dimensions: curriculum theory, the role of politics, and leadership identity, all of which are informed by sociocultural and political influences (e.g., neoliberalism), particular community contexts, and school cultures. In recent years, circulating discourses related to neoliberalism, neoconservativism, authoritarian populism, the new middle class, and new public management have had a profound impact on curriculum leadership identities and practices by circulating a particular set of discourses that have affected our common sense about what it means to be a good "curriculum leader." Teachers, administrators, and educational consultants often praise school leaders for their abilities to manage a veritable cottage industry of curriculum design and organizational reforms, data analysis skills, and abilities to quickly improve student outcomes and effectively market their schools. While many currently popular reforms, such as professional learning communities, are grounded in excellent empirical studies, accountability pressures have affected the ways in which these reforms are implemented in schools. In other words, school leaders and teachers often spend professional dialogue time on test-data analysis and pacing calendars that ensure coverage of state standards and standardized test items (often now translated to mean "the curriculum"). Educators are told, and often express the view that, "We need to focus our attention on what we can control in our schools" or "parent and community involvement are a bonus." All of these "good" (new professional) curriculum leadership practices now enhance and reinforce efficiency, productivity, and professional discourses with little regard for the role of politics, curriculum theory, education for the whole child, or compassion for those less fortunate in our communities. For this reason, I indicate that new professional curriculum leadership is highly affected by recent (conservative) cultural political shifts as these shifts play out in particular communities and schools.

Curriculum leaders need to have an ability to "read" and reread sociocultural and political influences and discourses and determine the elements of good sense and opportunities to make their schools and communities better places to work and live as well as to read the potentially unjust effects of these broader influences. Further, curriculum leaders must have a strong understanding of curriculum theory, including rational technical models, critical theories, and postmodern theories in order to recognize "new" rational, technical curriculum models or old wine in new bottles. In other words, curriculum leaders must take a critical perspective on curriculum theories as these are shaped by broader sociocultural and political influences.

These intellectually engaged curriculum leaders then use their understandings of curriculum theory and community relationships to develop culturally relevant, authentic, and rigorous curricula that contribute to holistic achievement on various kinds of assessments. They recognize the reality of accountability legislation (including elements of good sense regarding achievement gaps) and have skills to meet these requirements in ways that are in the best interest of their students. In other words, critical curriculum leaders use professional skills, but these leaders have the critical theoretical grounding and political awareness to consider professional discursive shifts and practices more fully. In the examples in this book, I focus primarily on principals as instrumental curriculum leaders; however, I agree with Spillane, Marks, Printy, and others who promote distributive, shared, or integrated leadership models. In my study, there were many instances in which students, teachers, parents, and community organizers exhibited curriculum leadership, both individually and in fluid, dynamic groups.

In the next section, I describe the communities featured in the study and examples in this book. Specific schools and principals are described in the next two chapters.

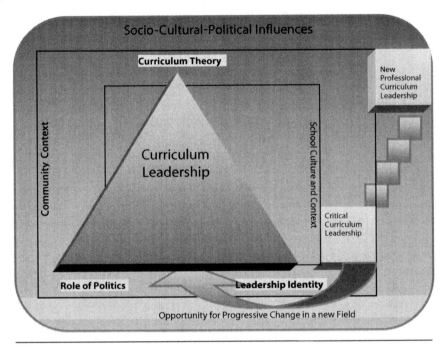

**Figure 1.1** Curriculum leadership model.

## Communities Featured in the Study

### *The Community of Treelane*

In the current political era, individuals and groups talk about and thereby enact curriculum leadership in face-to-face interactions that echo aspects of cultural politics from wider contexts. The schools featured in this book, Babcock and Pinehurst, boast classrooms and meeting areas that reflect Treelane's particular interpretations of the politics around state curriculum standards, teacher-proof instructional programs, and marketization rippling across the United States and other Western countries. With a clear but subtle effect, the two principals, teachers, parents, and students in my study sites challenge or foster the conservative restoration in different ways.

As its name implies, Treelane, a city in the Northeastern United States, is an appealing place to live. There are many parks in the city, there are many tree-lined streets, and the public schools are well regarded. Treelane is home to many large white-collar industries, several blue-collar industries, and a university. White flight from a nearby city has contributed to an increasingly diverse adult and student population in Treelane. Real estate prices generally are mixed according to school attendance boundaries. At the time of data collection, only about one third of the city's population has children in schools, and yet there is strong interest in education. In the past 5 years, several new private schools and charter schools have opened in the area.

Treelane has many small but active neighborhood associations with strong and sometimes competitive interest in their neighborhood schools and local civic government. The local media follow public debates about schooling and other civic opinions very closely. Many of Treelane's citizens assume responsibility in their neighborhood schools, volunteering in classrooms, and arguing for new programs before the school board.

Treelane had been overwhelmingly White in the past, but its population has become increasingly diverse over the past 10 years. Treelane's churches sponsor many refugees from Latin America and Asia. Blacks form the largest minority group and now make up 27% of Treelane's total population. The numbers have tripled over the past 15 years with most recent increases being from a nearby metropolitan area and from nearby states. Overall, about 53% of Treelane's school students are minority children, and the city's demographic shifts are reflected in the schools. About half of the Black adults who live in Treelane are employed in white collar jobs, and those who are parents are active in local schools. Many civic organizations and Treelane public schools promote racial tolerance. It is also important to note that Treelane's neighborhoods are not all rigidly segregated by race, but there are clear differences according to class. Census data document the predominance of middle-class neighborhoods: it is more common to see business owners and university professors living in affluent areas near the university; recent immigrants or arrivals living in the eastern part of the city, and poor Black newcomers living on the west side. Children attend neighborhood schools so housing patterns influence school populations at the elementary and middle school levels. The city's four comprehensive high schools draw from larger attendance areas so socioeconomic differences are less distinct.

Many Treelane residents work in the schools, university, or government offices, areas that offer some protection from economic stress. However, recent property tax increases, the general economic decline of the Rust Belt, and federal cutbacks in social programs are reflected in political campaigns as members of the blue-collar working class and lower middle class compete for fewer jobs.

The shrinking economy, rising prices, declining job prospects and related school enrollments, increased numbers of minority students, and an increase in the number of students qualifying for academic intervention programs have affected Treelane's school system and the community's attitudes toward it. Financial support for Treelane's schools remains high, but the school budget meetings have become more contentious. In particular, neighborhood school organizations, parents, and teachers have engaged in public debates over potential closing and merging of elementary schools as a means to deal with declining enrollment and the budget crisis.

Economic and political issues have also produced swings in district organizational structures. For example, in the late 1990s the district had initiated a decentralization plan with a horizontal decision-making structure, with decisions focused on curriculum and instruction. Each school governance council developed its own curriculum with some alignment to a district overall curriculum and then selected materials to meet curriculum goals. Previously, the district had strict centralized curriculum and textbook selection policies. While the school curriculums and materials purchases were subject to district approval, each school essentially followed its own course of study for students. Decentralization represented a major change in principals' instructional leadership duties. In 2000, however, the new superintendent proposed some recentralization in order to cut costs in student materials and operation costs, including merging some schools. Debates over potential merging of schools exposed some racial overtones as some community organizations suggested that the previous decentralization plan had produced schools segregated by race and class.

Debates over these economic and political factors have been clearly connected to curricular debates. School board meeting minutes and newspaper articles at the time contained questions about the effectiveness of academic curriculums, particularly in district use of "whole language" literacy. Concerns about particular school curriculums increased after the state mandated standardized testing in grades 3, 6, and 9 and the local newspaper compared schools within the district, the district to surrounding districts, and all to the state average. Some vocal parent groups have started to question the use of particular reading materials in those schools identified as "below state average" for two or more years since the enactment of the state testing policies (including both schools featured in the study). Curricular debates sharply intensified with the enactment of the No Child Left Behind Act and related curriculum and testing policies announced on my first day of observation in Treelane schools. It is important to note that while the principals featured in the study took different curriculum paths and constructed different leadership identities over time, their schools attained similar (high) student outcomes on state tests.

### The Community of Hillside

Like nearby Treelane, Hillside is an attractive community with a lot of green space, a thriving cultural center, and generally strong public schools. Hillside is primarily a blue-collar community; however, a major white-collar industry recently relocated its headquarters to Hillside, bringing many high paying jobs. Real estate prices are considered one of the lowest in the region. With increases in more affluent white-collar families, there has been a surge in parent involvement in the public schools and enrollment in private schools. Like

Treelane, neighborhood associations are very strong but with a strong ethnic identity. Many families have lived in Hillside for three generations. The Hillside schools featured in this book, Greenway and Elmhurst, reflect state and national trends for collaborative governance (professional learning communities) and pressures to improve student achievement amidst changing demographics. Hillside civic government debates are often heated, and newspaper stories about mayoral and city government races are often filled histories of contentious past elections leading up to the present one. Public debates about schooling are followed very closely by the local media.

Hillside's population is overwhelmingly White with diversity more evident in terms of differences between working class, a shrinking middle class, and a growing upper class. Blacks form the largest minority group with 22% of the population, a figure that has remained relatively stable. Recent increases in Asian and Latino/a families have increased the overall minority population in Hillside and those demographics are reflected in the schools. Overall, about 31% of Hillside's school students are minority children, and the city's demographic shifts are reflected in the schools. About one third of the Black adults who live in Hillside are employed in white-collar jobs. The city's three comprehensive high schools draw from larger attendance areas so socioeconomic differences are less distinct.

The Hillside community has a history of union pride with multiple generations of family members working in local factories. In the past 7 years, however, many of the blue-collar jobs have been shipped overseas, forcing some workers to take early retirement and many others to leave the area. Like Treelane, recent property tax increases, the general economic decline of the Rust Belt, and federal cutbacks in social programs leave many blue-collar working class and lower middle class workers to compete for fewer jobs.

The shrinking economy and lack of blue-collar job security, combined with increasing numbers of minority students have affected Hillside's school system, and the community's attitudes toward it. Economic and political issues have also produced organizational changes in the district. In 1998, Hillside's new superintendent initiated a decentralization plan, the last district in the region to do so. Like Treelane, each school governance council developed its own curriculum, with some alignment to a district overall curriculum, and then selected materials to meet curriculum goals. Eight years later, the district was still struggling with decentralization. In an early interview, the superintendent attributed the struggles to union resistance and budget cuts that prevented optimal staff development for administrators and teachers.

State-administered standardized test scores are relatively stable in Hillside, a trend that the new superintendent and the principals are determined to change with more data-driven decision making aimed at improved academic performance. Community members' voices are becoming increasingly vocal about job shortages, with more and more newspaper quotes from businesspeople and blue-collar parents questioning the schools' abilities to prepare children for a shrinking number of jobs. Some parents and a community organization concerned about many schools' literacy performance attend many school board meetings. In particular, some citizen groups and teachers have started to question the use of disparate elementary and middle school math programs that are not clearly aligned into the four city high schools. As in Treelane, curricular debates sharply intensified with the enactment of the No Child Left Behind Act (2001) and related curriculum and testing policies that were announced on my first day of observation in Hillside schools the following year. And like Treelane, Hillside parents, school board members, business council members, and educators expressed growing concerns about those schools identified as "below state average," including particularly the two schools featured in the study. Disjunctive school-based curriculums, increased accountability pressures combined with multiple, often contradictory community and school norms, policies, and the economics of Treelane and Hillside communities created a climate conducive for heated debates over curriculum content and pedagogical philosophy. However, over time, both of these schools increased student academic performance to proficient levels.

# 2

# New Professional Curriculum Leadership

This chapter explores the emerging new professional curriculum leadership identities of principals, using examples of the Greenway and Elmhurst schools in the cities of Treelane and Hillside. This chapter presents case study data from the principals of these two schools, Margaret Draper and Michael Grant (pseudonyms). I do not specifically link these cases with broader cultural–political movements, however; that will be part of my conclusions in chapter 7.

The curriculum leadership qualities of the two principals described in this chapter are in several respects similar to those discussed in the effective schools literature of the 1970s through 1990s and in some ways similar to the critical curriculum leaders described in the next chapter. Specifically, many educational administration scholars in that era identified principals' pedagogical expertise as a hallmark of effective curriculum leadership. Margaret Draper and Michael Grant are like all contemporary principals, in that they work in an era of high-stakes accountability and must have the curriculum content knowledge, pedagogical expertise, and leadership skills to raise student achievement quickly, often in school contexts challenged by poverty and racial tensions. A close examination of these two leaders' curriculum leadership identity formation in this context over time reveals that they have evolved toward a new professional management identity within their curriculum priorities and practices.

I detail Draper's and Grant's emerging professional identities as curriculum leaders and compare their interpretations of the meaning and practice of curriculum leadership with the findings of previous investigations. Although my theoretical frameworks differ from those used in previous studies to interpret the meaning, role, and practices of curriculum leadership, it is still useful to compare my results to data generated by James Henderson (2006), Joe Murphy (1985), Phil Hallinger (2003), James Spillane (2002), and others reviewed in the introduction. I differ from them less in the nature of the data per se than in my interpretations of the *meaning* of such data for the nature of curriculum leadership in the midst of recent (conservative) cultural–political movements. In other words, data reported in previous curriculum (or "instructional") leadership studies need not necessarily be interpreted within the learning and psychology frameworks in which they were generated. Instead, they can be used to illuminate a different understanding of curriculum leadership in the current political context.

In this chapter, I argue that "new professional" curriculum leadership emerges from beliefs about district and state mandates as expressed in other administrators', teachers', and parents'/community members' constructed meanings of and concerns about curriculum. It is this relational aspect of curriculum leadership identity that is important here. In the current era, new professional curriculum leadership formation does not develop only from leadership preparation or professional training. It is also forged in a dialectic with constructed perceptions of institutional authority, the meaning of curriculum, opposition to progressive curriculum leaders, and politics around racially based and class-based achievement gaps. All of this curriculum leadership formation takes place within a particular cultural configuration and political time, as illustrated in the following two cases.

## Case 1: Curriculum Leader Margaret Draper

Dr. Margaret Draper is the African American principal of an urban middle school in the U.S. Northeast with 17 years of experience as a principal. In 2002, Draper was recognized as principal of the year by a local reading association and described as a leader who "stays current in best practices for literacy instruction." Her school, Greenway, has a population of more than 1,200 students in grades 5 through 8, 95% of whom qualify for free or reduced lunch. Greenway is located in the high-crime neighborhood of Hillside, and many students complain that they have to cross through gang and drug problem areas on their way to and from school. Draper has secured several grants to increase technology in the school and provide after-school programs. Although parent involvement has historically been low, during Draper's tenure, parents have become more active in school programs. Dr. Draper is highly committed to closing racial achievement gaps in ways that provide poor and minority students with the best possible chance for higher education opportunities.

Draper and some veteran teachers recalled that prior to 2002 they used grass-roots, teacher driven curriculum development processes, meaning that Draper expected teachers to write goals or objectives for subject content, then to develop innovative instructional strategies to engage students in learning. She formed academic curriculum-writing teams, chaired by teachers and with a regularly revolving membership. Further, all staff members attended staff development training, which was most often scheduled during the day and always included a peer-coaching component.

In our first interview in the summer of 2002, Draper described her curriculum-writing process as "very organic," with goals developed and tested by teachers. In her view, curricula are "living documents, and assessment is an integral part. We are teaching students not curriculum goals." Teachers were aware of her curriculum philosophy, as one math teacher's comment illustrates: "I can really see how we're learning things that inform the curriculum. The curriculum does not sit on a shelf. We're always working on the framework with new research but we talk about what kids need almost daily. That's the curriculum." In the same first interview (fall, 2002), Draper described how she saw herself as a curriculum leader when she said, "I see myself as a catalyst or a motivator of teachers' best experiences and ongoing study that will develop the most interesting and relevant possible curriculum for our students."

## Case 2: Curriculum Leader Michael Grant

Michael Grant is the White principal of Elmhurst School, located in an area of Treelane characterized by changing demographics, which have moved it from being a largely middle class community to a mix of residents in the middle class, working class, and those living in poverty. Elmhurst School enrolls 800 primarily White students in grades K through 8; and only 3% qualify for free or reduced lunch. The state report card for Elmhurst reflects high student achievement in all academic areas. Yet middle-class parents continue to demand higher performance, particularly as their children compete for placement in nearby private and public high schools.

Grant has a master's degree, 12 years of experience, and is a former resident of a Treelane working-class neighborhood. When Grant lived in the neighborhood, he attended a different school due to differences in boundary requirements at the time. Grant has been recognized as a curriculum expert by state curriculum organizations. Like Draper, he is a proponent of differentiated instruction and shared decision-making strategies in curriculum development, and in the late 1990s, he established sophisticated, interrelated groups to develop content and humanities curricula. Although the district has guidelines for the selection and use of instructional materials, individual schools are given wide latitude to purchase materials suited to their students' needs. The flexibility to choose teaching resources, combined with collaborative study of current curriculum research, allowed the teachers to develop rich and unique programs serving particular student populations.

Grant has a long-standing interest in content literacy and in team-building skills. Early in his career, he served in a district with a strong norm of collaboration, and there he eventually became a district trainer in team-building and shared decision-making processes. Grant organized collaborative academic curriculum-writing teams chaired by department heads. Teachers served on the curriculum team for their academic department and took rotating memberships in the teams for other content areas. In our first interview (summer, 2002), he described the curriculum-writing process as "very collaborative, with goals developed and refined through team processes. If we don't all agree as a department and have some buy-in from other departments, we go back to the drawing board." Teachers talked about the curriculum process as "a team effort. Mr. Grant is very big on collaboration. Students are involved, too. We all have to agree on the direction, or we keep working on it until we agree."

As can be understood from the above interviews, in 2002 the principals at both Greenway and Elmhurst reported generally similar procedures and sentiments about how the academic curriculum was developed at their schools. Their comments are typical of curriculum leadership studies that conceive of curriculum development as a process through which principals, teachers, and sometimes parents and students identify content goals and objectives, relevant pedagogical strategies, assessments, and materials. Much of this mainstream curriculum/instructional leadership literature (e.g., Glickman, 2006; Hallinger & Murphy, 1985; Spillane et al., 2001) suggests that instructional leaders draw on their experience and study of exemplary teaching practices to inform the curriculum-writing process. Further, principals who are exemplary curriculum leaders facilitate the enacted curriculum when they supervise teachers in classrooms.

This is the starting point from which the study of principals Grant and Draper began in 2002. As both faced growing accountability pressures and policy requirements that affected the curriculum decisions in their schools, many of their instructional leadership identities, priorities, and attitudes began to change, as we shall see.

### Curriculum Leadership Expertise in Theory

Previous studies have suggested that effective principals take on the role of curriculum (instructional) leadership when they exhibit pedagogical expertise and other qualities deemed valuable to teachers and other members of the school community (e.g., Marks & Printy, 2003; Spillane et al., 2001). According to this literature, principals develop expertise through personal experience and study. By modeling how to develop pedagogical expertise through personal study and continuous growth, and by inviting teachers to engage in learning and growth, principals build leadership capacity and motivate teachers to foster high levels of academic performance in their students. Further, in some previous studies, principals were recognized for the supervision skills whereby they coached, evaluated, and supported teachers to attain excellent instructional skills.

Regardless of whether curriculum leadership is construed as an individual or collective construct, it has been argued that principals/curriculum leaders indirectly improve student outcomes. The most obvious dimension of the principal's instructional leadership authority in Murphy's (1984) seminal study, for example, is encouraging teachers to use current pedagogical perspectives to improve classroom practices and student learning. Effective principals set the school direction and goals for curriculum and instruction in their schools. And while Murphy does not specifically identify the source of principals' curriculum and pedagogical expertise, findings suggest that it comes from previous teaching experience, university courses, and workshops. The core leadership skill here is classroom supervision that fosters in teachers current information about curriculum and pedagogy in classrooms and schools, which in turn, improves student learning.

Although improvements in classroom teaching and student learning could be attributed to teacher effectiveness alone, several studies have suggested that the principal's pedagogical expertise plays a critical, albeit indirect role in school effectiveness and student performance (e.g., Hallinger, 2005; Leithwood, 1994; Marzano, Waters, & McNulty, 2005). More specifically, Hallinger (1984) suggested that principals' pedagogical expertise—derived from previous teaching experience and study, supervision techniques, and staff development skills—affects school climate and instructional organization, all of which shape teachers' behaviors and students' learning experiences. A follow-up study (Heck et al., 1990) tested this model and found support for its basic hypothesis: principals indirectly influence student achievement by creating learning organizations in their schools and by building a school climate and culture characterized by clearly communicated goals and high expectations for academic achievement and social behavior.

In a more recent example, Marks and Printy (2003) suggested that principals build instructional leadership capacity for systemic school change by *modeling* appropriate instructional leadership behaviors (e.g., ongoing professional learning and development of pedagogical expertise based upon research) and inviting teachers to share leadership responsibilities, which in turn, increases teacher commitment and innovation. Marks and Printy concluded, "When teachers perceive principals' instructional leadership behaviors to be appropriate, they grow in commitment, professional involvement, and willingness to innovate" (p. 5). Jackson (2000) used a mixed-methods approach to examine schools that consistently performed well on various assessment measures; he found that what he called an "interactive leadership model"—whereby principals invited teachers to lead curriculum improvement efforts and then worked with them in a shared instructional leadership capacity to develop instructional innovations—could improve student learning.

**Curriculum Leadership Expertise in Practice**

A common thread runs through these studies (e.g. Hallinger, 1984; Heck et al., 1990; Jackson, 2000; Marks & Printy, 2003): recognition of the principal as pedagogical expert and authority in the school. In my ethnographic study, both principals Draper and Grant had long been recognized as "curriculum leaders" because of their pedagogical expertise and ability to influence and support the use of current pedagogy in classrooms. When their districts launched what may be considered poorly conceptualized whole-language curriculum initiatives that challenged their expertise and authority, however, these two principals' reputations as experts began to erode, clearing the way for circulating conservative discourses to resonate and affect the principals' best instincts or what Kushmiro (2008) and Apple (2004) refer to as "common sense" about curriculum. As some scholars (e.g., Apple /1996, 2006; Pedroni, 2007) have argued, the conservative era (restoration), which includes neoconservative, neoliberal, and increasingly neonationalist perspectives, has been successful in imposing its ideology by circulating certain kinds of discourses to create a new "common sense" about curriculum and pedagogy in schools.

Despite Grant and Draper's initial attitudes about curriculum, when the district mandated whole-language philosophies and broader literacy trends that they did not entirely understand or support, the principals began to express resentment over the district's erosion of their instructional leadership authority. Grant's case was complicated by his role in the district's parallel mandate for collaborative decision making in site-based management. As Grant put it, "So now we collaborate on how to implement the district language arts mandate. It's a huge contradiction, and the teachers know it. I've been very involved in team-building and collaboration so I feel like a hypocrite with my own staff." To make matters worse, between 1995 and 2000, Elmhurst lost students to nearby charter schools that promoted direct instruction and phonics rather than whole language. Therefore, Mr. Grant and other school members were pressured to market their schools, with student achievement scores considered the best marketing tool.

Likewise, Greenway came under fire from a local education foundation that promoted "no nonsense" instructional practices. The foundation director was highly influential in the Hillside business community and frequently spoke at regional business association dinners. The foundation web site captured headlines from recent speeches, such as:

"It's time to get back to basics in our schools."
"Our schools are failing because they do not focus enough attention on academic achievement."
"Schools do not have sufficient competition like we do in business."
"Schools must produce results."

During this time, both principals expressed covert rejection of the district curriculum mandates, particularly in the area of literacy, opening the door for these leaders to identify with back-to-basics and standardized official knowledge agendas within larger neoconservative movements and the new right. Thus, unlike the principals/curriculum leaders of Murphy and Hallinger's (1985) earlier studies, principals Grant and Draper expressed resentment over experiencing diminished reputations for pedagogical expertise, a basic component of curriculum leadership in their schools. Basically, the impetus for the principals' attitude change and resentment arose out of institutional control over district curriculum mandates in the mid- to late 1990s that forced teachers to abandon their textbook programs and adopt "literature-based" practices that frequently led to parent complaints about inconsistent literacy practices, poor student spelling, and poor performance on state literacy test scores—all of which made the principals feel that they were losing control of curriculum leadership authority at a time when student demographics were changing, federal and state accountability pressures were increasing, influential parents and community members were demanding school reform, and district administrators were pressuring schools to compete for students in an open enrollment market.

In a closely related development, Draper and Grant resented district mandates over how they spent their instructional supervision time in schools. Whereas traditional instructional leadership literature has frequently identified instructional supervision as well within the principal's realm of control and influence, many contemporary principals, including those at Greenway and Elmhurst schools, were required by their district curriculum departments to spend inordinate amounts of time supervising classroom teacher teams in the development of thematic literacy and content area units that used authentic materials in authentic contexts rather than textbooks.

In both Greenway and Elmhurst schools, central office curriculum administrators then approved (or rejected) the thematic- and literature-based units so developed, meaning that the principals' and teachers' time might have been completely wasted. Further, district administrators visited their schools on a regular basis to evaluate principals on how they spent their time as instructional leaders. Inevitably, classroom supervision time and curriculum content decisions became key arenas of struggle. These two principals particularly resented their lack of control over curriculum decisions that affected their schools and the control that other institutional authorities—specifically central office administrators—had over their work lives in general. The following quotations exemplify these sentiments; although gathered in separate interviews, the quotations are integrated to show the similarity in the principals' perspectives:

Grant:  I don't like how the central office is managing curriculum decisions for the school now.

Draper:  Central office has become much more heavy handed in terms of curriculum these days.

RY:  Why?

*Grant:* They have control over what kinds of curriculum we use, or at least they try to. It used to be that as a principal you worked with your teachers like a family and developed the best curriculum and instructional strategies for your kids. All these mandates from central office have really tied our hands in some ways. We get the parent complaints, too.

*Draper:* There are curriculum meetings with teacher representatives across the district, and they are supposed to gather input at the schools and take it back to the district, but it really seems as though they do what they want anyway.... I actually started out supporting the direction of the district language arts curriculum, but it's really hard to support or complain at this point.

*RY:* If you feel like the central office is tying your hands as a curriculum leader in your school, why stay in this district?

*Grant:* My family is in this community, and my kids are at the age where it's hard to move them.... That's the main thing. I have to go along to support my home family, and as much as possible, my family at school.

*Draper:* I've been in this district for almost 20 years. It would really mess up my retirement to move at this point. Besides, many of my friends in other districts say that they are experiencing the same kind of thing.

*Grant:* The evaluation visits from central office have really almost become a dictatorship. They're supposed to develop you as "curriculum leaders," but it's almost like Gestapo coming in to make sure you're doing what *they* think is needed. If you just do what they want, even if it's pro forma, they don't come as often.

*Draper:* I'm really getting tired of [the curriculum director] coming around with the clipboard to make sure you're observing the teachers to do what they want for the curriculum. If you just fill out the [supervision] sheets and say what they want to hear...don't think...then you're usually left alone a little more.

*RY:* So who wins if you just do what you are told and go through the motions?

*Draper:* Well, central office wins really.... Or I'll win when I retire and come back and get on the school board.

*Grant:* Well, central office wins in the end...although I think the parent complaints are getting louder. This, too, shall pass.

*Draper:* I'd like to see central office get back to treating principals like the curriculum leaders of their schools. I'll give you an example: textbook selection. So the district office has a textbook selection committee for language arts. We all have to commit to the literature-based philosophy and go through training and then teachers can order sets of books to use for shared reading and guided reading and writing workshops. Well, that's all good, but if some of our kids really need more structured approaches, we have to get special permission and then the district will select the materials based on their approved list of "research" studies. If I'm supposed to be the leader and work with my teachers as leaders, and we best know our kids, why not give us an account and let us select program materials, and then, sure, go ahead and hold us accountable, but let us make decisions that best meet the needs of our kids.

Grant:    Why should we have to play "Mother, may I" for every little curriculum decision now? It's getting to the point where I can't order any materials for the school without writing a dissertation about how it meets the guidelines for whole language.

Generally speaking, Grant and Draper adhere to the district curriculum policies, and anyone walking into their schools would gain an impression of order in language arts curriculum and instruction. They challenge central office dominance over curriculum decisions only indirectly, such as by skipping a faculty meeting, having sidebar conversations in the district parking lot, and applying for grants to buy their own materials. They attend workshops that are not recommended by the central office because they support either a more bottom-up model of instructional decision making or decontextualized reading materials that emphasize phonics. It is significant that the principals generally *leave* the district grounds whenever they challenge central office authority, rather than confronting issues directly within the confines of the institution itself. Although the principals may talk quietly of insurrection in the district office parking lot, they inevitably (and resentfully) follow the central office procedures when they return to their buildings. There is, therefore, ongoing grumbling about district curriculum authority and how it plays out regarding control over their curriculum leadership time and decisions, but there are few direct challenges that could result in the kind of conflict that would break down district order and challenge the status quo.

## Shifts in Curriculum Meanings, Processes, and Leadership Identities

Principals Draper and Grant also described noticeable shifts in their attitude toward curriculum and what it means between their initial interviews in 2002 and their interviews in 2004. As we will see, both curriculum leaders came to support the value of externally developed instructional models and textbook programs. Both principals had been considered experts in grass-roots curriculum development (albeit using rational-technical models), meaning that they led their teachers in making decisions about content, instructional processes, and materials. As the district curriculum authorities exerted more control

over curriculum decisions, Draper and Grant became increasingly supportive of teacher reliance on textbooks and externally developed research-based
models. In fact, between 2002 and 2005, both principals developed strong
reputations as experts on these externally developed models. By 2005, neither supported pedagogical expertise derived from experience and personal
study, which previous studies endorsed as the standard of excellence (e.g.,
Hallinger, 1984; Hallinger & Murphy, 1985; Purkey & Smith, 1983). Instead,
they argued that any creativity in curriculum decision making must be coupled with accountability for performance on standardized tests. It is significant that the literature does not document such an approach to curriculum
leadership. Both principals also tended to connect their movement toward a
back-to-basics, utilitarian approach to curriculum with growing pressures for
accountability on standardized tests as well as the worsening economy (e.g.,
factory closings) and demographic changes (e.g., increased numbers of minority, working-class, and high-poverty populations) in their communities. Such
sentiments are echoed and reinforced by many teachers in both schools.

*Draper:*    I picked up a sample of the new SRA materials with decodable texts.
It's the only thing I can do for some of the struggling readers now.
Of course, I did not tell the district office, but I told the teachers we
have to keep it quiet.

*RY:*    What do you mean?

*Draper:*    Well, in my school, whole language is not working for a lot of kids,
despite what the curriculum office says about research. It's fine for
teachers to be creative and come up with lessons with these literature books. Some of our teachers are really innovative and effective
at creating their own units, but you have to have some consistency
in the skills for the children who come to school with limited readi-
ness, that kind of consistency today requires a textbook.

*Grant:*    Teachers are not prepared to deliver on the kind of curriculum initiatives for whole language that central office promotes. They come
right out of college and they don't have that kind of preparation to
figure out what kids need to learn. They have potential, but that
development takes a while. In the meantime, we are going to have
to get some kind of textbook to teach the skills, or this is all going
to fall apart.

*RY:*    What do you mean fall apart? Give me an example.

*Draper:*    There's a lot more pressure now to perform on standardized tests. The
state is coming out with standards and benchmarks. Our students
are going to be in trouble on some of these tests if we don't do something. I believe curriculum must be aligned with state standards, and
my role is to create accountability for that curriculum, but instruction is where the teachers' creativity comes into play.

*Grant:*    [Over] the last 2 years, our reading scores have stabilized and even gone down on some of the test sections, especially the items that deal with phonics. Well, no wonder! We're not teaching it any more, thanks to the wisdom of central office. At least now that we have state standards, we have consistency and defined skills in the curriculum. I think our teachers can be very creative with teaching the standards.

*Debbie (third-grade teacher in Grant's school):* I just sort of jumped into the whole-language movement in the mid-1990s, really enjoying picking trade books and teaching the whole class. I have to say that I've noticed a decline in students' abilities to use conventions appropriately, especially in grammar and spelling. We're dealing with a different, high-poverty and working-class population now, and they need more direct instruction.

*RY:*    What do you mean?

*Debbie:*    Well, in our school, we used to have a lot of stay-at-home moms that volunteered in school and really worked with their kids at home. Now a lot more kids come from homes with both parents working and they're busy, or a lot of parents have lost jobs when the factories closed, and they're trying to make ends meet by working two jobs. So the homework support and reading at home is just not happening. Kids need a lot more support when they come to school, and I don't think whole language is really meeting all their needs. Our test scores have gone down a bit, too.

*RY:*    What are you doing in the school to accommodate the changing needs of these kids?

*Marian (fifth-grade teacher in Draper's school):* Fighting mostly. Michael gets that we need to be more direct in our skills instruction, but his hands have been tied at central office. He really supports us to use whatever direct instruction strategies we need to use so that children learn the skills. I think we'll get more support now with all the talk about accountability at the state and federal levels.

*Bob (fifth-grade teacher in Draper's school):* I don't think we're really making the instructional adjustments kids need. I've talked to Margaret, and she agrees in many ways, but so far central office has not made any firm decisions about adding more direct skills instruction. Eventually, the curriculum office will have to change and implement more direct instruction on the tested skills.

I do not mean to imply here that all principals of schools facing similar pressures—changing demographics, declining test scores, and frustrations over district control of curriculum and textbook selection—necessarily become advocates for back-to-basics and neoconservative ideologies. It is noteworthy, however, that of the principals I interviewed during the process of selecting candidates for the in-depth ethnographies, many of those in districts characterized by centralized curriculum decisions and growing populations of children from working-class families and children living in poverty expressed a desire to implement more structured instructional programs and were far less aligned with progressive curriculum trends and internally developed curriculum processes. At the same time, a close analysis of interview data reveals opportunities to develop progressive educational approaches along with basic skills approaches. For example, if Grant and Draper supported progressive curriculum processes, such as cooperative learning or critical thinking that required teacher decision making and student initiative, they immediately coupled their support with concerns for basic skills and voiced equal support for creative programs that emphasized basic skills instruction.

*Grant:*   I have always believed that teachers are closest to instruction, and they should be involved in identifying curriculum goals for their students. As a principal, you want teachers to be creative with the curriculum, but now in this accountability age, teachers really need to be aware of the standards and make sure that they are teaching the standards and subskills.

*Draper:*   I think students benefit from teachers who are capable of making decisions about what students need to learn and have the knowledge to adjust their instruction to meet the needs of their children. We have so many new teachers now that don't really have the background to do that. They really need to follow the structure of a teachers' manual for a few years to get to know the skills that children need at each grade level.

By 2005, the principals and teachers rarely discussed the possibility of developing curricula and instructional processes organically, from the bottom up-practices that had been the norm in their schools for more than a decade from the 1990s to 2002. With regard to supervision, both principals struggled with growing district restrictions on their time and evaluation procedures. Both principals were adept at gaining control over their supervision time and placed a high priority on this. In particular, they filled out evaluation forms with language they believed would satisfy district curriculum authorities, in order to reduce the direct district oversight of their schools. These actions did not mean that they supported district curriculum initiatives, but rather were a means of passive resistance though which they attempted to reclaim their autonomy.

Another one of my studies of principals in challenging school contexts (Ylimaki, 2007), as well as studies by Henderson and Kesson (1999), and others who have examined curriculum leadership in the United Sates, suggest a similar pattern. Among curriculum leaders in challenging, high-poverty schools particularly, there is a tendency simultaneously to affirm and to reject teacher innovation. Henderson and Gornik (2006) refer to this as "curriculum work conflict"; I refer to it as a "lived tension." The point is that curriculum leaders do not entirely reject teacher-developed programs and progressive education while at the same time acting as if they do. In my previously studied urban schools (Ylimaki, 2007), for example, principals actively affirm the knowledge and the ideas of teachers. Their criticism of teachers centers on beliefs that the teachers are not trying hard enough, are not meeting professional obligations to keep up-to-date on instructional practices, or do not connect with their students. Yet the principals also have a strong sense that teachers possess expertise that is worthwhile for curriculum development and instruction. Despite this, the urban schools had a high rate of teacher transfer requests and little time was made available for teachers to work on curriculum development outside the parameters of district or school mandates. Thus, Margaret Draper and Michael Grant exhibit a contradictory set of curriculum meanings and curriculum-related priorities. They simultaneously embrace and reject teacher creativity and standardized curriculum standards.

Draper and Grant both appear to be moving toward a contradictory relationship with curriculum and policy mandates—fueled, as I will argue in chapter 4, by the school culture itself. Although the principals valued teacher innovation and curriculum decision making, there are other lived aspects of emerging "new professional" curriculum identity that may explain these tensions and contradictions. The principals typically attended and even participated in district-sponsored professional development workshops. Further, tensions and resentment over district curriculum mandates were not evident in my observations of district meetings. The principals might skip meetings here and there, but for the most part, they complied with district expectations for professional development and curriculum implementation in their schools. Similarly, Elmhurst and Greenway meetings and administrator-led professional development sessions were exceptionally well run. During numerous observations of district and school curriculum meetings over 4 years, I saw only one meeting at each school generate "out of control" conflict. The district curriculum administrator often had a strong preference about the outcome of any curriculum effort so discussions that cleared the way for dissent were quickly discouraged or even halted. Overall, breakdowns in district order were rare and tempered.

On the other hand, the two principals' voluntary attendance at professional development workshops and conferences declined by 63% from 1995 to 2000, then surged to 100% at the beginning of the 21st century, most likely in response to accountability pressures. Two additional trends make these changes in professional development very interesting. First, the topics of these most recent workshops included how to close achievement gaps, data-driven

**Table 2.1** Changes in Workshop Topics and Sponsors for Greenway and Elmhurst Schools

|  | 2002 | 2006 |
|---|---|---|
| **Sponsors** | Local Reading Council | Houghton-Mifflin |
|  | Local English Council | Scholastic |
|  | Local University Professors | Wright Group – Phonemic Awareness Workshops |
|  | Australian Literacy Expert Andrea Butler | Differentiated Instruction Consultant |
|  | Teachers College Literacy Project | Understanding by Design consultant |
|  | The Wright Group Balanced Literacy (holistic language publishing company) | Solution Tree (Professional Learning Community Workshops) |

decision making, spelling, phonics, differentiated instruction, and other aspects previously associated with traditional views of literacy acquisition and curriculum format. Second, as Table 2.1 suggests, the workshop sponsors changed drastically from a preponderance of professional organizations (e.g., reading associations) to textbook companies (i.e., Harcourt Brace and Houghton Mifflin), state education departments, and other companies recently founded to meet the needs of accountability. In other words, the content of workshops attended shifted dramatically from holistic literacy perspectives to packaged programs and student outcomes. Indeed, the language of "passing tests" and "meeting standards" increased and eventually dominated teacher and principal discourse in these schools, as the following excerpts suggest.

During the same period of professional development, Principals Draper and Grant gradually came to understand curriculum in more utilitarian terms: that the purpose of schooling was to provide students with 21st century learning skills that would yield good jobs and productive lives. Therefore, schools had to provide students with standards-based instruction and track their progress toward high performance on these standards and related assessments. Draper and Grant may have resented district institutional authority over curriculum decisions, but state and federal testing requirements—and related, externally developed curriculum and instructional models—provided them with a renewed curriculum leadership identity as professional experts in "scientifically based research programs," data analysis procedures, curriculum mapping, and related instructional models that would improve student achievement. They portrayed these identities as counter to the laissez-faire (progressive) curriculum leaders and practices that let students use class status and language proficiency as excuses for poor academic performance. In this process, they both turned their primary attention away from social problems in the neighborhoods surrounding the schools and focused instead on improving academic student performance within their schools.

### Greenway School Faculty Meeting, October 2003

*Draper:*  We need to cross-reference the list of skills taught in the reading series with the state standards and tested skills.

She then distributes an Excel spreadsheet with columns for recording the state standards next to student performance on state test items and objectives for each month of the school year. The entire faculty is almost completely engaged in looking down at the tables or writing in notebooks. A closer examination reveals that some teachers are surreptitiously grading papers; a few are actively engaged in looking at the standards and test-item analysis. Others are looking at the standards and test charts completed the previous year to see if there is a way to update data from the previous year rather than starting anew.

### Pinehurst School Faculty Meeting, September 2003

*Grant:*  Okay. We need to look at how our benchmark assessments align to our standards and curriculum maps. We'll look at them again at our next faculty meeting. [Some chatter]

*Sam (Teacher) to Marianne (Teacher):*  I think we can mostly use the alignment pages from the Houghton Mifflin series.

*Marianne:*  I think it's important to really look at what we're teaching in relation to the benchmarks. If we use the process the way it was intended, we can use the information to move the children forward. [Some louder chatter]

*Grant:*  Work on these charts between now and the next faculty meeting and we'll look at what you have at that point.

The important point to note in these examples is that, except for one teacher at Elmhurst School, the faculty members do not directly challenge either the form or purpose of the curriculum alignment activities. They respond passively, doing what they are told but not doing any conscious curriculum development at all. They fill out their curriculum maps and standards alignment forms (sometimes happily), but are not engaged in the curriculum decision-making process. Yet, this teacher disengagement coexists with a more positive valuation of curriculum development—namely, mapping and state-local standards alignment—than previous studies have revealed among teacher leaders. The more positive valuation plays itself out, however, largely in terms of growing teacher and principal acceptance of external curriculum models and the importance of state testing data.

### Greenway School Faculty Meeting, December 2005

*Draper:*  We have our benchmark assessments to look at first this afternoon. What do you notice?

*Evan (Teacher):* I notice that the children who have difficulty with the comprehension questions dealing with story structure, plot, characters, they also have difficulty with the writing portion of the exam.

*Sarah (Teacher):* Let's look at how students do with the story-writing benchmarks.

*Draper:* Good idea. We also need to make sure our benchmark assessments align with the text structure questions on the state tests. [Two teachers volunteer to examine and revise the benchmarks and bring the results back to the next faculty meeting.]

This extract does not have the flavor of instructional leadership studies (e.g., Hallinger & Murphy, 1985) that suggest principals and teachers work together to develop and align curriculum goals and instructional strategies, using their own pedagogical experience and expertise; indeed, even the most ardent supporters of the district's whole-language mandate recognize the value of state accountability policies that validate data-based decision-making and curriculum and assessment alignment procedures. As Principal Grant put it when discussing state testing policies, "I guess we need the tests to make sure that we are teaching the standards in all the classrooms." The significant point here is that principals and teachers at Elmhurst and Greenway schools express increasing affirmation of state standards and testing requirements for curriculum content and test data analysis. As we shall see in chapter 4, the principals act on this affirmation by communicating policy requirements and cultivating a professional school culture based upon productivity and efficiency.

### Elmhurst School Faculty Meeting, December 2004

*Grant:* Our first agenda item is test item analysis. Get out your test results from the spring testing. What trends do you notice on the reading section?

*Susan:* Most of our kids seem to be doing well on the literal comprehension sections, but the critical analysis across text sections shows less proficiency.

*Grant:* Why do we think that is?

*Bob:* Well, we have focused more on getting the basic skills back in order, and now we need to have students focus more on reading critically across tests.

*Grant:* Yes, we have a clear trend there.

*Beth:* McGraw-Hill is sponsoring a workshop on critical thinking skills for passing the state tests. It might be good for some of us to attend that. We would also get a look at their new series, and the language arts is up for adoption next year.

*Grant:*    I agree. I think we can free up funds for three of you and me to attend that workshop. Please let me know if you are interested by the end of the week.

*Greenway School Faculty Meeting, November 2004*

*Draper:*    We need to look at the highlighted items on the data from bench-mark assessments [designed to align with state tests the previous year]. Where are our kids doing well, getting 3s and 4s? [On these state tests, a 3 designates proficiency and 4, exceeding proficiency. Students must attain a level 3 in order to "pass."]

*Seth:*    Writing has gone up. We have more students getting 3s.

*Daryl:*    Yes, but spelling is also going down. If you look at the highlights in the reading section, I see a correlation. Students who scored 1s or 2s seem to have difficulty with spelling and phonics.

*Draper:*    Yes, spelling and reading pronunciation are parallel skills.

*Seth:*    There's a spelling workshop coming up. I think it's part of the Four Blocks Series.

*Draper:*    I like that idea because it builds on our writing strength. What does everyone else think? [Murmurs of agreement]

*Draper:*    I will look into bringing someone in to look at our Four Blocks model to help us incorporate more spelling within our writing and reading blocks. Does anyone know of a good presenter? We need to get this scheduled in the next 2 months so that we have time to get it underway before spring testing. In the meantime, work on incorporating the spelling and phonics skills into your cur-riculum maps and have them ready to present at our next faculty meeting.

There are two points to note here. First, the vast majority of teachers and these two principals, at least in their language, are not focusing on curriculum issues that extend much beyond "efficiently passing the tests." It is "getting a 3" that counts, not the necessity of critical thinking for democratic education, lifelong growth, or the joy of learning advocated by Dewey (1916/2008) and others (e.g., Page, 2006). Second, both Draper and Grant have resumed more managerial curriculum leadership identities in the alignment of state test stan-dards with curriculum *formats* in their schools, setting up staff development opportunities and making related instructional decisions with their teach-ers. At the same time, the discourses around these instructional decisions are all related to "passing tests" and "improving student outcomes." While this discourse is also evident in the more critical principals' schools featured in chapter 3, it is more salient between Grant and Draper. Indeed, as we will see in the next chapter, some principals with more progressive curriculum philosophies critique current curriculum and accountability trends because standardization and an overreliance on numerical data may be incompatible with democratic education.

The desire that students "pass the tests" is further apparent in the use of curriculum maps, a popular way to align state content standards and assessments with classroom instruction. Many teachers promote the use of curriculum maps to guide their instruction, but they do not employ curriculum maps to promote depth of learning or pride in building from knowledge to evaluation levels of understanding. Further, both of these are the articulated purposes of curriculum maps in many schools as well as currently popular literature (e.g., Hayes-Jacobs, 2005). As the following examples make clear, for some teachers, curriculum maps are simply a chore to be completed, and many teachers reuse maps from the previous year or actually copy from one other regularly in order to hand in something to the principal and central office.

### Greenway School Examples

*Social Studies Teacher Meeting, September 28, 2003*
Seth:      Did you get your curriculum maps done?
Mary:      No, I just have not had time. It's been a busy 2 weeks.
[Several other teachers also say they did not finish their curriculum maps.]

*Faculty Meeting, November 17, 2003*
Draper:    Did everyone get a chance to finish the curriculum mapping exercise this month?
Marian (*low voice to Jim, sitting next to her*):  I got a start, but it's not anywhere near accurate.
Jim:       I'm still working on last month's. I'm behind. I copied [teacher's] maps from last year. I'll work on it, but there's just no time.
Daryl:     Would you mind sharing when you're done? I'll share next month.

*Math Teacher Meeting, January 17, 2004*
Several teachers are gathered around a round table in the back of a classroom, passing curriculum maps back and forth so that they can copy from one another. Technically, teachers are supposed to document what is taught in each classroom on a monthly basis and then work together to compare how much time is spent on each standard and benchmark, then make necessary adjustments in order to cover all standards.

*Faculty Meeting, March 2004*
Draper:    Our goal for this meeting is to look across our curriculum maps and identify the standards that are not getting sufficient attention.
Seth (*to another teacher*):  Well, this would be a good idea if we all did it right and didn't copy off of each other's maps so often.

*Memo to Central Office Curriculum Director, May 2004*

We are pleased with our progress in curriculum mapping. The teachers worked hard to document their teaching objectives as they actually play out month-to-month in each classroom and for each academic area. Our goal for the summer is to refine these maps in light of our performance on the state tests and local benchmarks.

### Elmhurst School Examples

*School Leadership Team Meeting, September 28, 2003*

Beth: This map looks just like the ones [another teacher] turned in last year this time.

Roxanne: I know. I thought the same Terabithia unit turned up last year.

Grant: We're also missing maps from sixth grade, too. I'll put out a memo saying we need new curriculum maps by the end of the next week.

*Faculty Meeting, October 17, 2003*

Grant: Did everyone get a chance to finish the curriculum mapping? We really need them now.

[Affirmative murmurs can be heard throughout the room.]

*Bob (low voice to the teacher sitting next to him):* I had to copy mine from last year. I just didn't have time, but I think it's important to document our teaching month-to-month. I get that; I just don't have time to do it right.

Beth: I'm on the leadership council, and honestly, most of the maps looked a lot like last year's maps or the teachers' edition.

*Mary Lou (low voice):* I used the teachers' manual. [An examination of the curriculum maps reveals that the vast majority of teachers copied either from each other or the textbooks.]

*Faculty Meeting, March 2004*

Grant: We need to take a look at each other's curriculum maps and the standards and test items to see what we are covering in depth and what goals might not be getting adequate attention.

Beth: It seems like we've seen this before. We always have to hurry so much, it's hard to really think about what we're teaching.

Rebecca: I know. I think we all know our goals, but we have to do this.

Maria: Shhhh. We need these curriculum maps to cover the standards.

[Teachers look down at their curriculum maps and quietly make notes in the margins.]

*Memo to Central Office Curriculum Director, May 2004*
> Attached please find our curriculum maps for the 2003–04 school year. We also attach documentation for our cross-grade-level analysis of curriculum maps as well as our analysis of curriculum alignment with state standards. During the summer, we will use our analysis to revise our curriculum goals for the 2004–05 academic year.

In both of these schools, many teachers, like their principals a few years earlier, are not engaged in the processes of curriculum development learning. They are involved in the *form* of curriculum writing (mapping), but are not doing substantive work that addresses curriculum content and instructional decision making. These teachers may be writing curriculum, but they are not engaged in its substance at all. This dynamic holds true for both schools, although it is more pronounced at Michael Grant's school. Those teachers tend to write less curriculum, and instead to copy from other teachers, from teachers' editions, or from the Internet.

An adherence to curriculum form but not substance is apparent in classroom observations as well. Students are orderly, but there is little evidence of student engagement in learning. Like their teachers and principals, they copy each other's homework and dutifully sit through the classes, but they can rarely articulate what the class discussion is about beyond reading aloud from the "objective" or "big idea" statement posted on the board.

### Greenway School Examples

*Social Studies Class, November 12, 2004*   In Mary's class, students alternated with Mary in reading from the textbook. Everyone in the class was quiet and appeared to follow instructions. Yet, when Beth called on students to read aloud, they were often unable to pick up at the appropriate place.

*Reading/Language Arts Class, January 21, 2004*   Teacher Marianne passes out a story map with typical fiction components (i.e., setting, characters, plot) to accompany the selection in the basal reading series. She says, "You need to complete this story map by the end of the class period. If you do not complete it here, you can take it home for homework and we'll check it tomorrow. [Some students throughout the room chatter and giggle.]

*Math Class, March 8, 2004*   The topic of class is solving long division problems, and for a major portion of the period, the teacher (Bob) demonstrates how to estimate and then solve various math problems. Throughout the entire time, almost all students are looking at the demonstrations, but only a few students raise their hands and voluntarily respond to the teacher's questions about the division process.

### Elmhurst School Examples

*Social Studies Class, April 2004*   In Beth's class, students all read from the same book and complete a text structure frame. Everyone in the class is quiet and engaged in completing the structural frame. Yet when Beth calls on students to correct the frame, many have difficulty reading from the appropriate part of the frame.

*Reading/Language Arts Class, February 2004*   Seth (the teacher) passes out a story map with typical fiction components (i.e., setting, characters, plot) to accompany the selection in the basal reading series. Students sit quietly and work on the story map. Seth says, "You need to take this home, if necessary, and do your best work because it's going in your portfolio." [Students sit quietly; initially they start working on their story frames, but over time most begin talking to each other quietly, doodling, or texting each other.]

*Science Class, March 2004*   The topic is magnetism, and a major portion of the time is spent on the teacher Marianne's demonstration of magnetic phenomena. The class observes the demonstration, then students work in pairs to complete experiments with the magnets, testing what is and is not magnetic. Students record their observations on a worksheet, but only a few students raise their hands and voluntarily respond to the teacher's questions.

Notable here is that students do not directly challenge either the pace or direction of the classroom activities; they do not respond to each other or to the teacher in active discussions. Rather, they respond passively, doing what they are told. They are compliant but not engaged. Like their teachers do with their curriculum mapping tasks, these students turn in homework, but they do not really do their homework. Yet although both teachers and students are disengaged, many teachers and the principal express support for current trends that align the curriculum with standards because these activities have "raised standards and increased students' critical thinking skills and writing skills." Of course, I did not observe the schools prior to the standards movement to have any firm data on what happened before 2002. At the same time, the teacher and students' disengagement with curriculum is of concern, particularly when the curriculum maps indicate a prevalence of "critical thinking skills" and "teaching for deep understandings."

The picture that emerges here is that teachers and students are engaged with the form rather than the substance of curriculum content and instruction. Curriculum content is defined by state standards, and curriculum formats are geared toward consistent implementation of the standards. Yet, importantly, the state report card documents improved academic achievement for both schools. In this light, the emerging contradictions in curriculum directions and development processes can be clarified somewhat. These two principals experience a resurgence in curriculum leadership authority as they direct and model curriculum form (mapping and data analysis) activities that they believe will lead to improvements in student outcomes. In this respect, the principals engage in more curriculum development work than some previous investigations have found. On the other hand, the principals—along with the teachers—engage in the *form* of curriculum writing rather than the substance of curriculum content decisions, just as students engage in the form but not the practice of learning. Teachers copy curriculum maps, and along with their principals, elaborate the language of "passing tests," making "data-driven decisions," and ensuring that students "master basic skills." Teachers and students frequently express a lack of engagement with curriculum content and instruction just as both principals did when the district central office mandated practices outside of their time and interests. Yet, the principals and teachers assert the value of current curriculum mapping and accountability practices, often referring to dialogues regarding these topics as "professional learning communities."

The Elmhurst and Greenway school principals' emerging contradictory relationship with curriculum work is further complicated by concerns about racial and class-based achievement gaps. In particular, Dr. Draper said, "I push minority students and students living in poverty to achieve on the tests because they need these scores to get access to higher education. I know there's more than tests, and some of the work is not engaging or relevant for these students, but it has to be done." The contradictory attitude toward institutional authority and curriculum meanings described here characterizes all four principals in the ethnographic study and many others examined during the selection process, but it is most pronounced in the principals with emerging new professional curriculum leadership identities.

## Ignoring Cultural and Social Issues

A third element of conservative curriculum leadership formation is that both principals turn their gaze away from cultural issues and challenges surrounding the school to focus almost exclusively on data-driven academic improvements. Few previous investigations of curriculum leadership have examined how leaders approach issues of cultural diversity, class, gender relationships, and racism within and beyond the school. Rather, traditional curriculum leadership studies write about "building a professional learning culture" within the school as essential in order for curriculum innovation and instructional change to occur in classrooms (e.g., Jackson, 2000; Marks & Printy, 2003). Principals Grant and Draper actively build their school cultures around teachers' professional development and student learning; however, both also emphasize norms and values related to accountability and data-based decision-making processes.

Within both schools, there is also evidence that the principals have adopted a no-nonsense approach to student achievement, in which parent involvement and community partnerships are viewed as a luxury. In other words, both principals state that they need to focus their attention and resources on what they can control within the school in order to make a difference in children's lives. Consider, for example, the following arguments that were offered like mantras during monthly faculty meetings:

*Grant:* If we get parents in to help and we get community organizations to support our school, that's a bonus. We cannot depend on our tough, high-poverty, high-crime communities with all their problems. We have to provide students with everything necessary to raise student achievement. [Peer district principal] spends all kinds of time on working with parents in their homes so that they have books and strategies to read with their kids. That's all fine, but we need to put our resources into school and classroom libraries where we know our kids will actually read the books.

*Draper:* Our population is changing. We have some parents, often middle class, that come in and volunteer in our schools and show up for parent meetings. These parents work with their kids at home, but they are a minority. I'm not saying parents don't care, but they have so much to worry about trying to put food on the table and other things, we can't count on them anymore. We have to do everything in the school. If I focus my attention outside, I'm not putting attention where it needs to be: inside the school and creating a school culture in which everyone is focused on student achievement.

Both the Treelane and Hillside neighborhoods are segregated, with Whites living in different areas from African Americans and Latino/as. While the neighborhoods surrounding both schools saw growing cultural diversity and racial tensions, these issues were rarely discussed inside the school. In fact, principal and teacher comments in numerous meetings and personal interviews echoed the sentiment that "schools must turn away from problems like poverty and racial tension out there" and instead "focus on what schools can control." Most African American and Latino/a students at Greenway live in a large public housing project, located near an area of abandoned businesses and a closed factory; these project residents are living in poverty, and many have received public assistance for more than one generation.

Further, both districts require teachers to live in the district where they teach, but they need not live in the school attendance area. In fact, the vast majority of teachers at both schools are White, and only 5% of Elmhurst teachers and 3% of Greenway teachers live in the school attendance area. Yet, the human resources department confirms that many teachers were born in Treelane and Hillside or communities with similar demographics. As the following examples illustrate, significant underlying racial bias plays itself out in discussions of the uneven use of resources to close various achievement gaps, and to some extent, in comments about the lack of parent involvement and community engagement.

### *Elmhurst School Examples*

*Faculty Meeting, November 2003*

Bob: Our Latino and ELL populations are not making the same level of growth as our Anglo students.

Beth: Well, you know, we have so many students living in [a low-income, largely Latino area,] and these kids just don't get the support at home. The parents rarely come to conferences.

Grant: That's why I keep saying we have to provide kids with homework help in after-school programs. If the parents help, that's great. We can't fix what is out there. We have to focus on what we can change, and that's student achievement within the school.

### Faculty Meeting, March 2004

Grant: Let's look at trends in our data as disaggregated by race and SES.

Kim: Our parent room has really helped kids who need support with their homework.

Mary: How many of our volunteers are actually parents?

Kim: Very few. Last month I think we only had one parent; but does that really matter as long as our kids get help with their academics?

[Several murmurs of "no, that doesn't matter" can be heard throughout the room.]

Bob: Our kids can get help with their academics, but what about working with families and family literacy?

Grant: That's a great idea, but I think what we're saying overall is that we can try to reach out to families, but if they don't respond, we have to work where we can make a difference—in the school.

### *Greenway School Examples*

*Faculty Meeting, October 2003*

Draper: What trends do you notice when we disaggregate our state test scores?

Seth: I don't think it's as much racial difference. If we look at the scores of children at the lowest SES levels, they struggle with literacy.

*Daryl:*   They are already so far behind by third grade. We need to do more with early intervention, but you know we have to do it in the school because I know a lot of these parents just don't have the resources and time to work with their kids on a regular basis.

*Marian (quietly to another teacher):* What about making a difference in kids' whole lives? Have we come to a point where we ignore our responsibility for making communities better places to live?

*Margaret (does not seem to hear Marian):* I would like volunteers to work on a 21st century grant to expand our before- and after-school programs.

**Faculty Meeting, November 2005**

*Draper:*   Our 21st century grant is due for renewal. Dan, can you give us a report on progress from our current program?

*Dan:*   Well, we have great numbers on increased uses by African American students.

*Seth:*   It seems like we have more students but fewer parents.

*Dan:*   That's right, but as we've said many times, children need the help. If we can get parents in, especially African American parents from lower SES, that's great. We know we can't depend on that or fix all those social problems. We have to fix what we can, and that's student achievement.

Racial tension exists within the school, and it reflects racial tension within the surrounding community and within society as a whole. This is the perception of students as well as the perception of a few teachers during individual interviews. For example, several Greenway teachers admitted to feeling that ELL populations (primarily Latino/a) were using too much of the school resources, making slow academic progress, and diminishing the school's academic reputation and standing on the state report card. (This is not to say that teachers did not express concerns about slow academic progress of White students, but these concerns were not a central focus of the principals.) In contrast, on several occasions, both principals minimized problems with race, maintaining that "we teach all children equally, regardless of race, class, or gender." I never heard any direct comments about racial tension from the principals; however, on several occasions Dr. Draper and Mr. Grant and many teachers otherwise expressed empathy for children of color who were living in poverty and underachieving in math and literacy, and made more frequent assertions that they needed standards and tests to ensure high achievement levels for all students. The principals and many teachers also exhibited considerable fear and concern about second language learners and children from particular neighborhood areas lowering the overall school test scores, while at the same time asserting a protective stance that these children had a right to academic achievement. The following conversations in both schools illustrate these points.

### Elmhurst School Leadership Team Meeting, April 2005

*Grant:*    Our demographics have changed substantially in the last 5 to 10 years. At our school, we firmly believe that all children can and will learn, regardless of race, ethnicity, or socioeconomic status. And we really need to make sure *they* achieve well because we cannot exclude children in the state testing process.

*Beth:*    We really need to shift our instruction to provide more differentiation, because we have so many more kids from [a poor, high-minority] area that have moved into our school boundaries. *They* just do not come to school as well prepared and it's almost impossible to get the parents to come into the building.

*Bob:*    Our school is really changing. We've been working on differentiated instruction, but it's hard to watch the school go from excelling to high-performing and now we're likely to hit performing. It's hard to see the school status decline and not be able to keep up with the academics fast enough.

### Greenway School Leadership Team Meeting, April 2005

*Jim:*    We've really been working, but we know our third grade is not going to do as well on the state tests this year.

*Daryl:*    Well, that's not unexpected. Four years ago, we knew we had a class of kindergarten children that came in so much less prepared than in previous years. That's the same year [low-income housing] opened in our attendance area.

*Marian:*    That's also the year we had that large influx of Arab immigrants, along with a large number of other ELL populations. You can only make so much progress so fast, and we focus on that. We believe all children can learn, and we have high expectations for all kids, but this population can be a challenge.

In both cases, I noted that new professional curriculum leadership forms in part in reaction to constructed perceptions of "other" (progressive) curriculum leaders and in constructed relationships with popular curriculum model trainers and participants, experiences that clearly affected these principals' curriculum development processes and leadership roles. Consider, for example, the following conversation:

*Draper:*    Some of the principals and teachers are still into holistic practices... everything.... They write about whatever they want, and spelling is not always corrected. I'm sure the kids enjoy these kinds of instructional practices because they are not accountable for demonstrating that they know the skills, but I think as an instructional leader, you have to make sure that teachers are covering the standards and children are learning at high levels. I work with a lot of educators and nationally recognized trainers in UBD [Understanding by Design, a popular curriculum model], curriculum mapping, skillful teaching, and data-based decision making, and they really have inspired me to be deliberate about connecting curriculum skills and assessments, and holding teachers and kids accountable for performance.

RY: Do you mean that these other instructional leaders do not hold teachers and students accountable for the standards?

Draper: Not in the same way that we do at our school. Teachers are required to write the big ideas and standards and benchmarks on the board each day so the students know what they are supposed to learn. Any time I come into the classrooms, the students can tell me what they are learning. Some of the more whole language type leaders that I know, like [principal] at Elmhurst School, say that the teachers provide instruction based on where the children are.... That's fine, but how do you know that they are learning or not learning until they take the state tests and it's too late? You have to use data in this environment. These principals used to be cutting-edge, but I don't think they've really kept up with the latest research on reading and math that I've had to learn in the ASCD workshops that I now run for teachers in the area.

Grant: I don't like how some of the other principals are still into whole language and more laissez-faire approaches to instruction. They promote practices like critical thinking, and I agree with that, but some of these principals do not make it clear that they need to teach the standards. That's why we use a textbook series now. Some of our veteran teachers, and all of our new teachers, need that structure.

RY: Do you think that these more holistically oriented principals encourage teachers to teach whatever they want?

Grant: Well, they talk about how they incorporate the standards, but their test scores are not as good as ours, so I don't think they can be giving the standards the necessary attention. I don't think these principals and teachers have really kept up with the latest scientific research behind the standards. As I've taken on more and more training with UBD, I've really had to study more current research. I've become involved with these models, even doing training with these leaders. I think we've really started to make a positive difference in the state, and it's gratifying to think you can have influence even beyond your school.

**PROBLEM-POSING CASE:**
## Challenging Ideals of Curriculum Consistency

Elmhurst School Principal Grant and many veteran teachers have come to believe in the ideal of curriculum consistency. To this end, the principal announced a writing contest with prizes for the class that best exemplified the tested criteria on the writing component of the state assessment. Students from two different classrooms performed equally well. Mr. Grant and teachers from a neighboring school who served as judges independently rated the students equally on each element of the rubric. The judges unanimously agreed to declare a tie and award the prize, a trip to visit an author, to both classes.

Yet Mr. Grant wondered if the educational experience leading up to the writing product was the same in both classes. He knew that Mary Zanders, one teacher, was very detail oriented. She spent countless hours working with the students individually, and ultimately helped each student write an outline and key paragraphs for their papers. Mary Zanders gave everyone a copy of paragraph frames for their papers along with careful instructions, demonstrations, and editing at each stage of the process.

In the other class, teacher Tanner approached the writing contest quite differently. As soon as he heard about the contest, he engaged his students in prewriting strategies and reflective processes in order to select their topic. The class all knew that Kevin was expert at graphic organizers, so the class nominated him to model that prewriting strategy. Other students volunteered to share resources, peer conferencing, revision, and editing strategies. Before long, peer writing groups formed in which students read each other's work and made constructive comments for improvement. Kevin helped all students individually develop graphic organizers for their papers so that they could produce the best essays possible. Students shared their drafts and final essays with the whole class. The whole class celebrated when their classroom won the contest.

These two teachers created and taught a different curriculum for the same project.

1. How would you characterize these teachers' curriculum philosophies?
2. Was one of these learning experiences better than the other? Why?
3. What is the role of curriculum leadership in this project?

## Summary

In sum, these principals talk at length about what they perceive as a lack of standards-based instruction in relatively holistic or progressive schools. They differentiate themselves from such curriculum leaders and the practices within those schools in various ways. Both principals and teachers in these schools are portrayed as laissez-faire and less concerned with standards-based instruction and academic outcomes. It is also significant that the conservative curriculum leaders describe themselves as having higher levels of curricular and pedagogical expertise in comparison to their holistically oriented peers. Certainly, the principals' new curriculum leadership identities as "data-driven" leaders and experts in externally developed curriculum models are connected to an increase in academic performance in their schools. These principals use academic performance measures as a basis to denigrate principals who support holistic philosophies and practices and to portray themselves as better curriculum leaders in the current political era of high-stakes accountability. Thus, curriculum leadership processes that support holistic or progressive instruction are seen as inappropriate in an accountability era—in contrast to their own processes. Their own standards-based, data-driven curriculum leadership is, in contrast, seen as positive. In the final analysis, conservative principals elaborate their curriculum leadership identity in contrast to the ideologically constructed curriculum leadership identity of more progressive (laissez-faire) principals and teachers. Thereby, these principals set themselves up as professional curriculum leaders "other than" and "better than" their progressive peers in both groups. Furthermore, they identify with their peers who have promoted standards-led instruction and high academic performance for all students.

Certain elements of the emerging "new professional" curriculum leadership identity and roles at Greenway and Elmhurst schools, as described in this chapter, are similar to features noted in previous investigations (e.g. Hallinger, 1984; Murphy & Hallinger, 1985). In another sense, however, Draper and Grant are distinctive as curriculum leaders, in that they exhibit a more contradictory relationship with curriculum meanings, institutional authority (district and state), and struggling learners of color and low SES. In this sense, they are moving toward a new professional management ideology with regard to curriculum standards and expectations for high student academic performance. This rhetorical is congruent with the neoconservative agendas described by Apple (2004). (For a sample course activity in challenging this rhetorical, professional identity, see appendix B.) In the next chapter, I will explore two curriculum leaders who take another path: they experience an epiphany of critique about current policies and trends and, in the process, lay the groundwork for new progressive educational and social movements in their schools and surrounding communities.

# 3
# Critical Curriculum Leadership

In chapter 2, I discussed the emerging new professional curriculum leadership identities of two principals who (somewhat unconsciously) helped foster back-to-basics curriculum agendas and practices in their schools. This chapter introduces an emerging critical identity of curriculum leadership in two other schools. Grounded in the work of the Frankfurt School and curriculum studies (e.g., Apple 2004; Bourdieu, 2001; and Freire, 1993), critical curriculum leaders are ultimately concerned with dialectical relationships among suffering and oppression, curriculum content, cultural politics, and social inequities. They believe in the democratic imperative of curriculum leadership and work toward agency, growth, the empowerment of children and adults in their communities, while grounding curriculum decisions in curriculum theory and learning/achievement. Finally, critical leaders rely on public intellectual skills and discourse as an analytical tool aimed at social change. The unity of curriculum theory and leadership practice and the use of discourse as an analytical tool rather than a means of control, are also important to critical curriculum leaders.

In this chapter and the next three chapters, I examine the elements of critical curriculum leadership identity that emerged as important in the ethnography. In other words, I do not specifically intend to make a counterpoint argument with the conservative, new professional curriculum leaders of the previous chapter any more than I would make a comparison of women leaders to White male leaders (as the dominant norm). That would perhaps allow or even encourage the conservative discourse to be the dominant norm by asking the question, "How do critically oriented curriculum leaders compare with new professional, conservative ones?" Instead, I focus on elements that may or may not strictly parallel those for professional curriculum leaders who have become aligned with conservative ideologies.

## Critical Moments of Critique

To begin, the two principals featured in this chapter (Ms. Juidici and Mr. Hughes) experienced what Weis (1990) referred to as "critical moments of critique" about how the conservative restoration had (re) shaped common sense about the aims of "official" school curricula and the need for consistency, standardization, even teacher deskilling and poor quality intervention programs for struggling learners. These moments of critique evolved and occurred in waves throughout the study as the principals worked through and with conflicted feelings about current policies and politics. Like their peers in the previous chapter and in their own districts, these principals found themselves, at various times, using standards and testing policies to leverage improvements. On these occasions, the principals also reminded themselves and other study participants that they needed to question underlying motivations and actions that resulted from policy acceptance, particularly when the effects of these actions were potentially unjust for children of color, second language learners, and children living in poverty. In so doing, these principals purposely circulated counter (resistance) arguments about the compelling need for curricula that foster informed and compassionate democratic citizens. These two principals worked with and through others to develop teachers and children as public intellectuals who were academically strong and passionate about making their communities better places to live. Giroux (2001) uses Bourdieu's concept of public intellectuals when he argues for a political/activist role for educators.

Before I flesh out the principals' critiques of current policies and politics, I describe the principals in their school and community settings. Each descriptive section ends with a set of interviews conducted over a 3½-year period shadowing the principals/curriculum leaders as they worked with policy and developed curricula around the knowledge, dispositions, and skills necessary for children to become informed and compassionate citizens. As these leaders are presented in this chapter and in subsequent chapters of the book, the principals' perceptions of state curriculum policies and leadership guidelines are examined, in addition to the (counter or resistant) circulating discourses of democracy and social justice as well as "agencies" that are set in motion as principals navigate the politics of curriculum decisions in their schools and communities. In so doing, the political tactics and analytical tools that helped them fight back against these conservative discourses and processes are highlighted. Although this approach does not provide a generalizable model, it does give us a good sense of how curriculum (and the leadership thereof) can be reconceptualized in critical ways.

### Case 3: Angela Juidici, First-Ring Suburban Elementary Principal

Angela Juidici is a White principal of Babcock Elementary, a small suburban school in Treelane, a community in the Northeastern United States. Babcock Elementary is situated in an open field area just off a major intersection in Treelane. The building is well kept but modest, with one main entrance at the corner of one wall. Ninety-five percent of students are White, from low SES families, and qualify for free or reduced lunch. The remaining 5% include Native American,

African American, and Asian students. When I first visited the school, about a month into the 2002 school year, the halls were bright, clean, and painted with the school mission prominently displayed. Several other announcements were displayed on a bulletin board outside the principal's office. Most parents would be considered working-class in terms of income by virtue of their employment in a nearby automobile parts factory and a major steel factory. The average class size is 20 students, and many Babcock classrooms have parent volunteers on a daily basis. There are limited services for students with disabilities. Babcock Elementary opens the building to early childhood services as well as community activities before and after school.

On the first school visit, there was little evidence of student writing or any other authentic curriculum projects in the hall; most hallway displays featured commercially produced posters and seasonal art. Classroom instruction featured prepackaged programs in literacy and math, and I noted frequent didactic teaching and students sitting in rows completing individual assignments. In 2006, although there was more variation in teaching strategies, the hallways were generally filled with samples of student involvement in community service, such as writing to local newspapers and state representatives, and other authentic tasks. Many interviewees pointed to Principal Juidici's leadership as the catalyst for changes in the school curriculum philosophy and commitment to critical pedagogy.

The Babcock student population has been stable at about 380 students in pre-K-5 with 70% of students receiving free or reduced lunch. Per-pupil spending is far less than the state average, and although parents and community members are generally supportive of education, the school board meeting minutes contain frequent refusals to purchase new, expensive programs with a rationale that "it was good enough for us, so it's good enough for our kids." Student literacy and math scores are consistently above average on state tests; however, by 2005, Ms. Juidici clearly recognized that lower SES students were "trapped in test preparation and remedial courses that limited their opportunities and aspirations for careers beyond blue collar jobs in their hometowns and surrounding areas."

Ms. Juidici has a master's degree and 20 years of experience as a principal. She also has a strong background in reading through her training in special education. Juidici began her career as a first-grade teacher for 5 years and then became a special education teacher at Babcock for 7 years. Since the beginning of her tenure as principal at Babcock Elementary, Ms. Juidici has lived in the Treelane community with her husband and two children. While she attended a nationally recognized principal certification and master's degree program, the leadership literature used in the program primarily reflected structural functionalist perspectives on curriculum leadership through courses dealing with "instructional leadership and managing the instructional program" and "instructional supervision." Ms. Juidici also has a background in community organizing techniques from her undergraduate days at an adjacent state university.

In one of her early interviews (fall 2002), Ms. Juidici described her school and surrounding community as conservative, meaning that people here have strong family values, they go to church on Sunday, they work hard, and they save their money to buy things for their hunting camps and deer season. They don't like lots of changes and fancy programs in their schools because there is some suspicion of new educational practices that may take their children away from the community.

Several teacher interviewees likewise described the Babcock Elementary curriculum as "safe" and "structured," meaning that expectations and norms for students and adults were clear and consistent. Many interviewees stated that this consistency arose from a recent history of strife, angst, and conflict over "the whole language wars." For several years in the late '80s and early 1990s, many teachers were committed to a "whole language" movement that favored the use of authentic texts (real literature rather than textbooks) and authentic assessments, such as holistic scores of writing and running records/ observations of reading progress. Whole language was not implemented consistently, and many teachers just went through the motions of literature-based instruction and authentic instruction without deep understandings of the reading and writing process. The resulting declines in test scores led to outcries from more conservative elements of the community and the school board. Ms. Juidici was not on staff at Babcock at the time; however, this history of literacy curriculum struggles was still evident and fresh in many teachers' memories. In fact, the superintendent stated, "We hired Juidici to bring more traditional literacy practices back to the school." In 2003, the potential "consistency" of standards-based instruction was attractive to these teachers (and to Ms. Juidici) who wanted to "avoid a second round of reading wars at all costs." With this contentious literacy curriculum history in mind, Ms. Juidici agreed to serve on a reading standards committee at the state level.

Juidici:   I really was not very upset about the more traditional, skills-based curriculum practices supported in No Child Left Behind and state "instructional leadership" standards. Most of my career, I taught special education with basic skills kind of instruction. I became concerned about how these powerful interest groups like NRC [National Reading Council] and the state were becoming more involved in school curriculum decisions and really narrowing the curriculum to more academic subjects. That's the least of my concerns now, though.

RY:       What else are you concerned about more now?

Juidici:   For many more affluent students, a narrow curriculum might be okay because they get the enriching experiences at home. I can see who is going to be left behind. It's the poor kids…. It's not even subtle anymore. Several legislators and leaders of professional groups that testified at the hearings actually said that these tests are designed to sort kids in various ways in order to promote excellence. In my school, that means kids get sorted by SES and tracked into classes that limit their opportunities to aspire toward careers outside the hometown area. I knew I had to take some leadership and help teachers and community members be more informed about the politics so that they would not make a knee-jerk reaction and want traditional-skills based instruction like in the whole language wars.

### Case 4: Ken Hughes, Urban K-8 School Principal

Ken Hughes is the White male principal of Pinehurst School, which is located in an urban area. Pinehurst is a red brick two-story K-8 building on the corner of Low Street and Main Street, an address that signaled a declining neighborhood for more than 2 decades prior to the beginning of Mr. Hughes's tenure. Pinehurst's student population is 90% African American, with 90% of students eligible for free or reduced lunch. These school demographics held consistent throughout the 4 years of the study. The front yard of the building has been landscaped by community members and students with numerous flowers, shrubs, and green space, a far cry from the beer bottles and drug paraphernalia that confronted Mr. Hughes on his first day 11 years ago. The average class size is 24 students, but teams of English teachers, literacy coaches or special education teachers, and content area teachers often teach classes together. Pinehurst's hallways are bright and sunny with plants on the windowsills and student work displayed outside of classrooms and surrounding the office. The school has an active community organization room where students join with community members and parents in outreach activities, such as the community garden and sustainability project. That organization's work is documented outside of that room and throughout the school.

Mr. Hughes is in his late '30s with expertise in math and technology and 7 years of teaching experience. Mr. Hughes has his master's degree and is currently enrolled in a doctoral program at a local research institution. He is in his 11th year as principal at Pinehurst School. He began his career as a guidance counselor and then earned his master's degree in a program grounded in sociological theories and social justice aims along with a minor in educational leadership that included certification classes. Mr. Hughes describes himself as "an urban person" because he has always chosen to live in urban areas. His house is about five blocks of an easy walking distance to the school. However, in the same conversation, he quickly admitted, "I might be five blocks from the school, but my house is still a far cry from some of my students' homes with absentee landlords and drug dealers on the corner. Still, I walk past these parts of the neighborhood everyday just like my kids."

During Mr. Hughes's 7-year tenure as principal of Pinehurst (prior to the beginning of the study), the school was designated among the state's most improved with a steady increase in state test scores and with city real estate and crime statistics indicating a revitalization of the surrounding neighborhood. As a result, many (more affluent) parents wanted to send their children to Pinehurst, an act that required home residence in the school boundaries. The improvement in state assessments is also notable in light of increasing numbers of Pinehurst students for whom English is a foreign language.

At the beginning of the study, Mr. Hughes was working with his staff to apply for charter school status. His expertise in technology and the improvements in Pinehurst's test scores garnered him a state commissioner's invitation to sit on a state curriculum advisory committee. As with Ms. Juidici, Mr. Hughes's experience on the state committee along with work at his school helped him develop a critical awareness of how the circulating discourse of the conservative restoration had (re)shaped curriculum conversations in his school. As we shall see in chapter 6, Mr. Hughes's curriculum leadership challenges were highly affected by a particular challenge. In 2004, the district hired a new superintendent with a top-down leadership style and distinct (conservative) ideas about curriculum and testing.

*Hughes:*  At first, I really just felt like I was supposed to give feedback on the policies and how they would affect my school and students. As time went on, I realized I was starting to buy into this really logical argument that schools did not have standards and needed tests to be accountable.

*RY:*  What did you notice that made you realize you were buying into the argument?

*Hughes:*  I would find myself nodding when these different professional groups or interest groups testified at the state meetings about how schools needed to do more, that teachers had been doing too much experimentation with instruction, and that we needed to use test data to make decisions and differentiate instruction. Then I would find myself coming back to school and saying the same kinds of things. At administrator meetings, I would hear the same kind of ideas, and teachers were all talking about standards and tests at faculty meetings. The interesting thing is that it's not like they were afraid of the tests, but they accepted the argument that they needed to be more accountable. It's like these messages were making sense to me and everyone around me.

## Summary

The data suggest that critical curriculum leadership identity is moving in a more emancipatory direction than conservative curriculum leadership identities, meanings, and roles. Specifically, the critical curriculum leaders exhibit what might be called a moment of critique or epiphany about the dominance of conservative discourses. This nascent critique, however, is not at the moment reflective of a collective struggle around issues of curriculum and politics. Rather, these two principals/curriculum leaders tend to pose individualistic, private solutions to their felt notions that the growing neoliberal aims and forms of curriculum (i.e., standardized programs, instructional pacing guides, differentiated instruction) will not work for them and are, at the same time, somewhat unjust.

I will suggest here that critical curriculum leadership identity emerges in relation to that of constructed understandings about the dominance and detrimental social effects of broader cultural political shifts toward back-to-basics curriculum, marketization, and accountability pressures. As in the last chapter, it is this relational aspect of identity formation that will be highlighted. It is significant that critical curriculum leadership identity is not formed in relation to that of constructed ("other") conservative leaders as is the case for Draper and Grant. I will pursue this point later in this chapter.

Previous studies suggest that principals elaborate a curriculum leadership role that primarily emphasizes supervision practices, a role that has only been accentuated with increased accountability pressures (e.g., Blasé & Blasé, 1999; Murphy, 1984; Murphy & Hallinger, 1985). Academics (reading, math, science, social studies) assume a central position for principals' priorities and affective, democratic student development takes a secondary position. As some recent studies have shown, contemporary curriculum leaders elaborate what Glickman has called a directive "super-vision" role for principals in which they monitor the consistent use of "evidence-based" or standardized programs, constructing a curriculum leadership identity that serves, ultimately, to direct teachers' and students' efforts toward improvements in academic outcomes (Glickman, Gordon, & Ross-Gordon, 2009). Studies of supervision have been important in terms of our understanding of the way in which instructional improvements work upon and through curriculum leadership of principals (e.g., Hallinger, 2004; Marks & Printy, 2003; Tucker & Heinecke, 2003). Tucker and Heinecke (2003) also noted that principals spent increased proportions of time on supervision and evaluation (e.g., walk throughs to ensure consistent instruction of standards), instructional management and motivational techniques, such as "pep rallies" designed to encourage students to attend school and do their best on tests. By defining supervision as primary, today's principals/curriculum leaders reinforce what can be called accountability-driven leadership under which principals examine teachers' practices in relation to an objective set of guidelines, looking, for example, at consistent implementation of "official knowledge" in state standards or curriculum pacing guides. The reality, of course, is that generations of teachers have adapted curricula in a myriad of ways that are not always evident in supervision events.

## Critical Moments of Critique about Conservative Discourses

### Curriculum

The most striking point about critical curriculum leadership at Babcock and Pinehurst schools is that there is, unlike the case in numerous previous studies and in the conservative principal examples, little evidence of a professional, managerial identity or test-driven discourses. These curriculum leaders have, in fact, made democratic leadership and purposes of schooling primary rather than secondary efforts. Both of these principals desire to develop children as democratic citizens and community advocates, and they are clear that they intend to do so in order to extend the purpose of curriculum academic achievement beyond accountability and test scores. It is important to note that, like Draper and Grant in the previous chapter, Juidici and Hughes faced strong community pressures and commonsensical arguments to incorporate more emphasis on "basic facts" and improved test scores.

Over time, Juidici and Hughes recognized shifts in teacher and parent beliefs, gradually reflecting neoconservative and neoliberal ideologies as well as new public management identities. It is worth noting that this critique is reminiscent of the voices of female working-class students at Freeway High (Weis, 1990) and African American parents in Pedroni's (2007) study of school choice programs. In order to interrupt these circulating conservative discourses, Juidici and Hughes consciously decided to launch neoprogressive educational and social movements in their schools and communities. Further, both Juidici and Hughes stressed helping children develop as compassionate and thoughtful citizens. They talked about data and accountability, but their purposes differed considerably from the more conservative perspectives of Principals Draper and Grant in the previous chapter.

It is also noteworthy that only one principal's interview narrative mentioned "standards supervisor" first when talking critically about who they were and what they did as curriculum leaders. Both principals critically examined these commonly held district assumptions about teacher supervision, asking themselves and other educators "to what degree their own administrative practices contribute to the development of truth, freedom, or justice, and offered options for change" (Foster, 1986, p. 255). Only when I inquired about their role in policy implementation did Juidici and Hughes mention supervision at all. This is in striking contrast to the conservative curriculum leaders from the last chapter where the implementation of an envisioned "standards dominated" curriculum was foremost on their minds. This reflects an interesting contrast: new professional curriculum leaders envision supervision of standards-led instruction and data-driven curriculum decisions first whereas critical curriculum leaders focus first on the public sphere with the goal of developing children with democratic dispositions and public advocacy skills to make their communities better places to live. Consider, for example, the following quotes from Juidici (Babcock School Principal) and Hughes (Pinehurst School Principal) as they become aware of changes in commonsense perspectives about the need for official knowledge (standards) and back-to-basics curriculum and views of children as "future workers in a global society." The following headlines from the community newspaper exemplify this point:

"Schools fail basic skill tests."
"Over one-third of our schools designated as 'needing improvement' by the state."
"Children failing in global comparisons."

Although gathered in separate interviews, the principals' quotations are integrated to show the similarity in their perspectives:

*Juidici (September 2004):* I am getting more and more concerned about the changes in beliefs about the purposes of curriculum, the knowledge all children must possess, and how we think about children. I'd like to say it's the parents or community members. I have to admit that the biggest wake-up call for me was when I started nodding my head at a community forum where they had a speaker going on about how our children were just not as knowledgeable about facts as they used to be.

*Hughes (September 2004):* When the state first came out with standards in 2000, I thought it made a lot of sense to get more consistency in the schools. I think there's a point to that still, but I have been getting concerned about how that's all we talk about now are what the state thinks we should teach to all children regardless of their cultural knowledge and strengths of our communities. More than that, the standards that count are the tested standards. Period. Achievement matters, of course, but all of these shifts in our thinking about whose knowledge counts is also problematic. We are, after all, a democratic society.

*RY:* What did you notice? Can you give an example?

*Juidici:* I remember there was a time when our test results came back from the state, and I looked at the vocabulary section and saw that the score had declined over the past couple years. Something flashed in my mind about how schools were not teaching vocabulary skills as well as they used to. I don't even know where it came from, but I got really concerned and started asking teachers how they were teaching vocabulary.

For awhile, we were very focused on vocabulary. We started emphasizing our word walls more and checking the walls against basic vocabulary lists. Every time I went in the classrooms, I would ask kids to recite the words on the word wall. Children were organized in groups according to proficiencies in vocabulary. They were all getting better at reciting these lists and even spelling the words, but there were clear differences in the words and experiences that children from lower SES families experienced. So I had to start asking, "How can we teach vocabulary skills well and yet not privilege children from more affluent backgrounds?" This kind of organization is not getting some kids access to resources that they do not have at home. And while it's tempting to buy into the argument that we can't worry about the inequitable home life of kids and just get the high achievement scores, but that's just general talk. It doesn't acknowledge the ways that school and classroom structures have a place in these inequities.

Hughes: We had a parent who was on a board for this foundation that was into sort of a no-nonsense philosophy about schools that schools had to just deal with teaching kids to the highest possible level so that they could get good jobs in a global economy. She would go on and on at parent meetings about how the school needed to just deal with teaching the kids so parent groups should help with buying books and things like that…. In other words, don't get kids involved in community service unless they were in gifted and talented classes or something. Her mantra was "schools are for teaching the academics. If the kids excel and there's time at the end of the year, they can get involved in community projects. That stuff is a bonus."

In 2003, it was one parent talking this no-nonsense approach and then the next year (September 2004), it was some teachers talking the same way about the importance of the tests and how we needed to teach the standards and not worry about any extras. I would even find myself nodding as they were talking because it's just common sense. That logic has potential side effects, though, and I started to see them in the schools.

Hughes: Our population of students comes to school with strong forms of cultural knowledge that can be tapped. This knowledge is not "official" or recognized on standards and standardized tests. In fact, even in open-ended sections, the children are punished if they do not parrot certain language on the test rubric.

*Juidici:*    We have to realize that you can test specific sources of knowledge, but we have to start asking "whose sources of knowledge?" We may not be able to answer the question definitively or change the tests, but we must ask the question.

These questions and comments do not negate, however, the fact that in September of 2004, Juidici and Hughes also exhibited a somewhat contradictory relationship with broader cultural political shifts and commonsensical arguments about curriculum and school knowledge. They, too, accepted and rejected official knowledge of state standards and conservative cultural politics at one and the same time, although not nearly to the same degree that Principals Draper and Grant (from the previous chapter) did during that same timeframe. Juidici and Hughes also required teachers to incorporate more basic skills into their literacy and math lessons. Beginning around the spring of 2004, both Juidici and Hughes gradually changed their priorities and beliefs about curriculum in their schools.

### February, 2004—Babcock and Pinehurst Schools

*RY:*       How did you become aware of your concerns?

*Juidici:*   I think the eye opener for me was when we started grouping our children for reading instruction and they had to pass vocabulary tests in order to move on to the next reading level. We bought books where the teachers would use a script to teach vocabulary words. It had to be so boring to teach. That spring, our vocabulary scores went way up. So it's time to celebrate, right? But at the same time, I noticed that children were not enjoying their reading class and they were not as excited about writing their own stories as they used to be. So we have good vocabulary skills but what for? Because we had to disaggregate data and were concerned about our lower SES families, special education kids, and ELL students, they got the least amount of actual reading and writing time. The least got the least.

*Hughes:*   I noticed that we were so focused on the data that we were forgetting who our kids are and who we'd like to see them become as thoughtful, intellectual, and compassionate people. I was looking at our faculty meeting minutes at the end of the year, and I realized all we talked about was numbers and academic achievement and curriculum maps. These aren't bad things, but why were we not talking about kids in deeper ways? I also realized that all we were talking about at the district administrator meetings was student achievement and curriculum maps and other alignment procedures. There was no time left to talk about the arts, humanities, multiculturalism, kindness, and service learning in our communities. Aren't these things basic?

### Perceptions of Students

Principals Juidici and Hughes were critical of the notion that children should be considered future workers for a global economy, advocated for broader conceptualizations of children, and purposely cultivated students' agency to make decisions about their lives. Although the principals and many teachers in both schools were preparing students for state assessments, they nevertheless challenged the circulating discourses about children as workers for a new economy. Neither principal placed test results before democratic education and community service. The principals' perceptions are reflected in the following teacher quotes as well.

*Principals' Interviews (Spring 2005)*
RY:      Talk about your goals for state assessments.
*Juidici:*   We have goals from the state and the district based on what we need to do to make adequate yearly progress. Obviously, we have to monitor student achievement data as part of policy requirements. I have really found that if we engage children in their learning in a broad sense, students will do well in basic skills and state standards. At the same time, if we help children develop the academic and human skills they need to be thoughtful and compassionate democratic citizens, they will do just fine on the tests.
*Hughes:*   I've come to believe that we have to set goals with students as capable and thoughtful people with the intellectual skills and inner human qualities to make their communities better places to live. This goes beyond setting goals for the tests. We have to keep track of the data to make adequate yearly progress, and really the standards are so broad, it's fine to focus on them. If we educate and empower children to make thoughtful and informed decisions, they will do well academically.

*Teachers' Interviews (Spring 2005)*
RY:      What are your goals for the state tests?
*Chris Marlan (Babcock second-grade teacher):* Oh, sure. We've made a conscious choice as a school, though, that we want children to care about each other and to actively work on making their communities better places to live.
*Vicky Barker (Pinehurst eighth-grade teacher):* We do not ignore the tests by any means, but if you teach children to engage in learning in

authentic and intellectual ways, even the youngest children will see the relevance of the academics. They have to use basic spelling and phonics skills when they write.

RY: Do you see children competing for high-paying jobs out of their neighborhoods?

Chris Marlan: I think it's up to children what they want to do, but as caring people and citizens, it's up to them to make their communities better places. Whether they want to stay in the community or get a job anywhere in the world, that's up to them.

Vicky Barker: I think they can, but that's not the main goal. The main goal is to help children be thoughtful and compassionate people wherever they live. That means they do not abandon their neighborhoods but do what they can to help the people within them now and in the future.

RY: Do you want to leave this community and get a good job somewhere else?

Sam (sixth-grade Babcock student): I want to have a job that I enjoy, but right now I live here. My teacher says that I am a citizen of this community and I need to enjoy it and make it as nice as I can for me and everyone else.

Susan (sixth-grade Pinehurst student): Eight years from now, I'll graduate and go to college. I have a purpose for my life, but that doesn't mean I abandon my responsibilities here. I am part of this community and I need to use my skills and talents wherever I am.

In the next section, I explore the analytical tools and strategies that Principals Juidici and Hughes used to foster critical awareness of conservative discourses related to education generally and curriculum in particular.

### New Analytical Tools for Critical Curriculum Leaders

Juidici and Hughes's awareness of fundamental shifts in beliefs, thoughts, and feelings about curriculum prompted them to seek alternative analytical tools beyond those learned in their educational administration training. In order to interrupt these political shifts, the principals employed discourse as an analytical tool to challenge unjust curriculum and testing practices in their settings. Specifically, they used discourse to change conservative disciplinary practices of curriculum leadership, awaken school and community participants to discourse effects. They also identified and exploited fault lines among interest groups in conservative alliances and corresponding policy texts. Because discourse enabled the principals to challenge the ways in which school and community members were "living out" the deep assumptions of the conservative restoration, it will be discussed first and in the greatest depth.

*Discourse*

The primary analytical tool these principals used to expose and analyze current curriculum politics and policies was discourse. Scholars who write about the concept of discourse frequently draw on Foucault's studies of social institutions and the ways in which power circulates and shapes relationships within them. Foucault's notion of discourse (1977) suggests something more than oral and textual linguistic and communication practices often discussed in educational leadership literature (e.g., Bolman & Deal, 2008; Hoy & Miskel, 2007). According to Foucault (1977), discourses also include forms of knowledge constituted in social practices (like curriculum leadership and teaching) and organizational practices (like curriculum decision-making structures). As Clegg (1989) explained, "Because [discourses] are knowledge constituted, not just in texts, but in definite institutional and organizational practices, they are 'discursive practices': knowledge reproduced through practices made possible by the framing assumptions of that knowledge" (p. 54). Further, because discourses shape practices and practices produce discourses, some authors use the term *discourse-practice* to denote this circular dynamic (Anderson, 2009). Discourse-practices determine what counts as true or important or legitimate in a particular place and time. For example, becoming a good curriculum leader today means analyzing test data effectively, designing curriculum around standards, and improving individual student and school performance on standardized tests. "Good" principals seek to master these "legitimate" discourse-practices of curriculum leadership and promote them in their schools and districts, which, in turn, reinforce these particular kinds of activities with teachers. These activities begin and continually reinforce the circular nature of discourse.

The importance of certain good curriculum or "instructional" leadership skills (e.g., classroom supervision and curriculum development) at any particular time and place is a battle over competing discourses (Anderson, 2009). Anderson (2009) also reminds us that the battle over competing educational administration discourses is seldom carried out overtly and most often is not part of the consciousness of those who are shaped by it. Further, educational leadership training programs seldom interrupt this approach to professional socialization of administrators and unintentionally help to reproduce discourse practices, including "good curriculum leadership," through internship programs, applicant screening processes, and assessments. In addition, current curriculum leaders who have been socialized and prepared this way continue to reproduce and mentor new leaders and teachers: "This reinforcement through discourse continues throughout an administrator's career" (Anderson, 2009, p. 106).

In light of broader cultural political shifts toward a conservative restoration (Apple, 1996, 2004) and the educational leadership reinforcement of mainstream discourse, it is not surprising that state policy guidelines for "instructional" leadership draw on previous (traditional) discourses that have shaped the field of educational administration in general and "instructional"/ curriculum leadership in particular. Both Juidici and Hughes served on state committees charged with development of "instructional" leadership guidelines, an activity that brought them face-to-face with the meaning and practice of curriculum leadership in their own settings as well as on a broader (state) scale. At a largely intuitive level, the three principals analyzed discourse practices related to curriculum leadership, standards, and testing policy guidelines. Discourse provided the principals with a manner of questioning basic assumptions, regardless of their personal beliefs or philosophies about the topic. In other words, discourse as an analytical tool enabled individuals (curriculum leaders) to reveal the hidden motivations and meanings behind a statement in a policy guideline as well as curriculum language and practices circulating in the schools. By making assumptions explicit, school members viewed the "problem" (local experiences with policy mandates) from a "higher" vantage point and gain a comprehensive view of the policy implications and themselves in relation to that "problem."

In particular, discourse tools provided the principals with ways to name and describe the many and varied political influences that act on and are expressed in particular curriculum situations. These principals made a critical decision to examine discourse (language, texts, actions) related to current policies in open public forums because it exposed the political nature of curriculum decisions and cast leadership in an authentic light not often seen in their schools' recent practices. Examples in each case are provided below.

*Ms. Juidici*   In public meetings, Ms. Juidici enlarged policy language on charts or overhead projectors and then publicly questioned what each leadership characteristic really meant to children's lives. This involved making leadership explicit and open, which meant that she was able to interrupt circulating discursive practices of curriculum leadership. In the fall of 2003—before she became concerned about policy texts and practices—Ms. Juidici initiated vertical (cross-grade level) and horizontal (grade level) teacher teams to write curriculum maps to reflect actual instruction, levels of understanding, and tested standards. It is important to note that curriculum mapping and alignment practices are promoted and reinforced by state policy guidelines, ISLLC standards, active professional organizations, and her own district. Ms. Juidici became concerned when she noted a concurrent increase in use of decontextualized skills-based pedagogy and test preparation materials and a decrease in student engagement during her classroom observations.

Consider the following student comments (in the spring of 2004) that illustrate Ms. Juidici's and several other school members' concerns about the decontextualized learning experiences and curriculum differentiation. In

2003, Michael, a White male fifth-grader, punctuated these concerns when he stated, "I used to like reading class but now we read the same short stories over and over and we have to work on these extra books before and after school." Angela, a White female, gave a similar perspective from the vantage point of advanced classes: "I like reading class, but that's only because I read well. I'd hate to be in the low group with all these worksheets and after school sessions." Table 3.1 presents an excerpt from a fifth-grade curriculum map developed in 2003 with questions about underlying assumptions generated in 2005 (italic).

Ms. Juidici also made curriculum policies, language, and practices ("texts") explicit and open to challenge at her school and in her community. Specifically, at public school and community meetings, she displayed policy documents that supported conservative curriculum ideologies and the kind of curriculum mapping and benchmark assessments that had become a source of concern to her. Her displaying of these texts provides a model of how to challenge underlying assumptions of curriculum and leadership language and related practices, particularly those that reinforce behavioralist curriculum perspectives, such as teacher pacing guides and academic intervention services that separate children by test performance level (1s, far below standard; 4s, far above standard). In her words,

> I take policy documents into meetings now and we read and reread them, highlighting where there are hidden assumptions regardless of our own beliefs. We ask questions about what the assumptions are, who benefits, and who loses if we take the policy text at face value. So our plans now include some provision to make sure those who could lose are considered; they're at the table; we get feedback early and plan for how to overcome any deficits that could be in a strict policy reading and enactment. I never would have done that a few years ago.

Juidici also showed academic intervention service materials for students who scored at the lowest performance level and materials for students at the highest level. As one parent put it, "The smart get smarter." For example, one of the teacher's materials for the intervention class devoted 85% of instructional time to phonics and phonemic awareness and the enrichment class materials spent 85% of time on comprehension, critical thinking, writing, and literature response activities. The latter activities have been linked to continued improvements in literacy performance (Allington, 2002).

Teacher narratives from Babcock Elementary also indicated shifts in teachers' understandings about the underlying implications of curriculum mapping, differentiated instruction, and pullout academic intervention services. Lily, a third grade teacher, provided telling narratives over time:

**Table 3.1** Social Studies Curriculum Map – Fifth Grade

| Standards: The focus of this important first unit is on concepts and enduring understandings rather than on specific standards | Standards CG1a, CG1b, CG4, E3a Map Skills: Continued Mastery Information Skills: Continued Mastery / Application | Standards H1, Gb, E2c Map Skills: Continued Mastery Information Skills: Continued Mastery | Standards H1, H2, CG1 |
|---|---|---|---|
| Unit 1 Focus *Where do these unit objectives come from? Students' lives? Community needs? Textbooks? Tests?* Concepts Used in 5th-Grade Social Studies | Unit 2 Focus Effective Citizenship Introduction *Who defines effective? What makes someone a U.S. citizen?* | Unit 3 Focus Civil War: A Nation Divided | Unit 4 Focus Reconstruction: The Nation Reunited |
| In this unit students will be introduced to the unit connecting themes of: <br>• Beliefs & Ideals – *Whose beliefs? Whose ideals?* <br>• Conflict & Change – *How can we teach conflict that contributes to radical social change?* <br>• Individuals, Groups, Institutions – *Think about these in terms of race and gender (how beliefs about race and gender are socially constructed and institutionalized in the U.S.)* <br>• Location, Movement, Migration <br>• Production, Distribution, Consumption <br>• Scarcity <br>• Technological Innovation | Beliefs & Ideals <br>• Responsibilities of a Citizen <br>• Freedom in Bill of Rights – *What does freedom mean in a democratic society?* <br>• E pluribus unum <br><br>Production, Distribution, & Consumption <br>• Competition, Markets & Price – Impact on Behaviors <br>• *Housing as a commodity* | Beliefs & Ideals – *Who named these people as essential?* <br>• *Uncle Tom's Cabin,* John Brown's Raid & Their Effects <br>• Slavery & States' Rights <br><br>Conflict & Change *If conflict means revolution, war, violence, eradication…* <br><br>Individuals, Groups, Institutions Location Gettysburg *Locate stops on the Underground Railroad in the local community* | Beliefs & Ideals <br>• 13th, 14th, 15th Amendments <br>• Constitutional Due Process <br><br>Conflict & Change <br>• Effects of War on North & South <br>• Reconstruction <br>• Jim Crow <br>• Amendment Process <br><br>Individuals, Groups, Institutions Freedman's Bureau <br><br>Productivity, Distribution & Consumption Effects on S. Economy |

*Lily (September 2003):* I really did not understand why we were reading and questioning these policy documents. What were we supposed to do with that? Ms. Juidici showed us how we need to realize that there are assumptions and meanings behind the language and processes.

*Lily (September 2006):* I can see now how important it is for us to have these policy reading skills. We need to be able to be thoughtful educators in a political sense as well as a curricular sense and then we can show our students how to do the same.

Many other Babcock Elementary teachers talked at length about how they learned to question their own underlying assumptions about the popular terms in current policies, such as *tested skills* and *disaggregated data*. Fifth-grade teacher Stephen's narrative is also instructive in this point when he states,

*Stephen (September, 2004):* I don't really see why we have to spend so much time looking for the political layers in policies and our textbooks. What can we do about it anyway?

*Stephen (September, 2006):* I find myself echoing Ms. Juidici when I read descriptions of instructional programs and research when I'm working on my own. She's got me thinking things like, "What do they mean by differentiated instruction? Whose knowledge is the norm to differentiate? What are we differentiating and to whom?"

Very importantly, Ms. Juidici demonstrated courage as well as intuitive discourse skills that helped her lay bare subtler notion of texts beyond written policy documents and guidelines. She talked at length about how she put herself at great risk by challenging these guidelines in the community. In her words,

> The memories of how whole language stirred up the conservative elements of the community with all their concerns about how we were not teaching basic facts and skills made it risky to make curriculum concerns public. It has taken a tremendous amount of modeling and patience and also developing community leaders and teachers as informed citizens with the knowledge and skills to challenge and question what we are doing in the name of test scores and other benchmarks of curriculum leadership.

Ms. Juidici also led the creation of student-centered curriculum discussion groups that included students, teachers, and members of parent organizations. Curriculum discussion groups will be presented in detail in the next chapter, but briefly, these groups were developed from a list of student interests and community organization needs generated in the fall. These interests formed part of the broad themes and projects pursued throughout the school year and related readings were included in teacher reading groups and presentations at local organizations. Thus, student interests and community needs became the basis for a curriculum developed around authentic community service projects. Because the parent and community organizations had a stake in curriculum content and process decisions, they were also willing to provide volunteer and material support for student project/thematic units.

In 2002, Ms. Juidici talked about her school culture as "focused on learning and high expectations for all students and staff," a classic definition from effective schools literature on "instructional leadership" (e.g., Murphy & Hallinger, 1985; Purkey & Smith, 1983). By the fall of 2004, Ms. Juidici described school and community relationships as "centered on curriculum and learning." By 2006, parents were in and out of the school at all times during the day. The relationships among the school organization, curriculum, and the community were seamless. Over time, the school went from narrow, direct instruction programs, teacher pacing guides, and textbooks to a vibrant education center and with seamless community connections. In 2006, Michael (the student quoted above) stated, "I have a lot to read in my classes now, but the reading is to do the community garden project. I really love learning about sustaining the earth." It is also important to note that increases in Michael and his peers' state assessment scores paralleled this increased engagement in learning and community service. In chapter 6, I expand on these community and school curriculum decision-making processes.

Ms. Juidici clearly recognized the need to help all children, particularly those living in poverty, perform well on state tests. In her words, "The state tests are the standard through which children are judged. Good test scores give students opportunities for advanced placement in high school classes and eventually in universities. You have to help kids understand and use the testing systems to work for them." At the same time, however, she expressed her strong belief that the more critical examination of curriculum discourses fosters creativity as well as agency and intellectual growth like that advocated by Dewey (1916/2008). I will return to this point in chapter 6.

*Mr. Hughes* The longer Mr. Hughes sat on the state committee (and participated in the study), the more he became concerned about challenging the underlying (conservative) ideology of current curriculum policies. As he put it,

> I think I started to shake people up because I'd say okay here's the policy but now look at what these words mean in children's lives. When the policymakers make wording changes because of pressures from some kind of interest group or some common idea, we have to know how to name some of these hidden meanings. Otherwise, we are all vulnerable to the owners of test companies. More than that, I believe

there are far more negative effects on students who are less privileged than any test score is worth. (September 2005)

Like Ms. Juidici, Mr. Hughes often showed teachers and parents quotes from content standards or the new instructional leadership guidelines. He analyzed the underlying meanings of the words and their implications for leadership. In September 2004, Mr. Hughes described how he used discourse analysis in curriculum development:

> So I took these policy documents, which in many cases were just blah blah blah for raising standards, and I showed the evolving revisions at community forums. We asked two questions.... What does this mean in general for education of our children? What does it mean in our community? We also watched debates over these bills on the state version of public access television and talked about the assumptions behind the words.

Mr. Hughes presented curriculum leadership guidelines and talked openly about possible implications for children with teacher and parent groups. In his words:

> These guidelines tell me I do a good job of instructional leadership when I supervise teachers according to student performance on standardized tests.... If I do only that, then I validate teachers' perceptions that they are supposed to teach the tests or some common tested standards.

One community member described his response to Hughes's presentations thus:

> We like to keep our community sort of safe from outside crazy pressures, but as we watched these policy changes and the debates on TV, we could see that the outside craziness was coming right here. Some of our food canning industries and businesses were definitely being affected by pressures to compete. Our kids needed to be taught like workers in the marketplace, so we thought it was good to work on upping the ante for the curriculum a bit more.

See Mr. Hughes's think-aloud example about instructional leadership strategies in Table 3.2.

Mr. Hughes also challenged what he perceived as "unjust testing practices." For example, he helped teachers disaggregate test data according to race, class, gender, and language. Then he juxtaposed the school results (on a scale of 1 to 4) against community and area housing maps with housing prices along with the same information from larger communities nearby. Finally, he showed

**Table 3.2** "Sample Instructional Leadership" Standards

**Think Aloud**

**Standard 1: Knowledge of instructional leadership standards as related to curriculum development and continuous school improvement process**

1. Use a recommended curriculum design (e.g., Heidi Hayes Jacobs (2005), *Curriculum Mapping*; Wiggins and McTighe's (1998/2004) *Understanding by Design*; and *Thoughtful Education Resources*).
2. Use grade-level data on reading to identify strategies to align curriculum, instruction, and assessment.

When I read through these standards for my leadership, it makes me think that we need a commercial curriculum design that helps us align state content standards instead of designing our own curriculum and using the state standards to support us.... The instructional leadership guidelines tell us we can use any number of curriculum designs, but it's pretty clear when I read the fine print that they want us to use curriculum mapping that emphasizes basic skills instruction. I don't have a problem with basic skills, but I want our students to go beyond and be able to think critically and solve problems that we cannot yet foresee. Also, when I look at the curriculum maps, they really reinforce to me the smallest items of knowledge. There's no real expectation that our students are able to put these bits together. It's really important to align curriculum, instruction, and assessment, and a map makes sense to me, but this idea doesn't go far enough. We also need to make sure that what we teach and how we work in our schools fosters equity and cultural diversity in our communities. Children learn that what we ignore (like diversity) is not important to us. We need to take responsibility for cultural sensitivity and diversity as well as making sure students perform well on small bits of knowledge tested in state assessments.

**Standard 2: Knowledge of instructional leadership standard as related to research-based best practices**

1. Given school-based student assessment data on reading performance, use instructional strategies to facilitate students' phonemic awareness, phonics, fluency, vocabulary, and reading comprehension throughout the content areas.
2. Use scientifically based applications to effective teaching and learning.

Supporting effective teaching is a critical aspect of my job because our children deserve instruction that is developed and tested with the most current possible research. The problem is that the state is basically telling me that I need to give students a particular kind of instruction regardless of their learning styles or their prior knowledge. When we teach reading, we have to make sure students understand how letters and sounds work within words, but that's only a small aspect of what children need to be literate. If we spend all of our time on that one small aspect of reading, we ignore critical thinking skills, for example. There's also no mention of multiculturalism. Our community is becoming increasingly diverse, and we need to make sure all of our children see themselves in books.

**Standard 3: Knowledge of learning, accountability, and assessment standard as related to school and community relationships.**

1. Given data, use strategies to attain community support for your strategic plan.

This means I should develop a plan based on my own ideas without really drawing on students' interests, their background knowledge, or community needs. This also means I should make the decisions, with data and perhaps input, but I am basically supposed to "sell" you on what I think should be done for the school rather than leading a community group through democratic decision making about student/community needs and what we see as the best course of action for our future. We need to work together as a community to develop and implement the best possible curriculum plans for our children.

teachers and community leaders the difference in pedagogy and materials children receive based upon test results. Then he asked, "How does disaggregation of data help children gain access to more equitable opportunities? How does it hurt children?" As he explained, "Disaggregation of test data is important to see how students are performing...but [only] when you connect the dots to curriculum opportunities." Mr. Hughes concluded, "Unless teachers, community members, and students challenge their own beliefs and actions, their learning reproduces the existing dominant structures within themselves."

Mr. Hughes started to audiotape and transcribe various state meetings and local meetings of various stakeholder groups where test data were discussed. In 2003, the comments he recorded featured concerns about spending time and resources on test preparation. By spring of 2004, comments shifted to concerns about spending resources on the 1s—those children who had scored at the lowest performance level and who would be unable to pass the tests at a proficient level 3 by the next spring. He continued the recording practices through the spring of 2005 when comments shifted to "How to deal with the structures that tracked subgroups of children" (September 2005). Periodically, Mr. Hughes showed the transcriptions to teachers and parents, asking them to examine changes in the policy words and intentions over time. As he described,

> I've always believed, as educators do, that we need to provide the best educational opportunities for all students to meet and exceed their potential. After listening to all the debates on the Hill and even in my own school, I realize that there are some people who (probably unconsciously) believe that some students are only good enough to be blue-collar workers and others will be society leaders. We need to work to deliberately uncover some of those assumptions and try to change them in schools. That means bringing service learning projects into the curriculum. It means teaching about social conflicts and class issues, to make these social structures visible, so we can see and change them.

Many Pinehurst teacher interviewees talked at length about how these presentations, asking questions, and discourse analysis strategies helped them think more about their own beliefs, which in turn shifted their thinking about their practices. As Sarah, a math department leader put it,

> At first it didn't make a lot of sense to spend all this time asking questions about policies and school practices...after all, policies have to be implemented...but I have gradually found myself asking questions about teaching materials and practices in the same way we did in the feedback sessions. I can see a lot more layers in the vocabulary in these

teachers' manuals. It really has made me think more about my teaching practices.

Essentially, Mr. Hughes challenged the legitimacy of curriculum standards, tests, and practices that reinforced test-driven expectations for teaching and leadership. In the process, teachers, parents, and students gained the skills and confidence to ask their own questions. Teacher and community reactions to Mr. Hughes' discourse analysis strategies paralleled Henderson and Gornik's (2006) perspectives on curriculum theory:

> Curriculum encourages you to wake up and start asking questions about what may have been a taken-for-granted reality in your classroom, school, and life. A curriculum theory that embraces the "self," encourages all of us, students, educators, parents, and the broader community to participate actively in our own evolution. A curriculum theory that asks you to be receptive to new information, even if it is unsettling, and to reexamine old assumptions: to persevere in the attempt to understand, in spite of confusion; a commitment to learning and growth as *a way of life* always seeking to expand your awareness to understand the world around you, and to want all of this for your students as much as you want it for yourself. (p. 117)

In 2004, the district hired a new superintendent with a top-down leadership style and more conservative ideas about curriculum. Because Mr. Hughes had engaged key community leaders in the curriculum change process (and earned their support), he was gradually able to convince the superintendent to support the curriculum processes. Although Mr. Hughes faced challenges, he came to understand his role as political mediator (Anderson, 2009), to remind himself, students, teachers, and parents/community leaders, "They should not unwittingly surrender their judgment to the state, textbook company, testing company, or any other external authority. External authorities are helpful for learning, but it is up to curriculum leaders and their constituents to be active (or activist) learners and educators, to take responsibility for democratic education."

### Hegemony: Probing the Depths of Discourse

Over time, these two principals/curriculum leaders also recognized that the circulating conservative discourses (language and thinking about professional education practice) were deeply embedded in the consciousness and lived experiences of many school and community members. Both of the principals used some type of radical consciousness raising activity to awaken teachers and parents/community members to how current policies and politics perpetuated social inequities. In other words, the principals showed how the accountability policies that helped them increase teacher dialogue about data and leverage improvements were simultaneously reproducing the social and cultural inequities that plagued their communities. In various ways, these principals cultivated awareness of the ideas and practices that perpetuated these inequities and then worked with and through others to change these practices. In so doing, the principals probed the depths of neoliberal and neoconservative discourse in ways that laid the groundwork for new progressive educational and social movements (described in chapter 6).

Neither Ms. Juidici nor Mr. Hughes has studied the notion of hegemony to any extent. However, each principal in the study was completely aware of the complexities involved in changing school/community perceptions about curriculum that are "lived at such a depth, which saturates the society to such an extent, and which even constitutes the limits of common sense for most people under its sway" (Williams, 1977, p. 205). Apple (2004) expands on the point, noting that hegemony refers not to congeries of meanings that reside at an abstract level somewhere at the "roof of our brain." Rather, it refers to an organized assemblage of meanings and practices, the central, effective, and dominant system of meanings, values, and actions, which are *lived*. It needs to be understood on a different level than "mere opinion" or "manipulation."

These principals were determined to foster awareness of how they and their constituents were living out dominant (conservative) systems of meaning about curriculum content and practice on a day-to-day basis. In all cases, the principals employed a two-prong strategy to do so. First, they engaged in various activities to make teachers and parents deeply conscious (and critical) of the underlying suggested meanings behind the curriculum practices they were enacting on a daily basis. Second, these principals engaged their constituents in experiential activities designed to help them consider how conservative norms and arguments were playing out in their lives.

Principals Juidici and Hughes worked "out of the box" to get school and community members' attention about unconscious, and potentially unjust beliefs and practices related to standardized curricula and high-stakes accountability. It is important to note that both of them started at the personal, individual level, talking with students, teachers, and parents about their individual experiences with varying test performance levels and decontextualized curriculum practices. While these principals recognized the value of student performance data and responsibility, at the same time, they made sure that teachers and parents had the tools to recognize the underlying and potentially detrimental effects of circulating discourses about student test levels and standards attainment. Their desire to develop critical awareness about curriculum policy requirements prompted them to lead learning community discussions and planning sessions around the realities of how tests can sort children, particularly those living in poverty. Specific activities in each case are described below.

*Ms. Juidici*  During the study, Ms. Juidici held many individual meetings with parents, teachers, and community leaders, talking about the positive and negative aspects of accountability policies, curriculum content standards, and various popular curriculum design models. As she explained in September 2004, "I don't like to put people on the spot, but I decided it was important for me to be the one to make sure we all know how our language and practices are shaped by these policies." When I asked if people were receptive to those conversations, she stated, "Oh, not at all most of the time. Over time, I kept plugging away, asking, 'Have you thought about what it means when we say we have to sort children by subgroups and that we have to align our classroom teaching to the test?'" Juidici also noted that while many teachers and parents remained resistant, she began to see a greater openness to problematizing how politics beyond our school doors have such a great effect on our beliefs about accountability and curriculum standards within our schools.

Ms. Juidici also administered the state math test to her school board, various parent groups, and her teachers. She then showed them the state leadership standards dealing with curriculum, instruction, and assessment. In her words,

> I told them...okay, now you probably did not get all the answers right.... That's how tests are made—to sort children out. They have to put some really hard items in there. Anyway, if you had some trouble with a particular content area or part of it, this is what the state tells me to do.... I showed them the instructional leadership standard that sounds like good common sense.... Teach the kids to meet these tested items (that they were not expected to master anyway) and then I showed them the recommended teaching methods that were pretty out of date and disconnected from the learners' interests and lives. We need to do better.

School board members, parents, and teachers all talked at length about how they felt during these test-taking experiences. One school board member, Mark, put it well when he stated "It really got my attention about these tests and how we talk about the logic of teaching tested standards. We have to do something more for our kids and just really think about our curriculums and how they are crafted through politics as much as curriculum research. We need to be responsible to bring our students' interests and learning needs to the forefront" (September 2006). Mark's comments above stand in stark contrast to his comments in September of 2004, when he stated, "I think we need to get on board and make sure we're aligning everything to the tests. We have a lot of new teachers that need more structure."

When I asked him what changed his mind, he stated, "Well, we have leadership. Ms. Juidici is a teacher, and she's really helped us think for ourselves about what we're doing to improve learning." Many recent studies have examined curriculum leaders' practices that contribute to improvements in student learning (e.g., Jackson, 2000; Marks & Printy, 2003); however, these studies do not consider student learning in relation to deep meanings of political discourses in school language and practice.

*Mr. Hughes*   Mr. Hughes took a more audiovisual approach (i.e., photos and voice recordings) to enhance his explanations about shifts in curriculum discourse and curriculum leadership discourse. He frequently showed maps and photos of the community and played various tape recordings of teachers and others talking about standards and tests. I observed one meeting in which Mr. Hughes played a tape of various teachers and parents using the same words as a rationale for state content standards and tests. The voices varied, but the message was the same: "Schools never had standards before and our kids are in danger of not being able to compete as strong workers in the 21st century." After these presentations, one parent commented, "I think we need to be very thoughtful about the implications of decisions about what we teach. It's a little scary how none of the educators think they ever wrote curriculum. Mr. Hughes makes it clear that we are responsible for making decisions about what we teach all of our children."

Hughes also talked at length about how he purposely met with teachers and parents individually after presenting the photos and recordings to group audiences. He wanted to offer people an opportunity to talk about the experience and how they connected on an emotional level. Hughes argued, "The images were powerful, and I wanted people to be able to share if they were willing to do so. At the same time, I wanted to make myself available afterwards to follow up with any concerns." Out of these individual and group conversations came several activist projects, such as the school food bank project and the homeless education center.

### Identifying Political Interest Groups, Alliances, and Fault Lines

Juidici and Hughes observed the formation of alliances among various state-level interest groups as well as sources of compromise among these groups. They became increasingly skilled in the identification of ideas and key people who could be mobilized for social and educational changes. At the same time, these principals also noted that policies were constructed out of compromises and some of the compromises could be exploited to meet school and community needs and goals.

*Mr. Hughes*    As Mr. Hughes participated in a state-level policy formulation process, he became fascinated by the relationship between compromise and policy formulation. In his words,

> As I watched the state policy process, I could see how compromises became the final language of the document. In one instance, our committee had agreed tentatively on particular language about "core" academic curriculum, there were legislative hearings with certain interest groups. I watched in the hearing how the legislative committee came up with compromise language that actually made it possible for people to use more progressive curriculum approaches…at least if you knew where to look in the policy. I would not have caught that otherwise. In another instance, we saw major objections to analyzing test scores without consideration for subgroups [e.g., ethnicity and gender]. The next time we met, the language had changed to reflect a compromise about disaggregation of data by subgroups.

It is interesting to note that civil rights groups objected to standardized testing until the subgroup analysis was added to the NCLB policy. The irony is that subgroups have gained attention in instructional decisions, but the quality of curriculum content they received and instructional delivery of that content has been open to debate. Mr. Hughes shared his growing understanding of compromise with his teachers. He showed them a series of state policy meeting minutes and drafts that showed where the discrepancies were in their argument as well as how compromises were reached. As Dereck, a fifth-grade teacher with strong influence among his peers, explained, "It was actually pretty funny because Mr. Hughes showed us how to look at the language of these different groups and see how opposite they really were. We were afraid we were going to have to give up our community organization room because it did not fit the goals of No Child Left Behind. We realized that we could craft our language to fit what we felt was best for the children."

Hughes and many other educators have recognized that standards language and related curriculum practices can be interpreted in multiple ways, as standardized, traditional curriculum and as more constructive, enduring understandings, and as "moral decisions that touch the core of what it is to be human, to live in community with others, to find meaning and purpose, and to create a more just and peaceful world" (Henderson & Kesson, 1999, p. 45). Hughes used his growing understandings of state politics to help teachers, parents, and community members approach standards with political savvy.

*Ms. Juidici*    Ms. Juidici purposely worked with community leaders who could actively counteract the conservative arguments that were most tenuous in the community. These leaders were asked to make presentations at Board of Education meetings and at influential community organization meetings. As Apple (2004) argued, one tactic to forward the agenda of a radically democratic social and education project might be to carefully discern fault lines within the hegemonic alliance where potential tensions among the different discursive positions might be exacerbated.

In these cases, the principals/curriculum leaders began to examine policy documents, curriculum materials, and daily interactions about teaching and learning with critical lenses, intent on finding and exploiting tensions in the requirements that they considered unjust. As such, there were also parallels between the principals in my study and the principals studied by George Theoharris (2009, 2009) and Scheurich et al. (2004), who demonstrated the value of testing data to identify inequities and quality programs. However, the principals in my study also used political analytical tools (e.g., discourse and hegemony) to challenge underlying assumptions about testing data. In so doing, Juidici and Hughes were able to illuminate the depths of hegemony; its effects on the social and economic inequities that had plagued their communities; and lay the groundwork for a renewed commitment to democratic education.

### Back to Basic Democracy

The fact that the principals do not minimize democratic aims for their curriculum leadership is in sharp contrast to data collected in other studies by Houle (2006) and Daly (2009). Houle, for example, argues:

> The principals' perceptions of their instructional leadership duties were, first and second, classroom supervisors and lead learners. Several of the principals expressed concerns regarding the time that would be necessary to observe teachers, give them feedback, and work with teachers in the professional growth phase. Democratic education and advocacy for multiculturalism were not mentioned. These issues caused the university facilitators to focus the bulk of the remaining monthly sessions on the areas of capacity building and personal growth and renewal. (p. 148)

The principals/curriculum leaders in Daly's (2009) study similarly had notions of the primacy of accountability policy responsibilities: test data analysis and classroom walk throughs for supervision. As Daly notes, "Schools under review for poor test performance—typically staffed with new and uncredentialed teachers—become more highly regulated as they move further into the improvement cycle. Principals in these schools limit professional interaction and collaboration in lieu of data analysis, curriculum mapping, and classroom supervision…" (p. 259). Evidence from these schools also suggests that if school climates are more open, then educators may be able to successfully negotiate sanctions and so increase student improvement (Mintrop, 2003; Mintrop & Trujillo, 2005).

In certain ways, curriculum leaders/principals Juidici and Hughes are markedly different from curriculum ("instructional") leaders in these other studies and from principals Draper and Grant in the previous chapter, particularly in terms of their concerns, priorities, and how they see themselves as curriculum leaders. Although Juidici and Hughes sometimes assert that they worry about students' academic performance and that they wish to have some consistency in curriculum implementation, these concerns are never asserted first, and generally only as a concern "out there," when they have to explain curriculum choices to the school board, or when they hear that the local newspaper is about to publish state test score comparisons by district and school. Rather, Juidici and Draper are far more concerned about the potentially deleterious effects of the commonly accepted discourses about back-to-basics curriculum and children as future workers in a global economy. The primary point, however, is that Juidici and Hughes see themselves as curriculum leaders who must assert strongly that they must guard democracy and foster the development of compassionate and thoughtful democratic citizens first before considering the results of state tests. In other words, the construction of a test-driven curriculum leadership identity is minor, rather than the reverse. Juidici and Hughes elaborated any kind of conservative curriculum ideology only on a few occasions over a 3½-year period, and they always talked about the problems associated with these ideologies in the next breath. I never once heard informal discussions or formal interviews that wholly embraced the conservative modernization or intensified professionalism as defined by new public management (NPM). Significantly, unlike the principals in Daly's (2009) study or the principals in the previous chapter, Hughes and Juidici do not construct data-driven curriculum leadership identities as a means of coping with the current accountability context. Rather, these leaders see test performance as means for students' access to higher education and other opportunities.

Juidici and Hughes frequently talked about themselves as leaders helping students develop democratic dispositions and ideals like respect, caring, and cooperation. As Juidici put it, "I need to make sure that children realize that they are part of a broader community, and their individual growth is critical to." Likewise, Hughes suggested, "We're living in an era where society would tell us we should restrict curriculum choices, but we have to remember that children are our future, and it is imperative that future citizens strive toward their highest ideals, not just high test scores." At the heart of democratic leadership rests a sense of what it is to be human and a deep respect for the cultivation of common human good and the individual's freedom and need to act according to one's own direction. In its ideal forms, democratic leadership contributes to leaders' and others' growth toward human potential (Woods, 2005). Dewey wrote: "A society which makes provision for participation in its good of all its members on equal terms and which secures flexible readjustment of its institutions through interaction of the different forms of associated life is in so far democratic" (1916/2008, p. 99). In the following examples, we see how participation in community service projects contributed to students' growth as democratic citizens in their schools and communities.

### Examples: Fourth-Grade Science Class, Babcock School

Students in Mrs. Minor's English class worked in small groups and analyzed city reports about lead in the soil of a particular neighborhood. As the economy declined, many older houses with lead paint were abandoned and eventually torn down. Lead paint soaked into the soil and eventually into plants. Their assignment was to create a plan to clean up these neighborhood areas, meaning they had to read their textbooks, city reports, and other resources and use what they learned to develop their written reports. Further, the children presented their reports to a parent group and members of a city council.

*Mr. Ricks (parent):* I was astounded at the quality of the children's work. Their papers were well written and informative. They also gave a very passionate and professional presentation about how they wanted to clean up the soil with a natural product and then plant flowers in these vacant lot areas.

### Examples: Fourth-Grade English Class Presentation to the Site Council, Pinehurst School

*Rob Martin (student):* We have a diverse student body in our school now. We think it's important for our school to reflect our multicultural student body. Our class would like to join with the art club to design a mural and paint it on the wall that you see when you first come to the school. [Students had read a set of multicultural literature and developed a written proposal for the site council.]

*Ms. Martin (site council leader):* We were so impressed with the multicultural mural proposal that we approved funding and support for the art teacher to work with a group of students on Saturdays. They designed and painted the mural, and it took several months to finish, but in the end it is absolutely beautiful...a shining moment for our school and our community. We invited parents and community members to come to an open house. Children wrote about the process and displayed their inspirational multicultural literature books as well as photos and stories they wrote about local heroes/

citizens. It is important to note in both examples here, Babcock and Pinehurst students are developing agency as well as academic skills. I will return to this point in chapter 7. Although students in both schools have ambitions outside of their communities, they feel empowered and responsible to the human conditions in their neighborhoods and communities. The student and teacher interviews and observations, in many ways, echo the principals' elaboration on the meaning of curriculum leadership by 2006. The curriculum work described above contributed, in many ways, to shifts in the meaning and practice of curriculum leadership over time.

RY:    What does curriculum leadership mean to you?

*Juidici (September 2002):* Curriculum leadership involves those activities related to ongoing curriculum writing, implementation, professional development, and supervision skills that improve learning in schools. I guess most of all I see myself as a good supervisor who knows enough about curriculum and instruction to give feedback that helps teachers continue to grow. I see myself as the lead learner in a professional learning community where we talk about how our children are doing in the curriculum, identify our goals, develop the best instructional strategies to meet those goals, and then provide assessments that inform decisions about student learning as well as continuous curriculum development.

*Juidici (September 2006):* Curriculum leadership is a way of building community relationships that support social equity and learning for all children and adults and that create a more equitable, democratic society. Now more than ever, curriculum is political. It's my role to stand in the gap, help teachers and parents cut through all of the rhetoric and accountability pressures, and teach what is important to children's lives. And we have to fight back when these external pressures keep us from doing what is right for children. I see myself as a guardian for public education in ways I never did before.

Over a 4-year span, Ms. Juidici made a fairly dramatic shift from a curriculum leader who espoused traditional pedagogy and prioritized classroom supervision roles to one who espoused social equity and democratic education and saw herself as a guardian for public education. She knew that such a shift required political knowledge and skills.

RY:    What does curriculum leadership mean to you?

*Hughes (September 2002):* Curriculum leadership includes practices that focus everyone's attention on curriculum and instruction, build a strong learning culture, and maintain high expectations for all students and teachers.

In the above quote, Mr. Hughes gave a nearly textbook answer, naming leadership components also identified by Hallinger and Murphy (1985).

*Hughes (September 2006):* Curriculum leadership is a way of being and modeling that helps cultivate freedom, equity, and the future for a democratic society. Now, more than anything else, it means that informed individuals or groups learn to stand up to some of the detrimental politics that distract us from what students and adults learn to be compassionate and productive citizens. As a curriculum leader, I have to teach school staff and community members how to question and challenge some of the ideas that everyone is parroting about curriculum, teaching, and learning. At the same time, I have to remind myself that children who have the least privilege need to succeed in the tests so they have access to higher education and other opportunities. At the same time, I have to remember that children are members of the community, and part of their learning experience must draw on their cultural backgrounds and work toward community transformation. I guess I'm saying that I see the complexities of leadership today, and I have to be able to walk in a number of worlds at the same time.

Like Ms. Juidici in the previous case, Mr. Hughes recognized the good sense in some elements of current policies and the need for subgroups to perform well on state tests. In certain respects, Mr. Hughes's responses indicate more complexity and nuance in contemporary curriculum leadership that must, as he put it, "walk in a number of worlds at the same time." Overall, however, Hughes saw his role as a leader who provided teachers, students, and parents with the political capital to be critical advocates for their rights in a democratic society.

In spite of differing curriculum philosophies early in the study (2002), both of the principals experienced similar moments of critique about the ways in which conservative discourses and policies were (re)shaping common sense about curriculum, teaching, and learning in their contexts. Mr. Hughes had been committed to progressive curriculum philosophies and authentic pedagogies from the beginning of the study whereas Mrs. Juidici shifted toward progressive educational beliefs during the course of the study. However, regardless of particular curriculum philosophies, the principals both had clear shifts in curricular beliefs and related practices that Allington (2002), Shannon (2001), and others have associated with the so-called conservative era. Beyond mainstream perspectives on educational leadership (e.g., Hallinger, 2003; Leithwood & Riehl, 2005; Murphy & Hallinger, 1985; Spillane et al., 2001), this chapter is grounded in the principals' view that curriculum leadership is critical and requires new analytical tools to interrupt the particular set of (conservative) ideologies that are contributing to unjust practices in their schools.

It is noteworthy that Juidici and Hughes's critical curriculum leadership identity, critique of current education discourses, and related commitment to democratic education, are not produced in relation to a constructed conservative curriculum leadership identity. These critically oriented principals/curriculum leaders do not elaborate an identity in relation to new professional or conservative leadership the way many contemporary educational leaders do, including Draper and Grant in the previous chapter. They do not, at Babcock and Pinehurst Schools, set up conservatives as "other" as they form themselves. This is not to say that critical curriculum leaders are not affected by the broader (conservative) ideologies; they may well be. Rather, it is to suggest that the critical curriculum leadership does not emerge in self-identity in relation to a conservative "other." It does emerge, as I have suggested throughout this chapter, in relation to a personal concern about fundamental shifts in common sense about curricula and a concurrent commitment to democratic public education and progressive curriculum ideals.

---

PROBLEM-POSING CASE
**What Children Learn Unconsciously—Babcock School, 2003–2004**

Seth was a first-year teacher in a sixth grade middle school classroom. Like all the other teachers of his unit, Seth had responsibility for one differentiated (homogeneously) grouped reading class. The school reading program was designed such that students worked in ability groups and progressed through a series of leveled, vocabulary controlled books. As part of the class, students also worked individually thorough a series of worksheets that accompanied the leveled books. In this way, students were to learn basic vocabulary and comprehension skills with the class, but individuals were free to "move up" or "move down," depending on their oral reading and worksheet performance. The idea was that the teacher could give individual attention to those children who needed it and still help children progress through groups with proficiency levels aligned with levels on state tests. Seth thought this system made sense. He liked the differentiated nature of the program and that instructional activity was clearly aligned with standards and state assessments. His primarily working-class students seemed to like the system, too. They were rewarded by evidence of their progress on a weekly basis.

By March, though, Seth began to be uneasy about the direction his reading class was taking. He felt that he was not really teaching his students.

They were just doing worksheets on their own. He had expected to be able to work one-on-one with students. Instead, he found he spent almost no time on individual teaching. Seth spent much more time on group lessons aimed at state standards and test items. The class was generally orderly and quiet, yet some students seemed to be progressing much too slowly. Seth was concerned that his inability to work with these students individually was a contributing factor. He talked with his department head, a veteran teacher recognized as a model teacher at the state level, and she requested a peer coach (reading specialist) for him. After one of her classroom walk throughs, the reading specialist advised Seth to balance the whole group skills instruction with more literature circle groups. Seth spent much of his after-school time preparing for literature circles, and students responded well. Meanwhile, the state tests were looming only 2 months away.

Seth's worst fears were *not* confirmed when the state test results came back. He was surprised to find that, despite his concerns, all the students made progress. In fact, several students moved from 2s to 3s (just below proficiency to actual proficiency). It had appeared to him in class that many students were not really learning, and yet they were able to score well on the state tests. At the last faculty meeting, the principal demonstrated how to "read" underlying assumptions behind policy and program texts as well as common ways of talking and thinking about policies/programs. Seth took her advice and really examined his program. He "bit the bullet" and asked students what they were learning from the differentiated program. Their answers revolved around themes of "how to do skills" and "how to get work done quickly."

Seth shared these responses with other teachers and began to wonder aloud about the underlying aims of the differentiated instructional program. Was the program designed to teach working-class children how to complete routine tasks quickly? If so, what were the implications for the students' futures, particularly for racial- and ethnic-minority children living in poverty? Naturally, these questions generated heated discussion and serious deliberations among the teachers. Over the next several months, Seth considered and reflected on the underlying assumptions of this program and of similar skills-based instruction occurring throughout the school. He began to think about how to tap into his social justice commitments, which he had not previously used to inform curriculum and instruction. As Seth raised these issues with his peers, he not only opened the door for serious debates and conflicts, but he also found out that he was not alone in his concerns.

---

**Questions**

1. Make up an ending to this case.
2. How would you characterize this school culture as it relates to the reading curriculum and classroom instruction?
3. What would you do to encourage this kind of reflective practice, questioning processes, and teacher dialogue if you were the principal?

---

## Summary

This chapter presented two cases in which principals/curriculum leaders influenced teachers to question underlying assumptions of (conservative) discourses, develop a sense of agency, and renew their commitments to democratic education. I have argued here that the principals' emerging critical curriculum leadership identity exhibits a beginning challenge to the conservative modern restoration. They are envisioning curriculum leadership very differently than researchers such as Hallinger, Murphy, and Heck conceptualized and that their predecessors or principals in the previous chapter did. For Juidici and Hughes, curriculum forms and commonsensical assumptions about the importance of instructional consistency, standardized curricula, and accountability are not primary; informed and compassionate democratic citizenry and community advocacy are. If the conservative restoration rests, in part, on commonsensical arguments about the utilitarian purposes of schooling, the necessity of accountability and competition in the open market, and the control of curriculum content as basic (official) knowledge, principals Juidici and Hughes represent the emergence of a critique about those arguments. They understand and articulate the fact that too many negative consequences result if you focus all attention on a back-to-basics or externally developed curriculum to the exclusion of depending on your teachers' professional knowledge and students' cultural funds of knowledge and abilities as active, engaged learners. This means that, as curriculum leaders, principals must work with and through teachers, parents, and students to challenge current discourses related to standardization  and accountability to state tests and engage in long-term efforts aimed at the development of growth in public intellectuals (Giroux, 2001). These principals do not suggest the "instructional consistency" and accountability-driven solutions offered in previous investigations and chapter 2.

In this sense, then, Juidici and Hughes's curriculum leadership identities embody a critical moment of critique of an underlying premise of the conservative modernization: that being the notion that schools must teach a particular set of knowledge, thinking skills, and values in order to prepare students for work in a global, market-driven economy. In so doing, Juidici and Hughes question the idea of curriculum as standardized "official knowledge" for a market-driven economy, which, as I suggest in chapter 2, "new professional" curriculum leaders affirm.

The potential for such a critical moment needs to be considered carefully, and I will pursue this at some length in chapter 6. I will also tie this evolving critique to the possibilities of neoprogressive educational and social movements in chapter 7. At this point, I propose that while the critical curriculum leaders' identity suggests a glimmer of critique, informed by both ideological pressures and economic changes that have contributed to suffering and oppression of marginalized groups in their communities, the critique does not necessarily presuppose collective action. Rather, it tends to suggest the individualistic private solutions for these schools and communities instead of a broader political struggle designed to change the prevailing conservative order around curriculum.

As I have suggested here and in chapter 2, "new professional" and critical curriculum leadership identities are, in certain respects, working at cross-purposes: the "new professional" principals envision consistent, standardized curriculum and instruction for workers in a global, 21st century economy and critical curriculum leaders exhibit a challenge to those aims in some important ways. In other respects, there are important similarities in the quest to prepare children as academically talented, productive critical thinkers for a future, global world. Several questions must be asked. In what ways do the school and community cultures block or encourage the formation of new professional and critical curriculum leadership identities? What are the effects of new professional and critical curriculum leadership on curriculum development in schools and social movements in the surrounding communities? In the next three chapters I take up these questions. Chapter 4 focuses on the way in which the routines and rituals of the school culture are related to curriculum leadership identity formation of principals.

# 4

# School Culture and Curriculum Leadership

As I noted in the last two chapters, based upon my research and other related studies (e.g., Anderson, 2009; Daly, 2009; Henderson & Kesson, 1999; Johnson & Johnson, 2005), new professional and critical curriculum leadership identities are closely connected to perceptions about the purposes of curriculum and learning. New professional curriculum leadership emerges in relation to constructed and somewhat contradictory commonsensical beliefs about the utilitarian purposes of education, related efficiency and productivity discourses, test-driven curriculum dialogues in "professional learning communities," and the need for competition and critical thinking skills in a global work environment. Although new professional, efficiency-driven curriculum leaders frequently express empathy for the children behind the achievement gap numbers, they focus much of their efforts on instructional consistency in core academic subjects and give less attention to students' interests, the broader culture, or social justice issues. In some contrast, critical curriculum leaders recognize the reality that test scores are important to children's futures, but they also criticize the unjust effects of the tests on children—critiques that influence their beliefs about the purposes of curriculum (e.g., emancipation, growth) and leadership thereof. Changing what principals and teachers take for granted as "common sense" about standardized curricula and test preparation requires tapping into a different set of values that they already hold but have not yet connected to curriculum leadership roles. All of this curriculum leadership identity formation takes place within a particular school culture and political time, as illustrated in this chapter.

This chapter is organized into four main sections: "Reconsidering School Culture," "The Nature of School Culture under Conservative Curriculum Leadership," "School Cultures and Critical Curriculum Leadership," and "Problem-Posing Case." Each section highlights the ways in which teachers and students embody and enhance the curriculum leadership identities and practices described in the previous two chapters. Aspects of school culture are examined and illustrated with data from my ethnography and from other scholars' research studies. The chapter concludes with a problem-posing case for further consideration of school culture and curriculum leadership.

## Reconsidering School Culture

Deal and Peterson (1994) defined school culture as "an inner reality of beliefs, attitudes, and norms" (p. 6). Culture influences everything that happens within a school, including norms, values, rituals, and symbols. In the current political context, inner realities, beliefs, attitudes, and norms related to curriculum and assessments are also influenced by shifts in broader cultural politics and in what we take for granted as common sense. In recent years, conservative discourses have penetrated school cultures and altered inherent attitudes, beliefs, and norms. It is time that these so-called inner realities—assumptions, norms, and values—of school cultures be opened to critical analysis and reconsideration because school cultures exist in a dialectic relationship with external cultural politics, curriculum reforms, and other policy trends. In the next section, I explore particular elements of school culture that enhance and embody new professional curriculum leadership. The section that follows illustrates what happens when curriculum leaders critically examine underlying assumptions of current test-driven curricula and tap into social justice values and cultural background knowledge to change their school cultures and, ultimately, their curriculum leadership identities and practices.

## The Nature of School Culture under "New Professional" Curriculum Leadership

New professional curriculum leadership has two major effects on school culture. First, the school's culture embodies and enhances the principal's contradictory attitudes toward education and curriculum. These contradictions show themselves in the ways curriculum is developed (described in the next chapter), knowledge is distributed in classrooms, and decisions are made (and sometimes controlled) by school leaders (teachers and principals) whose common sense has been deeply influenced by a particular set of circulating discourses. Both the treatment of curriculum content and the enacted rituals of control at school and classroom levels serve to contain any real struggles to superficial layers (often numbers), preventing meaningful issues from being discussed in any depth, and at the same time giving the appearance of orderly professional dialogue. The messages circulating in the school reinforce that student outcomes and learning are of singular importance in today's political environment.

Second, school personnel encourage the creation and maintenance of separatist identities along professional and critical lines, thus promoting the construction of the "other" discussed in chapter 2. For example, many vocal Greenway and Elmhurst schoolteachers assert that professional curriculum leadership and related curriculum practices are superior to all others. Subtle contradictions continue, however. Regardless of the principal's personal philosophy, individual (progressive) teachers—and the fact that the schools themselves are the sites of larger social struggles—keep critical curriculum leadership and progressive education alive to some extent within these and many other schools.

### Contradictory Attitudes about Curriculum

Over the past decade, curriculum discourses in education have been dominated by themes of accountability and basic-skills instruction, as well as somewhat contradictory reforms related to authentic assessments, cultivating deep curricular understandings, and critical thinking. Today's principals are under tremendous pressure to ensure that their students uniformly attain high scores on state tests. At the same time, principals are educators, most often former teachers, who have professional knowledge about pedagogy and curriculum philosophy. As such, they often recognize the importance of divergent thinking skills, reflection, giving voice to students, and other holistic practices seldom emphasized on tests, even while they continue to assert the importance of testing. This contradictory attitude is embedded in Grant's and Draper's curriculum leadership identities and practices (see chapter 2), and not surprisingly it filters down to the classrooms in Greenway and Elmhurst Schools. Teachers frequently talked about the importance of critical thinking skills and deep understandings, particularly for children from lower-SES backgrounds. Yet they prioritized consistent instruction in basic skills (e.g., vocabulary, phonics, spelling, note-taking, test preparation skills) in actual classroom practice. Grade-level team meetings and faculty meetings were frequently devoted to test-data analysis and curriculum-data alignment activities. The principals' roles as curriculum leaders revolved around establishing regular times for data dialogue and professional development about a host of "best practices," often provided by external consultants. Although many teachers privately acknowledged their personal discomfort with labeling children based on standardized tests, using standardized curricula, and differentiating instruction, the more vocal, veteran teachers expounded at length on children's weak literacy achievement, but the principals quickly squelched any public dissent. Faculty meetings were efficient and orderly, but grade-level team meetings were often filled with unspoken tensions related to curriculum and testing policies. These school tensions are also expressed and felt in many U.S. schools and classrooms today.

Contradictions were even evident at the level of the school mission statements, which articulated the importance of "high standards, critical thinking, and challenging academic success." In practice, however, teachers and students often discussed curriculum content in positive but highly utilitarian terms—it leads to a better job in the global economy. The principals, teachers, and parents almost uniformly expressed the attitude that the primary purpose of education is to prepare children to obtain higher education for what they consider to be stable employment. In spite of privately expressed concerns about test-driven curricula, teachers and administrators at Greenway and Elmhurst Schools gradually adhered to the dominant discourse about tests and 21st century workforce education, as was apparent in both their individual interviews with me and my classroom observations. Consequently, the teachers' instruction evolved over time (2002–2006), as they increasingly adhered to the form rather than the substance of curriculum, their instruction became increasingly flat and packaged, and many teachers became demoralized. The following examples clarify this point.

*Sixth Grade Social Studies Class, Greenway School, November 1, 2004* The teacher, Mrs. Miller, gave a long explanation of the electoral system, campaigns, and the election process. She then directed students to read a chapter in their social studies books and answer the odd-numbered questions at the end, saying, "Answer the questions, and then I can see if you understand everything about the elections. Take about 30 minutes." When students were slow to begin, Mrs. Miller reminded them to start reading, and then commented, "If the auto plant were still open, you wouldn't have to worry about reading and comprehending at such high levels. It's not likely to be there when you get out of school either. Now you have to be prepared for more advanced jobs, and reading is a big part of that." When students had finished, Mrs. Miller called out each question by number, then called on several students to share their answers.

*Sixth Grade Social Studies Class, Pinehurst School, January 26, 2005*
*Mr. Scott (talking to his class):* Why does level of education prevent people from getting a job? If you look at the classified ads today, you see that almost all jobs require a high school education. Most good, high-paying jobs also require college, sometimes more than a bachelor's degree. Each time you get more education, you can try to get more jobs. If you have a college education, it doesn't mean you'll absolutely get a job, but you have a lot better chance. The people who live in poorer parts of town have less education, and few of them have well-paying jobs.

During faculty meetings, the teachers and principals frequently affirmed their commitment to teaching for deep understanding and critical thinking. Yet when they tell students that schooling is useful for strictly utilitarian reasons (to get a job in a changing economy), they are in fact downplaying individual student growth and the substance of the curriculum. The nature of classroom instruction is, indeed, very telling, with virtually all classes taking the form of top-down distribution of knowledge. Although this pattern may not be particularly unusual—and in fact, several studies have documented its presence in U.S. schools long before the recent accountability mandates (e.g.,

Daly, 2009; Johnson & Johnson, 2005; Ylimaki & McClain, 2006)—the situation at Greenway and Elmhurst Schools is extreme in certain ways. Teachers tend to tell students exactly what they should learn, down to outlining content and dictating exact answers to open-ended questions. In other words, teachers do not stop at telling students exactly how to outline information in a textbook and where to put punctuation marks; instead (via teachers' editions) they actually control the very form of the outline and the information in it. It is no coincidence that similar outline formats appear on the state exams. Students are not encouraged to construct the information on their own. This method of content presentation is highly routinized in many U.S. schools and classrooms. The type of knowledge presented in the classroom leaves little room for students to interact with that knowledge. And simultaneously, teachers' mandated instructional materials, curriculum lesson plans, and pacing guides give them little latitude to engage students, even if more student interaction occurs. In the next example, another teacher taps into her deep-seated values and beliefs about literacy education.

*Seventh Grade Language Arts, Elmhurst School, December 1, 2004*
*Ms. Pulla:*  Part of the exam we take in May is the writing exercise. There is no reason why you can't get a high score on the writing exam. There is no way to really study for it, but you can get used to the expectations. [She passes out a writing notebook relating to an excerpt of *Bridge to Terrabithia,* which students read aloud as part of their reading series.] Don't copy from the passage in the book, but tell in your own words what you think the ending means. Now you have 5 minutes to put your answer down.... Okay. Let's go through your answers. Don't be upset if you don't do well when I give you feedback. We'll do this five or six times each month, and you'll learn the system of how to improve your score.

This observation reveals the teacher's intense efforts to prepare students for the state exam to be taken in May, an exam that according to federal and state regulations all students in this class must take, regardless of language proficiency or disability. In this sense, the excerpt is not striking—similar events occur in many schools. What is important, however, is Ms. Pulla's follow-up discussion on taking the writing test. The precision with which she instructs students on *how* to format their written responses in their notebooks is striking.

*Ms. Pulla:*  Okay. Open your notebooks up to page 13 [in their reading series] and get your notebook out. Skip a line and write "Writing Test"— suggestions on how to answer the main point of the question. There are four parts to this: Number 1 (period). "Write the topic sentence, usually the first or last sentence of the paragraph." Number 2, next page, page 14, "In the next three sentences, you should underline three detail sentences about the topic sentence. Making all of the detail sentences align with the topic sentence is the most important."

Even though the "big idea" is for students to write critically, the directions are given in such extreme detail as to preclude any independent thought, as students are told what to underline, where to put the period, and so forth. This example was not idiosyncratic; similar instances occurred in a number of classes at both Greenway and Pinehurst Schools, as the following examples make clear.

*Seventh Grade Social Studies, Greenway School, January 5, 2005*
*Mrs. Lake:* Put down in your notes, "Unit I, Part 3." Put down "House of Representatives [she spells R-e-p-r-e-s-e-n-t-a-t-i-v-e-s], one part of Congress."
*Jerry:* What do we write after that?
*Mrs. Lake:* Just write the definition from page 45.

*Sixth Grade Science, Pinehurst School, March 11, 2005*
*Mrs. Clarkson (after a 20-minute lesson on photosynthesis):* Take out your notebooks. On page 3, copy the concept web from page 38 of your science textbook.
*Marianne:* What do we put in the circles?
*Mrs. Clarkson:* Write the definition of each concept from your book.... Look for the words in dark print.

These examples demonstrate that even while many veteran teachers in both schools espoused beliefs in "teaching for deep understandings," critical thinking, and rigorous curriculum content (Wiggins & McTighe, 1998), they simultaneously privileged consistency and order, making use of the pacing guides and packaged materials in which decontextualized skills instruction is the norm. In the end, equilibrium or harmony within the school culture and consistent instruction override creativity and divergent thinking skills. Many of the most frequently cited theorists in educational administration advise leaders to control conflict because controlled conflict is associated with creativity and educational change (e.g., Fullan, 1999; Parsons, 1963). In other words, some conflict can lead to innovative ideas and change, but the preferred state of organizations is order and equilibrium. The mindset at Greenway and Elmhurst Schools is perhaps more extreme—suppressed conflict related to curriculum implementation. Further, the way the teachers deliver instruction is encouraging students to be passive and wait to be instructed in how to do each step the "right" way. It is not an accident that many of the teachers see the principal as a curriculum leader who expects the same kind of efficient but acritical curriculum work from them. In the end, many school members (teachers and students) are discouraged from independent thought in spite of the fact that they work in "professional learning communities." This is the situation in many other U.S. schools today.

### Rituals of Control

Control emerges as a theme in relation to more than curriculum content knowledge and delivery. It is also salient with respect to teachers' labor overall, particularly the activities of new teachers and those teachers with more progressive philosophies. It is the particular areas in which this control is exerted, as well as its public nature, that is important to note. In many U.S. schools, there are ongoing struggles among educators who support progressive philosophies, educators who believe progressive approaches are inadequate to meet students' academic needs, and administrators/teacher curriculum leaders who assert control over these conflicts and related curricular inconsistencies. Such struggles have intensified in the wake of recent accountability and curriculum reform policies that appear to support conservative-style ideologies (Johnson & Johnson, 2005).

In my curriculum leadership study, the struggle emerges in relation to three key areas and is largely confined to those areas: (1) teachers' lesson plan books; (2) pacing guides in teachers' editions accompanying packaged curriculum materials; and (3) classroom walk throughs to monitor the use of pacing guides. Many veteran teachers and advocates for basic-skills curriculum talked at length about how they want consistency and control over what other teachers are doing. Such advocacy reinforces the formation of new professional curriculum leadership identities.

What is most important is that the communication and interaction between principals and teachers parallels, to some extent, that between teachers and students. By this I mean that principals engage in a form of ritual control over teachers' conflicts and creativity in ways that do not necessarily affect the content of curriculum or distribution of knowledge. Similarly and ironically, many teachers control the substance of students' writing in an effort to teach "critical thinking" skills required on the tests. The principal appears to have control over teachers but may, in fact, have very little meaningful control. At the same time, the assertion of control over plan books, curriculum pacing guides, classroom observations, and data analysis forms enables the principals to appear as if they are doing something to improve student achievement. Clearly, contemporary principals must be concerned about student outcomes, yet this emphasis on control over curriculum-related *forms* more than curriculum content and learning (which is what the principal and teachers claim their school is all about) parallels the emphasis on form that emerges in the classrooms. Thus, *form* becomes more important than *substance in both the imparting of knowledge and principal–teacher relations.*

It can also be argued that this emphasis on curriculum *form* in Greenway and Elmhurst Schools serves to further reinforce the principals' emerging professional (data-focused) attitude toward general education curriculum and school knowledge. There are at least two dangers here. First, when form becomes the substantive curriculum for general education, all children are being poorly served in certain ways. This situation is most harmful for working-class children of color and for children living in poverty, who often lack the resources to gain that substance elsewhere. Second, if exemplary teachers stress order and form in their classrooms, principals with less instructional expertise and experience may well stress order and form in the curriculum (this is, however, dialectically linked). Indeed, Linda McNeil (1998) makes this very point in *Contradictions of Control*. Further, the ritual of control, or the appearance of an orderly curriculum, may unwittingly encourage students, like their teachers and principal, to engage with the form of the curriculum rather than the substance. This is not to suggest a set of linear relationships; each of these components exists in a dialectical relationship with each of the others, and these relationships are influenced by the circulating discourses of broader ideologies and cultural political shifts as these play out in particular community contexts. I expand on this point in chapter 6. For present purposes, this emphasis on form coexists with all the distributed and received messages regarding the importance of educating students in basic workplace skills for today's global economy.

### Lesson Plan Books

A key area in which control over teacher creativity and professional decision-making authority often surfaces is lesson plan books. Administrators frequently examine lesson plan books to ensure that teachers are using curriculum maps, covering the curriculum (state standards), recommended instructional practices, and otherwise planning effectively. Accountability pressures have intensified these evaluation practices, and many schools or districts require teachers to use specific planning formats, content standards, and instructional practices. Curriculum design programs that emphasize higher-order thinking skills, or "big ideas" (i.e., Wiggins & McTighe, *Understanding by Design*) are common topics at teacher orientations and faculty meetings. Although *Understanding by Design* (1998) and similar curriculum design models emphasize teaching for deep understanding and critical thinking, the ways in which administrators attempt to control or standardize teachers' use of these programs can have the opposite effect.

At Greenway School, for example, during a weeklong professional development session on *Understanding by Design* (in 2005) and during the orientation prior to the first day of the 2004–2005 school year, teachers were given a set of materials to guide their lesson plan development, with the understanding that they would be responsible for turning in to the principal plans in this format. Homework policies, classroom discipline, lesson plan formats (where to write the "big idea" and objectives, student activities, and assessments), classroom discipline policies, state content standards, and attendance procedures were all covered. Directions to teachers were fairly specific, as is illustrated by the example that tells them where to write "big ideas" on their lesson plans (the directions were given to teachers at orientation, and the example below is based on a first draft produced by a teacher committee):

> It is a good practice at the beginning of lessons for teachers to provide students with an overview of the big ideas that will be covered for each unit, including standards of academic content that will be required in the course. Such matters as the number and frequency of tests, methods of grading and reporting the test results and homework policies are valuable information for the student. Students should be expected to keep this information outlined in their notebooks.

Here the use of teachers' plan books emerges:

> Keep lesson plan books in the top drawer of your desk. It saves time and lessens confusion when a substitute teacher has to fill in for you. Plan books will be checked weekly. *They should be submitted to the principal as outlined in plan book guidelines.*

At this orientation, the principal told teachers that she would check their plan books weekly on Fridays and make any revisions prior to the beginning of the next week. The books came with an attached handout covering in detail how to write lesson plans in the expected format, with examples of the appropriate way of writing "big ideas" and related behavioral objectives. The instructions specified that plans should be clear and connected to the state standards. New teachers were given a special orientation regarding how they should write and turn in their lesson plans. The teachers at Elmhurst School, and indeed at many schools throughout the United States, are expected to adhere to similar policies.

Most important, perhaps, is the fact that each teacher is directed to submit lesson plans each week. Of course, teachers need to know what they are doing and plan accordingly, but the lesson planning mandates go way beyond ensuring that teachers are prepared. Interestingly, few teachers argued with the requirements in either public or private interviews, instead maintaining that it was their responsibility to develop lesson plans aligned with basic skills on state standards and tests. At the same time, some veteran teachers, many of whom had been leaders in the more progressive whole language movement, resented the principal's encroachment into what they considered their arena of expertise. For their part, Grant and Draper expressed concerns that teachers would not maintain fidelity to the state standards and the curriculum maps unless they were monitored directly. They justified their intense oversight largely in terms of the necessity for substitute teachers to know what to do in case of teacher absence; several teachers in both schools, however, told me privately that the principals always put more pressure on new teachers and on teachers who were loyal to the whole language philosophy.

There are larger issues to consider here. What does it mean for a teachers' committee to write documents that encourage the principal to exert control over teachers down to the level of checking lesson plan books? Such monitoring is not in any sense meaningful involvement in the curriculum development process by either teachers or principals, because it is not clear that plan books, even if completed in the specified formats, have any relationship to actual teaching or learning. Completing the plans is simply a ritual engaged in by vocal teachers and administrators as a way of asserting the appearance of order and control. In fact, focusing on lesson plan books contains any real struggle over the curriculum to a superficial level, as struggle over curriculum becomes flattened and defined as a struggle over plans (whether plans are written correctly, contain the correct elements, and so on).

Reportedly, some teachers resent principals' encroachment in the area of plan books (e.g., Johnson & Johnson, 2005; Weis, 1990). As teacher-ethnographers, Johnson and Johnson (2005) documented the trivial tasks they were forced to perform, such as coding plan books with district mandates. As Jeff Markam, a veteran whole language teacher at Elmhurst School, put it, "A lot of the comments on the books don't make any sense when I'm actually teaching, and then sometimes, I have to go looking for my plan book to teach on Monday morning." Likewise, Melanie Brooks, a relatively new teacher at Greenway, stated, "I don't mind getting feedback on my teaching, but it's all about paper control with the plan books. It actually screws up my planning because I plan before I know what the students need, in order to turn my book in on time." The point to note is that tensions among teachers, and between some teachers and the principal, emerge largely in relation to rituals of control over teachers' professionalism and creativity in their work. This resentment is not unlike the principals' resentment over the district whole language mandates described in chapter 2.

### Curriculum Pacing Guides

Principals Draper and Grant also required the use of curriculum pacing guides in order to ensure that teachers "covered" the tested academic standards sufficiently prior to the administration of state exams in May. Instructional pacing policies were covered during the opening-day faculty meeting in the fall of 2003. These pacing guides listed exact dates for teaching all units throughout the academic school year. Directions to teachers were fairly specific, as the following excerpt from the "Introduction to the District Pacing Guides" demonstrates:

> Elmhurst School is committed to improving academic standards and student performance. Based on the varied levels of performance found in classrooms, it is evident that support can no longer be relegated to only the students with the lowest performance. The key to increased student achievement lies with the school's ability to maximize all resources towards a common goal. With that in mind, realignment of resources and collaboration among District, Regional Centers, and School Differentiated Accountability (DA) staff in analyzing data and creating common action plans is critical. To positively impact student achievement across all schools, the consistent implementation of the core curriculum within the context of the [State] Continuous Improvement Model is essential. To this end, School and District administrators collaborated on the development of the template for the Pacing Guides and Instructional Focus Calendars ensuring the implementation of these materials School- and District-wide. In addition, lessons plans were developed by subject area administrators (e.g., English, Math). All of these materials are aligned to the District-wide administration of the interim assessments and the [State] Assessment Test. The consistent implementation of the core curriculum will maximize the impact of professional development provided and deployment of resources to your classrooms.

This level of directiveness with regard to instructional pacing is mirrored in many school districts because of the growing number of school officials concerned about instructional consistency related to tested curriculum objectives. Teachers may resent such restrictions on their professional decision-making capabilities and use of students' cultural capital or backgrounds, but it is difficult for them to complain publicly, particularly if they do not have tenure.

Principals Draper and Grant introduced curriculum pacing guides early in the fall of 2003. Grant justified them to the teachers in this way:

> Our new pacing guides were done during the summer to provide a viable and guaranteed curriculum. While the Curriculum Alignment Maps provide a broad structure to our curriculum, they do not give a clear sense of *emphasis or pace* to cover the content and develop necessary skills. In fact, last year many teachers argued that the Curriculum

Alignment Maps were not focused enough, and they didn't know "where to begin" to cover so much material. The Pacing Guide brings a sharper focus to the key elements of the Curriculum Alignment Maps: Enduring Understandings, Essential Questions, specific power standards, and it provides an instructional calendar for an effective pace.

In other words, these school members have attached a high value to standardization and instructional consistency.

### Classroom Walk Throughs

At the same opening-day faculty meeting where the curriculum pacing guides were introduced, the issue of walk throughs also emerged. The purpose of walk throughs was described as being to "check periodically that teachers are using the pacing guides appropriately." Draper told teachers: "Beyond formal supervision, expect periodic classroom walk throughs in which the principal and academic specialists will check to see if the classroom pacing guides are being used appropriately and if children are engaged in classroom instruction."

Teachers were also told at this meeting and in a follow-up memo that they had to have their curriculum pacing guides and lesson plans on their desks at all times. Each teacher was assigned to the principal or to a district academic specialist who would walk through the classroom, first on a weekly and later on a biweekly basis to check for use of the state standards and coverage of curriculum objectives on the appropriate dates specified in the pacing guides.

In this context, curriculum supervision becomes analogous to getting a meal at a fast food drive-through. The walk through process implies that principals or district administrators have a depth of curriculum knowledge that would allow them to formulate an almost instantaneous opinion of teacher instruction and student learning simply by walking from one end of the classroom to the other a few times.

Unquestionably, professional teachers need to have the knowledge and skills to make instructional decisions about teaching curriculum content and to plan accordingly. But in a scenario such as that described here who is responsible for the daily instructional decision making: principals, district administrators, specialists, or classroom teachers? Where do students' interests, cultural knowledge, and needs fit in? Some teachers—mostly the teachers with relatively progressive philosophies—maintain that this is their area of responsibility and see the principals and other administrators as infringing on their professional arena. At the same time, progressive educators tend to trust the learner and the learning process, seeking input from students when they make curriculum choices, an orientation hardly permitted, far less encouraged, under such close monitoring (e.g., Allington, 2002; Shannon, 2001).

Principals Grant and Draper fear that teachers will not attend to their responsibilities for content coverage and must, therefore, be monitored and controlled. Such fears are not uncommon or unfounded in some instances, but there are few attempts to problematize values of instructional consistency and order in Greenway and Elmhurst Schools. Indeed, much of the mainstream curriculum ("instructional") leadership advises administrators to use consistent procedures in their teacher evaluation processes but fails to problematize the underlying political issues that fuel these fears and behaviors.

### Making the "Other"

A second set of messages in the school revolves around an assumption of separatist conservative and progressive spheres, and the normality of certain types of behaviors and attitudes related to this separation. Such separatism is clearly a part of the curriculum leadership identities discussed in chapter 2. Greenway and Elmhurst Schools, however, enact certain routines and rituals to legitimate such separatism. This is true for both conservative perspectives about back-to-basics curriculum and concerns about preparation for work in the new economy, although there are occasional progressive counterdiscourses within these two schools, which I will discuss at a later point in the chapter.

To begin, it is important to note that separate curriculum spaces exist in the school, and that those teachers with conservative curriculum philosophies invade the progressive educators' spaces, whereas progressives never invade conservative spaces. Within the school, this parallels the traditional allocation of space whereby the principal comes and goes from classroom scenes (teachers' spheres), but teachers tend to remain in the classroom space. This division of space within the school was apparent to me when I made initial contacts with teachers in the spring of 2002 and was reinforced at faculty meetings over the next four academic years. As the following examples illustrate, vocally traditional teachers occupy specific spaces within the school. The faculty lunchroom is also separated by virtue of where people who are philosophically aligned choose to sit.

*Visit to Elmhurst School, September 9, 2003*   On this date I made my first visit to the faculty lounge and department workrooms located down the hall from the principal's office. The lounge contains two tables, and teachers have informally assigned seats for lunch. The veteran teachers and those teachers who are traditional and more vocal in opposition to whole language sit at one table, whereas teachers who are vocal in support of progressive education sit at the other table. When I inquired about this division a few months into the fieldwork, Ms. Marfel (a staunch supporter of progressive practices) said,

"Yeah, that gives us more opportunity to talk freely." I asked if people ever go to the other side, and she said, "The newer teachers who are more into basic-skills teaching and traditional practices come over here if they want to visit with a friend. Sometimes the department chair comes over if she wants to tell us something. We never really sit on the other side."

The same pattern of separation for conversation was apparent during the orientation meeting and in faculty meetings. Over time, however, as some teachers transferred and others shifted their philosophical orientation, the conservative teachers increased in number and the number of progressive teachers decreased substantially. As a result, the separation began to break down.

*Teachers' Lounge, Greenway School, October 10, 2003*  Many teachers were already in the lounge at 7:30 a.m. The teachers who had been vocally supportive of the curriculum pacing guides and increased attention to basic literacy skills were at one set of tables, and the teachers who were supportive of whole language were in a different group. It was clear that this was a deliberate separation of space.

Throughout the next four academic years, this pattern persisted at both schools, albeit with fewer numbers on the progressive side. The few teachers with progressive or whole language orientations sat apart from the majority of faculty members and complained to each other that the principal and most teachers encouraged basic skill and drill over meaningful learning activities. Although there were clearly separate spaces for traditional/conservative and progressive teachers, it was also clearly acceptable for the conservative staff members to invade progressive spaces. For example, the conservative veteran teachers frequently stopped by the "other" table. Yet, I never saw the progressive teachers at the more traditional, even "conservative" tables.

Significantly, teachers' interactions within these spaces tended to focus on their personal rather than work lives, albeit with a hint of complaint about workload and administrative control here and there. Little of the talk revolved around curriculum or students, although there was discussion about the principal. When teachers talked informally about curriculum or pedagogy, they most often focused on program implementation and test preparation activities. These patterns are evident in the following conversations.

*Elmhurst School, March 24, 2004*

*Jeff:*    Well, I had to search out my lesson plans again this morning.

*Maria:*   Mine were in my box, but I really could not make a lot of sense out of the comments. Well, I guess they make sense if you are intent on drilling kids on how to parrot objectives and fill out forms.

*Jeff:*    Well, anyway, I'm spending my weekends playing with my son.

*Maria:* I know what you mean. When we had to develop our lesson plans from the ground up based on the students' needs and our own ideas, it took a lot more time. I've taken up mountain biking.

*Jeff:* Oh, that's great. Where are you biking?

*Maria:* Mostly on the trails near the lake. I was thinking while I rode on Saturday about how many of our PLC (professional learning community) meetings are devoted to data analysis. It's fine to know how students are doing, but what are we really assessing and what are students learning?

*Jeff:* I know. All we hear in this school now is how we need to make performing plus status or how students need to move from one level to the next. I think we're losing our understandings of the reading and writing process. I worry about the new teachers really just parroting these terms like "big ideas" and "critical thinking." That's just teaching by the numbers, kind of like my son painting by the numbers.

*Greenway School, March 20, 2005*

Christina: I can't wait for break next week. After going to the Skillful Teaching [supervision strategy] workshop last week, I just felt like I was so behind with my lesson plans.

Mary: I'm anxious to get a week off, too. You know, when we get back, we'll have to get ready for [the state tests].

Christina: Yes, it will be back to chocolate break time.

For the traditional, conservative teachers at Greenway and Elmhurst, separatism encourages the construction of a progressive (i.e., laissez-faire) "other," in the sense that their own identities are formed in terms of a constructed notion that they are "good" (traditional, professional, or conservative) educators devoted to the improvement of academic achievement and 21st century learning skills. Whatever progressive elements exist within their identity structures tend to be only minimally encouraged by school members and the culture as a whole.

As I have suggested throughout this chapter, rituals of control permeate the school culture. Ingersoll (2006) writes about rituals that control teachers' work in relation to the hierarchy of administration and teachers' work in school organizations. At Greenway and Elmhurst the principals engage in this ritual when they check lesson plans and curriculum pacing guides, and teachers engage in a similar ritual with respect to the form of curriculum content. Students, in turn, work to "pass tests" and participate in the control ritual by being orderly and completing their test preparation materials on time. Johnson and Johnson (2005) noted similar student and teacher behaviors in their ethnography of Redbud Elementary School in Louisiana. The notion that *curriculum* (i.e., academic achievement) *must be taken seriously* is distributed at the same time as these rituals are enacted at Greenway and Elmhurst, leading the principals, teachers, and students to embrace and reinforce a fundamental contradiction. The means by which curriculum content is distributed, received, and monitored cannot possibly encourage the school community to focus on anything other than form. Although many would agree that students need to perform well academically in order to gain access to higher education and well-paid employment, the almost single-minded devotion to tests is problematic. Like Principals Draper and Grant, most educational leaders are not prepared to facilitate the critical discourse analysis and dialogue necessarily to critically examine underlying assumptions of test-driven policies and other curriculum trends. Yet critical dialogue and analysis skills are essential to open the door for transformative educational practices in schools and communities. I will return to this point in the last two chapters.

## School Cultures and Critical Curriculum Leadership

Many educational administration scholars since the late 1980s have examined school and leadership practices generally through critical lenses (e.g., Brunner, 1998; Capper, 1993; Dantley, 2005; Foster, 1986; Grogan & Andrews, 2002). These scholars nearly universally point to the importance of critique, transformation, and empowerment; yet, few have specifically attempted to examine curriculum leadership through critical lenses. Henderson and Kesson (1999) are two of the few scholars who have taken a critical approach to curriculum leadership work. Based on an analysis of curriculum theorists such as Pinar (2003), Henderson (2001) argues that school members must engage in serious, wise deliberations about curriculum issues with the ultimate purpose of helping students attain a democratic and moral way of living.

These critical aims and aspects of curriculum leadership are encouraged and supported at Babcock and Pinehurst Schools, the other two schools in my study. First, the school cultures support and enhance the principals' and influential teacher-leaders' critiques about the potentially unjust effects of neoconservative curriculum philosophies. Further, teachers work to become comfortable with open, authentic dialogue and even conflict with regard to the curriculum and their decision-making processes. Principals and teachers recognize contradictions in their beliefs about curriculum and support each other's struggles over curriculum aims and content. They use professional learning community structures as opportunities to critically analyze current curriculum and accountability policies, communicate about curriculum across grade levels and with community members, and talk openly about their struggles with curriculum decisions, particularly as these relate to require-ments about testing ELLs and other marginalized populations. Thereby edu-cators at these two schools find ways for social justice and students' interests to coexist with testing requirements. Messages distributed and received within the school reinforce that democratic education and social justice are primary concerns served by attention to academic achievement.

Second, Babcock and Pinehurst teachers tap into social justice and dem-ocratic values not usually considered during curriculum development and knowledge distribution in classrooms, thus eroding common sense about the primacy of standardization, basic skills, and workplace education. Like the situations at Greenway and Elmhurst, however, contradictions do appear in the school culture. Overall, however, as the following discussions of Babcock and Pinehurst Schools illustrate, critical curriculum leadership is enabled and encouraged within the school by teachers who recognize and connect with larger social struggles in their communities. Further, the teachers at these schools see their principals as curriculum leaders who challenge the status quo and continually pursue democratic education, which in turn, fuels critical curriculum leadership identity in the principals and other school members.

### Critical Deliberations about Curriculum

There is growing interest in identifying learning structures that foster profes-sional development and dialogue among teachers and other school members (e.g., Louis & Kruse, 1995; Mitchell & Sackney, 2009). Although these pro-fessional learning structures have provided educational leaders with many understandings about how to involve teachers in decision making and pro-vide opportunities for teacher reflection, professional learning communities do not necessarily lead to open dialogue and critical deliberations about con-troversial curriculum issues. In practice, norms of collegiality often prevail and decisions revolve around how to implement district, state, and federal mandates; how to increase test scores; and the pace of classroom instruction. Critical deliberations and serious conversations about the assumptions inher-ent in these tasks are often deferred or quickly resolved.

At Babcock and Pinehurst Schools, there are frequent, critical delibera-tions about the current curriculum, how it relates to the global economy, and its effect on working-class families and women. These range from discussing how categories on state tests (advanced, proficient, below standard, and seri-ously below standard) mirror economic differences between working-class and affluent families to identifying the reasons why women still do not receive equal pay as men. Significantly, these conversations about educational beliefs are connected to recent accountability and current policies.

*Faculty Meeting, Babcock School, January 28, 2004*
*Juidici (principal):* What are we measuring on state tests?
*Jim (2nd-grade teacher):* Academics—reading, math, science, and social studies.
*Juidici:* Yes, and what do students need to perform well on these academic assessments?
*Jim:* Knowledge and skills.
*Mary (4th grade teacher):* I would say it's tested knowledge and skills. They have to perform well enough to get a "proficiency" level on the tests. That way they don't get tracked into academic intervention services.
*Adam (2nd grade teacher):* That's really nothing new, if we think back to how long school officials have been figuring out ways to differentiate kids and instruction according to ability levels.
*Juidici:* Yes, and think about what else was happening at that time. Schools were modeled after factories, and in educational administration, principals were modeled after managers who kept track of time on task and geared all efforts toward improved efficiency.
*Mary:* Yes, but I think tests have always privileged males and more affluent children overall, and that hasn't changed.
*Jim:* Look how well I've been served. I'm still struggling to pay my student loans and everything else.
*Adam:* That's because we're not in employment categories like doctors, lawyers, and Wall Street executives.
*Mary:* Just think of the pressures kids face today.

*Faculty Meeting, Pinehurst School, February 2, 2004*
*Hughes (principal):* What are the assumptions of the district and state curriculum guides?
*Jan (sixth grade teacher):* I think it means that what we value is what we test, and what we test is what we value.... Here "I" means basic academics. Kids have to perform well academically, but is that all there is? [Murmurs of agreement]
*Robert (seventh grade teacher):* The tests drive everything now, or at least they try to.
*Hughes:* Well, the state requires that we administer these tests—that's true. I also think it's problematic if we do not think about the implications of what we're saying and doing when we comply with this policy in our curricula. What if we were testing athletic prowess? What if that were the basis of testing? How would we talk and act differently with our students?

*Tim (seventh grade teacher and Teacher's Union president):* Why are we spending time on this conversation? Teachers' time is valuable.

*Hughes:* Yes, that's why we're having serious intellectual conversations during our faculty meetings. We need to be thoughtful about our role in differentiating students according to these tests. So, what if we were testing athletic skills?

*Laci (sixth grade teacher):* I agree—we're professionals, and we have to talk about these issues related to the test. Well, that would mean that some of my girls' basketball participants would be considered better than the "top male kids" in the advanced classes.

*Robert:* Yeah, and we're so used to dividing kids, we'd divide them by athletic ability—the clumsy ones in one class and the graceful ones in another class.

*Tim:* Think of the best jobs in this country. They'd be the ones for physically strong people rather than brainy, white-collar people like doctors and lawyers and Wall Street CEOs.

I observed conversations like these regularly during faculty meetings in both schools. Over time, both principals pushed the teachers to debate the roots of efficiency, intelligence, and inherent class differentiation in state tests. As teachers critically examined the roots of state tests and related curriculum practices, they developed more critical awareness of their own beliefs and practices; of the unintended consequences of state tests on teacher and student morale; and of how they contributed to social inequities. Further, teachers often discussed and debated whether workplace goals ought to be the basis for curriculum, and in particular, the history of gender inequities in the workplace. Significantly, male, female, and racial- or ethnic-minority teachers and staff members were equally comfortable initiating these conversations.

*Lunch Period, Elmhurst School, November 23, 2004* Cheryl (an African American third grade teacher) was talking about the salaries of single, female teachers: Starting salaries in business are much larger than starting salaries in education. Single women just can't live on that kind of money. Men come in as teachers and can advance into administration much easier for more dollars. Teachers, just because they are women, don't make the same money after 15 years. It used to make me so mad [she was a single mother when she started teaching]. These male teachers [where she used to work] used to make so much more money when they advanced into AP jobs. I was 22 years old and making $20,000. Male administrators couldn't survive if it weren't for female teachers and secretaries.

Many other times throughout that academic year, this topic surfaced among female teachers. Jane, a White math teacher, took up the issue of gender inequality during numerous lunch conversations, faculty meetings, and in a later interview I conducted with her. She offers a feminist analysis of why pay for female teachers and secretaries is low:

> I have had male students say to me that they do intend to be elementary teachers and they've asked, "How much do they [teachers] make?" Now, that's the disappointing factor. Since it is basically—out there in the real world—dominated by women, and it is a traditional women's occupation its traditional pay is low because it is not considered equal to male work and that is a very poor perception of the males that control the school world because they couldn't function without those teachers who may not have a master's degree but have to take more specialized certification to move into administration. They [secretaries] are not paid what they are worth. In the end, most boys decide they want to go into the corporate world so that they can make more money. Teachers just do not get paid what they're worth unless they can quickly move into administration.

*Babcock School, February 2004*   In the teachers' lounge, three females (two White and one African American) were complaining about how the male principal and assistant principal want women to take care of them, and that those are often women who work in low-paying jobs. For example, the principal and male teachers expect them to clean up the teachers' lounge and do other menial chores:

*Cindy:*   They have wives who take care of them at home, and women teachers who take care of them at school.

*Marta:*   Imagine what the school would look like if it were full of men. What a mess!

This example reveals that female teachers in this school feel comfortable with a cross-racial discussion about gender and class inequality, and particularly, low pay for women and minorities. The second topic of growing and sustained critique among teachers is the perception that affluent families want poor servants, as the following two case examples illustrate.

*Pinehurst School, November 2005*   Three female teachers were complaining that powerful and affluent businessmen from the suburbs were willing to partner with schools and run them like businesses, but did not have the courtesy to spend time in those working-class neighborhoods and schools.

*Eden (White teacher):* They expect schools to train everyone at a high academic level, and then they expect certain kids to clean up their yards and their homes.

*Jan (African American teacher):* It's true. [The chairwoman of the Education Trust] talks about equity, but she's really talking about training kids to work in the factories she owns.

*Michelle (African American teacher):* There's all this talk that schools need so much reform, but in the end, it's really that schools need more testing.

*Marianne (White teacher):* The businessmen come in like knights in shining armor to fix the schools with their no-nonsense approaches and commonsense ideas, but they're really just more interested in control of education.

It is important to note that there are only two male teachers in the school, which probably contributes to the women teachers' comfort in critiquing local businessmen. In addition, separate racial and economic spaces are maintained in the community. Some of the women criticize both the fact that minorities and women earn less than businesspeople, and that businesspeople expect to have control over the urban schools that will train the children they expect to become working-class factory workers and domestics. Importantly, these teachers openly speculate about the relationships among economic disparities, race, and gender as part of their everyday conversations. As the following examples make clear, teachers frequently referred to the segregation in the community and speculated on how this might relate to achievement gaps.

*Pinehurst School, September 28, 2003* The meeting with language arts teachers was interesting. I introduced myself, talked a bit about my study, then asked them to make comments. Nick said that students would react differently to school depending on what part of the city they came from. All the teachers agreed there were "two worlds" in their community, and that these worlds needed to be bridged. One world had lush, green lawns and large, newer homes, and the other, in the city, had rental properties and rundown homes. Cheryl recalled how Mr. Hughes had correlated high state test scores with regions of the community, and the staff agreed that closing achievement gaps required more than data analysis and test preparation. She added, "We need to close achievement gaps because they are part of a social justice issue and a community need" (field notes).

Cheryl's comments were considered seriously on multiple occasions. When teachers and administrators create norms of serious deliberation about curriculum issues, the way is cleared for neoprogressive educational and social movements.

*Sixth Grade Social Studies, Babcock School, April 15, 2003* Before administering a test, Michelle, an African American teacher, was telling her students about urban planning. She asked, "Is everyone familiar with Miller Road?" Most students nodded affirmatively.

*Michelle:* What do you notice about the population on either side of the road?
*Ramona:* Yeah. Once my grandma, she said, "You don't go on the other side of that road much. The Whites live over there. This is our side."
*Ms. Stark:* Legally, she could have, but she would likely have been very uncomfortable. It was a bit different if you made a lot of money, and now it's not quite as overt. The pattern is still there.

No one would dispute that the neighborhoods in the community where Babcock School is located are largely racially segregated (and the same is true of the Pinehurst School community). The large housing project "on the wrong side of the tracks" (i.e., Miller Road) is virtually all Black and Hispanic/Latino, whereas the areas surrounding the school—the areas with green lawns and newer homes—are entirely White. The community segregation plays out in the school demographics as well. The preceding two examples illustrate how the school cultures at Babcock and Pinehurst have developed norms that permit serious conversations about social, racial, and economic inequities, both among the staff and with students. These conversations embody and support critical curriculum leadership formation in both schools, often leading to open conflict and debates. Much of the mainstream education literature advises educational leaders to limit conflict because controlled conflict is associated with creativity and change. Yet in practice, educators often halt conflict too quickly, before the point where change can occur. In Greenway and Elmhurst Schools, conflict is actually suppressed. Because Babcock and Pinehurst educators usually resist the urge to shut down conflict in the name of maintaining order, they are able to expose potentially unjust effects of testing and standardization, particularly on children of color and from low-SES backgrounds.

*Conflict*

Teachers at Babcock and Pinehurst Schools regularly engaged in serious conversations and open debate. Further, they deliberately incorporated controversy and conflict into their lessons. For example, they presented students with alternative beliefs and theories about academic subjects. For example, they highlighted the serious disagreements that exist over scientific methodology, goals, and theories by assigning students different perspectives and having them engage in serious debates.

*Sixth Grade Science Class, Babcock School, October 2005*

*Teacher:* What kind of debates over climate did you notice when you read your science book?

*Don:* Well, some people thought that climate problems or global warming were just made up, and other people thought that climate problems were a serious emergency.

*Mary:* I'm not sure the textbook didn't come down on the side of the people that thought climate problems were real.

*Barb:* I think so too. The authors did not really disguise that much.

*Don:* I read an article for the extra assignment that was written by people in Al Gore's company or whatever it is, and it was pretty convincing. [He reads from the text]

*Seventh Grade Social Studies, Pinehurst School, November 2005*

*Teacher:* What did you learn from different perspectives about the Iraq War?

*Bill:* It seems like there was not a lot of real evidence to justify going into war.

*Sarah:* Was it that there wasn't evidence, or that they presented evidence to Congress that looked like it justified the war?

*Bill:* That's a good way to explain it.

*Mara:* I think the book didn't really get into that enough.

In these examples, conflict is overtly addressed in the curriculum and is not hidden from students. That is, teachers feel comfortable with conflict, and conflict takes place in the context of strong mutual respect for different points of view. Likewise, conflict is viewed as healthy, not dysfunctional, and is continually present during faculty meetings and various decision-making processes. Teachers in both Pinehurst and Babcock Schools talked at length about how their principals encouraged ideological difference, individuality, and various fluid subgroup identities at the school. The subgroups were fluid in that they were described as temporary alliances on particular issues or situations.

Subgroup membership changed frequently and shifted over time, depending on the particular circumstances. In this culture, the principals promoted *shifting leadership* across the curriculum groups and subgroups—encouraging the emergence of multiple voices, knowledges, and debates. To be clear, leadership roles shifted among multiple members of the group, depending on the situation, who had particular interest in or knowledge about the issue at hand, and group membership at the time. During meetings, teachers prompted each other to "say what you really mean" or "push on that idea more." As one Babcock teacher put it, "Conflict is emotionally hard to listen to in a public debate, but it's necessary for people to get real and talk about issues that go somewhere."

By way of example, in one typical Babcock School faculty meeting, Principal Juidici told those in attendance that she recognized they had concerns about the literacy curriculum, and she asked everyone to speak publicly about their perspectives. Her secretary taped and later transcribed their perspectives on large charts for display during the next meeting. In the follow-up meeting (allowing reflection time between the meetings was important), Juidici read each perspective, treating each with the same level of respect; similarly, the group honored and seriously considered all points of view. The next day, Juidici asked if any of the teachers who had not attended the previous meeting would like to hold another meeting to deal with this agenda item. In response, a veteran English teacher called three subsequent, well-attended meetings. Juidici reminded that teacher to extend personal invitations to people with differing perspectives on the issue. A site document analysis of minutes from the three later meetings revealed that, indeed, people with different perspectives attended and shared openly.

The fifth meeting in this series was attended by many more teachers, who added their perspectives to those gathered during the first meeting (again, these were recorded on the wall charts). Some of these new perspectives aligned with those already on the charts, while others offered new twists and ideas. All solutions proposed (in some detail) were recorded and later distributed by Juidici's secretary. Principal Juidici was aware that teachers had diverse responses to and opinions about literacy—responses and perspectives she "needed to hear" in order "to understand where people were coming from and learn how to work with this textbook and ELA achievement problem." As Juidici listened respectfully to individuals who had previously been marginalized in literacy decisions, the established order regarding "how we teach reading around here" began to erode and change. Several teachers also commented that her openness toward differing opinions helped heal contentious histories among staff members. Under Juidici's leadership, Babcock School aimed its literacy efforts and resources toward targeted groups (i.e., African American males, Latinos, and English language learners).

Early in my data collection, the faculty began examining the literacy gaps between African American males and their peers. In addition to showing lower achievement, African American males were disproportionately placed in detention and alternative high schools; meanwhile, disproportionate numbers of White males were in advanced placement classes. The faculty held discussions of the reasons for these differences and instigated a pilot program grounded in African-centered pedagogy and literacy. In particular, two African American male teachers were trained in how to infuse an African-centered curriculum into language acquisition and instruction, with the goal of increasing literacy proficiency.

After 3 years, the findings of external evaluations (related to the whole school and to the pilot program) were mixed, but the recommendations for improvement stated that the pilot classes (which were small, containing 10 to 12 students) should be continued. In order to maintain the small class sizes in the pilot program, most other teachers (who had primarily middle-class students) were required to increase their class sizes to 30 students (from 22–24). Because of scarce resources (materials, assistants, number of faculty), maintaining the small class sizes in the pilot classrooms placed a strain (heavier grading responsibilities and workloads) on the teachers who had 30 students. Thus, to those with disproportionate workloads, the recommendation that pilot program classes remain small was an affront.

Teachers were split over whether or not to continue the program. Some noted that the pilot program segregated students. Yet these discussions, although heated, remained focused on issues not personalities. Participants did not label or blame individuals or groups for the tracking and segregation issues. At the same time, Principal Juidici worked through the conflict over segregation and racial tensions with an eye on social change. By the end of the school year, the achievement gaps among Whites, African Americans, and Hispanics had narrowed slightly, and the school was recognized on a statewide list of "most improved schools."

*Empowerment and Transformation*

By openly debating curriculum decisions, particularly those that affect marginalized groups, school principals, teachers, and students affirm the significance of liberation/empowerment/praxis. Educational administrators, a critical view argues, should "empower" and "share power" with staff, students, and community (described as "followers") and, in turn, "transform" society (e.g., Capper, 1993; Foster, 1986). One way administrators empower others is by helping oppressed individuals and groups become aware of their oppression. The assumption is that administrators understand the nature of oppression better than the people who are experiencing oppression can, and therefore can empower them and "give voice to the voiceless" (Tierney & Foster, 1991). If we educators are to accept our commitments seriously, we must have a special concern for helping to liberate society from the various conditions of oppression, particularly those of ignorance and illiteracy. Freire (1970/1993, 1973/1998) has shown that misery, oppression, ignorance, and illiteracy are more than societal embarrassments, in that they are necessary ingredients for maintaining poverty. The Babcock and Pinehurst educators have assumed the responsibility to pass on to students knowledge and skills that empower the many rather than the few, and in so doing, to foster a more just and compassionate world. This view is in keeping with Dewey's (1916/2008) concept of education as the process by which we can make a world. Principals Juidici, Hughes, and their staffs purposely empower students and teachers to cultivate awareness of oppression and work toward social change within their communities, as the following examples make clear.

*Fourth Grade Science Class, Babcock School, 2004–2006*   In the previous chapter I described the incident whereby students used data from soil analyses to develop urban neighborhood revitalization plans. Their soil analysis projects revealed high lead content in the soil as a result of the demolition of dilapidated homes in the neighborhood. The class created a plan to clean up the affected areas, which required reading textbooks, city reports, and other resources, then applying what they learned to draft written reports. After the children presented their reports to a parent group and members of the neighborhood council, several community leaders organized a neighborhood cleanup event. Parents, the principal, teachers, community members, and local environmentalists worked with the students to clean up the soil with a natural product and then plant flowers in these vacant lots. In 2005, Babcock School and the local community organization won a state award for community revitalization.

*Sixth Grade Social Studies Class, Pinehurst School*   Students were concerned about city plans to eliminate funding for a city park near the school. Many of the students had been visiting the park since they were in kindergarten. Further, because the school lacked green space, teachers often used the park for science activities and recreation trips. At students' request, the social studies class wrote letters to the city council, requesting the opportunity to present their case at an upcoming city council meeting.

*Ben:*   If the city eliminates funding for the park, it will be rundown, and we will not have the nice park place to play and do science experiments. We want to protest to the city council and see if we can make a difference.

*Leila:*   If the park gets rundown, it will be full of crime and no one will be able to use it.

The teacher encouraged the students to research the issue thoroughly and write to city council members. Because she was responsible for a particular set of state standards dealing with research skills, she had students document their efforts in a particular way. Further, she had students revise their letters multiple times, making the message clear and free of errors.

*Mr. Makin (city council leader):*   We were so impressed with the students' proposal that we tabled closing the park. Of course, the budget will need to support the park and that remains to be seen over time, but the children really made a good case.

*Principal Hughes:* We have come to realize that we cannot develop students' human feelings and interests in a few weeks after we teach the tested skills. We can, however, teach academic skills.

In both preceding examples it is noteworthy that Babcock and Pinehurst students are developing agency as they learn the academic skills required by state standards and tests. I will return to this point in chapter 5. Although students in both schools have ambitions outside of their communities, they feel empowered and responsible to improve the human conditions in their neighborhoods and communities, meaning that they will be good citizens, wherever they end up living.

The next section presents a problem-posing case to help you explore how a teacher challenges new professionalism and, in the process, violates cultural norms.

---

**PROBLEM-POSING CASE**
**"Why We Learn"—Violating School Cultural Norms**

*Greenway School, September 18, 2004*

In the second week of school, Samantha, a young fifth grade teacher with recent teacher preparation in progressive education and a social justice orientation, asked her 10-year-old students to write about "why they learn." The overwhelming majority of students wrote about learning in order to compete for a high-paying job. Given this result, Samantha was concerned about students' lack of intrinsic motivation for learning. When she shared the letters with her colleagues, however, she realized that most teachers agreed with the students. Several teachers also pointed out that the writing samples evidenced poor literacy skills in general, comments that initiated a heated disagreement among teachers, who were divided over the relevance of student comments in relation to growing concerns about literacy achievement. Dr. Draper showed teachers literacy data from the past 3 years indicating a downward trend in measures of reading vocabulary, critical thinking, spelling, and phonics skills. Although a few teachers agreed with Samantha and expressed their allegiance to the whole language philosophy as a way to foster effective literacy education, most were more concerned about test scores. Without realizing it, Samantha had violated unspoken school rules about keeping the primary focus on basic skills within the curriculum. All of the teachers agreed that they needed to make the curriculum more rigorous in terms of critical thinking even while they were espousing beliefs in basic skills instruction.

Conflict among teachers fueled Draper's concerns about student achievement and inconsistent basic skills instruction in the school. In response she launched a curriculum-alignment project in which teachers were expected to turn in their plan books and use data-driven curriculum pacing guides to ensure coverage of basic skills. She also looked for professional development programs and materials that would ensure more consistent basic-skills instruction in all classrooms. Draper listened in earnest when the CEO of the local Education Trust talked about the lack of instructional emphasis on facts and basic skills and the miseducation of students for a global workforce. She joined a regional curriculum association that presented a series of workshops on standards alignment, curriculum design models, and test preparation. She also sent several teacher-leaders to *Understanding by Design* and *Success for All* trainings, and these teachers subsequently trained the full faculty.

By the fall of 2005, the curriculum association (and local educators) recognized Dr. Draper as a "data-driven" leader with the knowledge and skills to improve student outcomes in her school. Dr. Draper gradually began to identify herself as distinct from "laissez-faire" whole language advocates because of her search for ways to make the curriculum more rigorous and, at the same time, consistent across all classrooms. Although school faculty meetings were generally orderly, and supervision records suggested more instructional consistency in classrooms over time, those teachers who embraced whole language philosophies believed that they had been marginalized in curriculum decisions and largely occupied separate spheres in the school. Veteran teachers with years of experience in literacy instruction were very vocal about their concerns related to children's proficiency in basic reading and writing skills.

### Questions

1. What do the teachers do to encourage or block the formation of new professional curriculum leadership identity (see chapter 3)?
2. To what extent does the school contribute to or inhibit this identity formation?
3. Which aspects are inhibited and which are encouraged?

**Summary**

As I noted in the last two chapters, based upon my research and other related studies (e.g., Anderson, 2009; Daly, 2009; Henderson & Kesson, 1999; Johnson & Johnson, 2005), new professional and critical curriculum leadership identities are closely connected to perceptions about the purposes of curriculum and learning. New professional curriculum leadership emerges in relation to constructed—and somewhat contradictory—commonsensical beliefs about utilitarian purposes of education, related efficiency and productivity discourses, test-driven curriculum dialogues in "professional learning communities," and the need for competition and critical thinking skills in a global work environment. Although new professional, efficiency-driven curriculum leaders frequently express empathy for the children behind the achievement gap numbers, they focus much of their efforts on instructional consistency in core academic subjects and give less attention to students' interests, the broader culture, or social justice issues.

In some contrast, critical curriculum leaders recognize the reality that test scores are important to children's futures, but they also experience moments of critique about the unjust effects of the tests on children—critiques that influence their beliefs about curriculum and leadership thereof. Changing what principals and teachers take for granted as "common sense" about standardized curricula and test preparation requires tapping into a different set of values that they already hold but have not yet connected to curriculum leadership roles. All of this curriculum leadership identity formation takes place within a particular school culture and political time, as illustrated in this chapter.

# 5

# Curriculum and Development Processes

Curriculum reform movements and testing mandates that promote "the right knowledge," teacher deskilling, and competition can promote new professional curriculum identity formation in some rather important ways, as discussed in chapters 2 and 4. As curriculum leaders define themselves in opposition to what they call "laissez-faire" (progressive) teaching practices, encourage the use of standardized curriculum materials and instructional strategies, aim all school efforts toward improved test scores, and compete for good students in the open market, their curriculum work (perhaps unconsciously) becomes part of a larger conservative movement. Along a different path, as discussed in chapters 3 and 4, critical curriculum leaders' personal concerns about fundamental shifts in common sense about curriculum and a concurrent commitment to progressive curriculum philosophy and ideals lead them to critique current education discourses and become committed to democratic, neoprogressive education. In order to promote critical curriculum leadership, curriculum development processes must ask a particular set of questions (Kliebard, 1992) and support a critical consciousness about broader cultural political shifts and their effects on teaching and learning in schools and communities (Gramsci, 1971).

This chapter examines relationships among curriculum content decisions, development processes, and broader cultural politics; what teachers and students see as the positives and negatives of current curriculum practices; and the ways in which these factors may contribute to a school/community culture that encourages emerging critical curriculum leadership. My intent here is not to criticize leaders who use standardized curricula and decision-making models, but rather to examine how broader social, cultural, and economic institutions interact and intersect in current curriculum decisions and so encourage alternative, critical curriculum leadership identities and actions.

It is no accident that the larger part of this chapter is devoted to neoconservative discourse related to standardization, consistency, and test preparation. Although many teachers support progressive philosophies, especially in language arts and social studies, they often remain silent. Many of the curriculum issues that emerge as categories are, at heart, conservatively oriented, and teachers and administrators typically have more to say about them. It is also significant that even in schools where principals and other members of the school community have a critical orientation toward curriculum, many progressive teachers keep quiet about their views, suggesting that progressive curriculum content, pedagogy, and politics have been forced underground in many contemporary schools. This observation dovetails with the presence of separate spheres in schools, as described in the last chapter, where traditional and emerging conservative educators feel comfortable invading progressive teachers' space but progressive educators almost never invade conservative spaces.

That conservative voices dominate educational discourse is in itself significant for the argument I present in this book. Conservative, new professional teachers and administrators dominate the space and discourse in many schools, reinforcing once again the ethos of conservative superiority. Progressive educators' relative silence can be attributed to the ways in which the school promotes separatism and superiority of conservative philosophies. Future research needs to focus more directly on progressive teachers in order to probe the knowledge behind their silence. At the same time, critical curriculum leaders of all kinds can and do find their voices, tap into underlying social justice values, and thereby interrupt circulating conservative discourses related to inequitable distribution of "the right knowledge" and cultural reproduction in schools. The latter part of this chapter provides specific examples of how principals, teachers, students, and community members develop curriculum in ways that do exactly this. The chapter concludes with a problem-posing case that explores tensions related to contemporary ideals of standardized curricula and consistent instruction. First, however, I explore varied curriculum meanings, purposes, and development processes in the current political context, using examples from the literature as well as my own study.

## Meanings of Curriculum

*Curriculum*, as I use the term in this book, refers not only to the official standards, written curriculum maps, or courses and related instructional activities but also to the contextualized meanings, underlying (conscious and unconscious) assumptions, activities, and organization of the educational program created by teachers, students, and administrators. Although the No Child Left Behind Act and other related policies have significantly restructured curriculum content and assessments in schools, educators and students still make curriculum decisions on a daily basis. And as Michael Apple (1992) has persuasively argued, such decisions are political acts, deeply affected by broader cultural–political movements, traditions in education, and social and economic institutions.

More specifically, curriculum is the content of education—what is taught and to whom—the meanings of which are inextricably linked to broader social, political, and economic institutions. Each individual constructs the meaning of curriculum through a dynamic interaction among his or her underlying assumptions, sociocultural and political influences, the content targeted in the written curriculum, and the contexts (school, district, state nation) of the particular educational program and timeframe in which he or she is situated. The keys to critical curriculum leadership are the abilities, first, to raise consciousness about the underlying assumptions behind curriculum and, second, to develop curricula in ways that inspire new progressive educational and social movements.

In the current era of accountability, schools must maintain official written curricula that identify specific objectives for each grade level or course and how they align to state standards and tests. Educators and students draw on their personal philosophies, assumptions, and content knowledge—shaped by macrolevel cultural–political shifts—to develop, interpret, and enact these written curriculum documents within a particular school and community. In a school with a history of administrative concerns about making adequate yearly progress on state tests, for instance, a principal's comment that "we need to prepare for the state tests" could mean that teachers need to emphasize basic skill curriculum targets and use more test preparation worksheets in their classrooms. The same comment would have quite a different meaning to teachers in another school with a history of less pressure about test results. In the latter scenario, the test preparation comment might arise as school and community members dialogue about how to maintain a calm and productive atmosphere in homes and at school during testing week. Although the content of these two curriculum-related conversations is the same in both schools, the purposes and constructed meanings of curriculum are quite different: giving teachers fair warning about test performance expectations and curriculum delivery in the first scenario versus offering support for a calm atmosphere and optimal test performance in the second scenario. Further, as noted in chapters 2 and 3, the ways in which teachers interpret and respond to the principals' comments over time affect the ways in which they view the principal as the formal curriculum leader of the school. In this chapter, I invite you to consider curriculum in this broader sense in order to recognize how much of what school and community members do and the underlying meanings and assumptions behind what they do, is important curriculum work.

## The Nature of Curriculum under New Professional Curriculum Leadership

Recent accountability mandates, back-to-basics, and new public management (NPM) movements have renewed interest in classic theories of curriculum as mental discipline and related rational, technical development processes (e.g., Schwaub, 1978; Tyler, 1949). Updated versions of Tyler's (1949) rationale are now packaged in standardized, "teacher-proof" materials designed to cover particular content knowledge and quickly raise standardized test scores. As I discussed in the introduction, Tyler created a rational, technical method for curriculum development in which educators think first about aims and objectives, second about the kind of subject matter or experiences most likely to help students achieve those objectives. They then pair the objectives and instructional practices programmatically and finally, evaluate the results of the curriculum in some way. Many contemporary schools and districts follow a similar rational process in the development of "pacing guides" or *Understanding by Design* (Wiggins & McTighe, 1998/2004); however, the design is typically "backwards," in that it begins with summative assessments (e.g., state tests), then identifies daily curriculum content objectives or standards, instructional strategies, and formative assessments that all align with the summative assessments. Such curriculum design modes are intended to promote higher levels of thinking and understanding among learners; however, many educators rely on state standardized test items as the ultimate goal of understanding, and thereby (unconsciously) reduce the depth of understanding by virtue of the standardized tasks required. Although popular curriculum models like maps and pacing guides ensure instructional consistency and standards alignment, scripted curriculum designs have also led to low teacher morale and rote memorization of fixed subject matter defined in adult terms, with little regard for broader social and cultural inequities or even making the subject matter meaningful and relevant to children (Wohlstetter, Datnow, & Park, 2008).

Further, research has consistently shown that low-income students and students of color consistently underperform on high-stakes, standardized tests (e.g., Madaus & Clark, 2002; McNeil, 2005; McNeil & Valenzuela, 2000). Research also highlights how high-stakes testing dominates pedagogic discourse in the United States (Au, 2007), and furthermore, controls curriculum content, in that high-stakes standardized tests have defined what counts as legitimate school knowledge: a knowledge domain is considered legitimate only if it is on the test (Au, 2008). In other words, this aim for legitimacy has narrowed the curriculum to tested subjects and tested knowledge.

High-stakes tests also exert considerable control over the form that content knowledge takes in the classroom, as teachers emphasize specific facts or pieces of knowledge that appear on tests (Pedulla et al., 2003). Such tests also leverage control over teacher pedagogies, as teachers increasingly rely on teacher-centered, lecture-based pedagogies in order to keep up with the content and knowledge forms required by tests (Au, 2007). Au (2008) argued that these two phenomena associated with high-stakes tests are linked; that is, race and class inequalities and increased restrictions on pedagogic discourse. The following two examples illustrate curriculum narrowing, inequities, and pedagogical shifts and how these phenomena are shaped by macro- (sociocultural and political) and microlevel (local) politics and recent emphases on efficiency and productivity in professional curriculum practices.

## Politics and Historical Practices

School norms and curriculum decisions are closely linked to community politics and historical practices. In two of the schools I studied, politics clearly affected hiring, diversity policies, scheduling, and curriculum committee representation, all of which affect the designation of curriculum, development, and instructional delivery systems.

### *Hiring*

Greenway School employed 85 teachers and staff members in the 2002–2003 school year, and roughly the same number in 2005–2006. Similarly, Elmhurst employed 74 teachers and staff members consistently between 2002 and 2006. Personal data regarding hometown communities and schools attended were available for 85% and 90% of teachers in these schools, respectively. Whereas the local community is 70% minority, the teachers at both schools are overwhelmingly White, although diversity has increased somewhat in recent years: Greenway has six African American and two Latina teachers, whereas Elmhurst has three African American teachers. Of these, 64% of Greenway teachers and 79% of Elmhurst teachers are female. There are no male teachers of color at either school. These demographics stand in contrast to national trends of increased hiring of minority teachers.

Data regarding teachers' hometowns and school attendance are particularly revealing, in that teachers at both schools are predominantly local: *74% of the faculty (both male and female) grew up in Treelane and Hillside or attended schools with similar cultural demographics.* Further, the majority grew up or has lived in these communities for many years and attended regional universities. These facts suggest there is likely to be relative congruence between home and school influences on curriculum and learning in these communities. At all four schools in my study, many teachers recognized the localized nature of the teaching force and that they shared similar working-class backgrounds with their students. Further, even in the conservatively oriented Greenway and Elmhurst schools, many teachers expressed appreciation for multiculturalism and interest in culturally relevant pedagogy. They quickly followed up, however, with concerns about taking time away from academics and test preparation. Several teachers comment on this.

*Greenway School, November 17, 2003*  Ramona talked about the localized nature of the faculty and about their concerns for children while, in the same breath, she expressed deep concerns about test scores.

*Ramona:* Almost all the teachers are from the area. Everybody knew somebody in order to get the job. That's nice in that we know the kids' parents and their grandparents oftentimes. We want these kids to succeed, to get out of the factories or off the streets. In some ways, that means we should teach in ways that are authentic and meaningful, but the kids also have to do well on these test scores to get anywhere…. Unfortunately, the principal and other vocal teachers think that means skill-and-drill test prep.

*Sarah:* Yeah, my first day on the job I met old friends from high school in the faculty lounge. I had not seen these people in years. It was like old home week. Right away, I thought, "I know their kids, too. They will be in my classes." It's become a problem sometimes because I think they should be taught a certain way. Dominating them with skill and drill on irrelevant information doesn't help.

Yet, drill is exactly what Ramona and Sarah did with their students. In fact, by the 2004–2005 school year, they believed skill and drill was the right thing to do, using discourse related to 21st century learning, standards, and testing as a rationale for doing so. In the next section, I explore the school's political history and why teachers' increasing reliance on worksheets and other teacher-centered pedagogical practices prompted a shift in the principals' concerns and thinking about curriculum.

*Ramona:* It's all sort of an incestuous hiring process at Greenway.

*RY:* Is it accidental that so many teachers were born and raised in the community?

*Ramona:* No, the school board likes to hire teachers from the community. Teachers often know someone in order to get hired. In fact, many of the teachers are related to each other.

*Elmhurst School, February 1, 2004*

*Darryl:* In order to get a job at Hillside Schools, you have to sub for several years, and then in the end, you have to know someone. In many ways, it makes for a very political environment, but it also helps us know our kids and where they came from.

*Mary:* It's sort of a patronage system. It's like you have to pay your dues by subbing and then, as long as you know somebody, you can get a job in the school. So we all know each other, and often the kids, when we start.

*Darryl:* I think it's good in a way to build community, but the downside is you don't get any kind of infusion of new ideas or perspectives.

Many Greenway and Elmhurst schoolteachers were White, and a very high proportion of them grew up in working-class homes and had parents employed at the local steel or auto parts factory. These teachers used education to move into the professional realm of teaching. In fact, job application materials and my teacher interviews indicated that many teachers had worked part-time in factories and local businesses while they attended college and in the summers. Several teachers commented that they were told to mention their connection with established community businesses during the interview process in order demonstrate an ongoing connection to their communities. As the teachers themselves pointed out, the hiring process is very political, but at the same time, new teachers enter the school with personal knowledge and concern for the children and their community.

*Cultural Diversity Policies and Practices* Both districts had instituted diversity policies with regard to teacher hiring, but are only beginning to see limited success. Staff members in both schools are still overwhelmingly White. And although some teachers are interested in culturally responsive teaching practices as an excellent strategy to help "our children" learn—and indeed some use multiculturalism very effectively in their own classrooms— these efforts are marginalized at Greenway and Elmhurst Schools. As Ladson-Billings (2009) points out, White teachers can effectively teach minority students as long as they use culturally responsive and high-quality instructional practices. Greenway and Elmhurst schoolteachers often exhibit these instructional characteristics, but school and district leaders have made few efforts to promote and expand culturally responsive teaching practices. Rather, the principals and district leaders support and promote as lead teachers those faculty members who excel in efficient classroom organization, test preparation, quality instruction defined in a Skillful Teacher (externally developed model), and productivity in high student achievement levels. The following examples are more revealing in this regard.

Cindy:    I've really tried to incorporate cultural traditions into my teaching so I draw on the children's background knowledge. I don't see that as a separate effort from preparing students academically.

RY:       Is culturally responsive teaching a priority in the school?

Cindy:    Well, no, I can't say it's a priority. I've never been asked to share what I do in terms of building in cultural activities. We sure hear from teachers who are good at "preparing for writing tests" and things like that.

Pauline:  I've lived here all my life, and I grew up and played with some of my students' parents. I know something about their cultural back-ground, and I feel like I want to honor that.

RY:       Is this a typical sentiment in the school?

Pauline:  It may be a typical sentiment, but it's not really promoted by the administration or team leaders. It's like, "That's okay as long as you cover the tested standards the way they are tested." The testing politics affects everything we do now.

Clearly, as Au (2008) noted, testing dominates instructional decisions in both schools. Teachers experience some tension over whether to apply culturally responsive practices in their classrooms or prepare students for tests in more decontextualized ways.

*Scheduling*

At Greenway and Elmhurst Schools, politics infuses scheduling at the school much as it affects teacher hiring and grade-level assignments. Something as apparently neutral as course scheduling is highly contested in these environments. It is subject to negotiation and has nothing to do with seniority or school rules, whether one teaches early classes or has after-school duties, or whether one teaches intervention courses or advanced academic (differentiated) classes (which require less preparation). Academic considerations are irrelevant in the assignment of teachers to specific classrooms: *the assignments are political and closely connected to accountability pressures.* That is, they are simply a matter of who knows whom and who can manipulate the system to improve their chances of meeting accountability requirements by getting academically stronger students, as the teachers themselves recognize. From the time many new teachers enter their first teaching assignments, they are part of accountability-driven decisions.

*Greenway School, March 2004*

RY:          What do you mean you got the short end of the stick in negotiating what you teach?

*Marianne:* Here board members can go to the district office and get favors for their friends or punish the people they don't like. They are going to tell me what to teach. You have no choice when you work at this school.

RY:          But how does a board member have a say in what you teach? The board doesn't determine scheduling and duties, does it?

*Marianne:* The board tells the superintendent. The superintendent tells the director of curriculum, and the director tells the principal. I complained to the AP, who is also a friend of mine, and he said, "Well, you know, the district plays politics with the board."

RY:          What is the advantage of teaching a particular segment of students in a grade level and of having early duty?

*Patrick:*   To teach advanced groups is much easier. You don't have to worry as much about test scores, for one thing. You also have time to prepare and don't have to stay after school. It's all politics, and it's been this way for years. Accountability just makes it worse. That's how they get the schedule set up.

*Elmhurst School, November 2005*
RY:        How much scheduling do you control as team leader?
*Principal Grant:* I make recommendations, but the final decision lies with the district office. I develop the master schedule, but the district can make changes any time they want. It is not unusual for there to be last-minute changes that come from the district office.
*Sheila:*   Well, in our school, we have a rotating schedule for duties. If you can get out at 2:30 rather than 4:30, you can have time with your family or even work a second job. One of our teachers sells real estate after school. The PE teacher also works as a security guard after school.
RY:        Are there any disadvantages to getting out at 2:30?
*Sheila:*   Not really. The other advantage is that if you control the schedule, you can get the easier classes to teach or the easier student groups. You get the high groups of kids, and they go to humanities classes at 2:30. The kids who struggle have to stay in intervention after 2:30, and their homeroom teachers have some responsibility for that.

Treelane and Hillside are historically political towns, and teachers' comments at both schools suggest that politics intrudes *directly* into the educational process at the levels of hiring and scheduling: who gets hired, who teaches what levels at the school, who teaches at which school, how many planning periods teachers have, who teaches the advanced students, and so forth. Historically, scheduling has primarily affected teachers' working conditions, such as whether they have time to pursue outside interests or work a second job; more recently, however, accountability has redefined the importance of scheduling in terms of who gets the advanced students that bring up test scores. In other words, this is a highly inbred teaching force with a long history of currying favor with influential school and district leaders as well as school board members, and this behavior has been reinforced as accountability pressures increase. It is important to remember at this point that these teachers do care about their students' futures and want to provide the best for "their own." Interestingly, most do not see these interests as incongruent; they simply accept "the way we do things around here."

### Curriculum Committee Representation

Local politics also permeates committee representation at school and district levels. Greenway and Elmhurst teachers talk at length about how teachers are selected for school and district committees. At Greenway School, for example, Principal Draper regularly asked for volunteers to serve on various committees; many teachers, however, viewed committee assignments as rewards for promoting the principal's or district's agendas and for high class performance on state tests. Greenway teacher Nadine Sanderson's comments are typical: "I know how teachers get selected for committees. Committees are for teachers that go along with the administration and support their agendas, mostly related to accountability." Elmhurst fifth-grade teacher Cindy Elliot added, "I never get picked for committees because the principal knows I have a different idea about how the reading program should be developed." Politics related to committee selection naturally affects curriculum content as teachers with contrary discourses and diverse knowledge bases usually excluded from curriculum decision making. In the 1980s and 1990s, district curriculum committees had a lot of power in making curriculum content decisions for all schools across the district. As we shall see in the next several sections, decentralization and accountability pressures only exacerbated the district and community politics over scheduling, committee assignments, and curriculum content decisions/development procedures. I further explore issues of dominance related to accountability and curriculum content decisions in the next section.

### From Grass Roots to Controlled Curriculum Content and Processes

In the 1980s and 1990s, it was not unusual for district and school curriculum committee members to write their own content goals and objectives, instructional strategies, and assessments. In such organic, grassroots processes, teachers, specialists, and sometimes local university professors developed curricula "from the ground up," using teachers' experiences and professional study to inform the official curriculum document. And although many school organizations relied heavily on packaged textbook series in these curriculum development processes, particularly for literacy and math, the primary selection criteria were often teachers' experiences and judgments rather than ideology inherent in federal policies and alignment with state tests. In recent years, as the following examples attest, many schools have come to rely much more heavily on state standards and test items to drive curriculum content decisions and development processes.

### *Greenway School*

In 2002, Principal Draper of Greenway School used teacher-led, organic curriculum development processes that supported teachers as decision makers who were capable of writing their own curriculum content from the ground up without reliance on state standards and other packaged materials. For example, she talked about how she incorporated professional development into her curriculum committees to help teachers develop deep understandings of their content area. Over time, however, her comments reflected growing concerns for instructional consistency and basic skills instruction. As her fears over accountability gradually took over her philosophy, she increasingly relied on state standards and skills checklists in externally developed instructional programs for curriculum development. She talked at length about how state policy requirements and concerns about skills development convinced her to focus on the tests. In fact, recall that Dr. Draper became a regional expert known throughout the state and district for her curriculum standards and technical knowledge of testing. As she stated, "We used to have teachers write curriculum from scratch and then align their curriculum with textbooks and other materials, but many teachers did their own thing. With all of these tests and the local pressures for accountability, we really need strategies like pacing guides to ensure that teachers are teaching the tested standards. And when accountability policies demand high student incomes in a short amount of time, you have to be the kind of professional curriculum leader who supports teachers to make the most efficient use of time and materials." Teachers also noted these curriculum changes.

*January 2003*

*John (sixth-grade teacher):* We are really taking more of our curriculum direction from the standards. It's not bad because many of the standards address critical thinking and higher-order skills. It's not all just decontextualized skills or literal comprehension. We meet as curriculum committees, but most of the content is decided by the standards. We just have to figure out when the standards should be taught.

*February 2004*

*John:* Our curriculum has definitely been taken over by the standards and the tests. We map out the curriculum month by month for each grade level, but it's really determined by the state. I remember when we used to write curriculum based on our experience and our own study of the research, and then we would pick textbooks that met our needs.

*February 2005*

*John:* We met last week as a committee to analyze our Dibbles assessments and see how our current scores align with the state tests. We're doing better on the state tests, and I think the curriculum pacing guides and practice tests have really helped. Our curriculum is stronger in certain ways. It's more tightly aligned with state expectations and assessments. I have to say there's a more narrow focus, strictly dealing with tested academic subjects, much less input from teachers, and no input from students.

Between 2002 and 2005, John clearly noted changes in his role as a teacher/curriculum developer. His curriculum writing responsibilities went from decision making to test data analysis. By 2005, John had little memory of his role in writing official curriculum documents in the school. Further, his comments reflect an assumption that curriculum must contain "the right knowledge" derived from state standards, externally developed textbook programs, and other sources outside of teachers' and students' personal experiences. By 2004, the original 2002 curriculum committee had been narrowed to include teachers who were skilled in standards alignment processes, and these teachers' consciousness about curriculum practices was shaped by commonsense interpretations and beliefs about the importance of standardization. Apple and Jungck (2004, drawing on Gramsci, 1971) explained this situation as follows, "Hegemony acts to saturate our consciousness so that the educational, economic, and social world we see and interact with, and the commonsense interpretations we put on it, becomes the world tout court, the only world" (p. 5).

### Elmhurst School

*October 2002*   In 2002, Principal Grant also used an elaborate curriculum development process. Before he began serving on a state advisory committee, he developed a technology-based, integrated curriculum with teachers. For more than 3 years, teachers at all grade levels worked on a framework of curriculum goals and expectations. Teacher groups met every 2 weeks to read professional literature and record their understandings about learning as well as their expectations for children's development across the grade levels. Teachers also kept reflective logs about instances where students generated their own expectations for learning. At regular curriculum meetings, teachers were asked to share their understandings and expectations, and to juxtapose them against those of scholars and their own students. Principal Grant also modeled for teachers how to examine their lists, readings, and teaching materials for evidence of research-based practices. Importantly, students were included in these curriculum development groups and the resulting documents. Across grade levels, students generated lists of their expectations for learning as well as their current interests and community needs. As Tim, a sixth-grader explained,

> All of us wrote down what they thought they were interested in and what they thought they needed to be able to do to make their communities better places to live. The ideas were typed on a graph, and three of us worked with our teacher to find patterns or common ideas across all the responses. We brought the responses to a teacher committee, and the teachers used them to write school curriculum goals.

Linda, a sixth-grader, added,

> It's cool to see our ideas incorporated into "Big Ideas" on the chalk-board. [Teachers write curriculum expectations as "big ideas" on the chalkboard each day.] Sometimes you see the goal [written] just like we wrote [it], and sometimes the teachers ask each class to adapt the goal so that it meets our needs now or it meets the needs of a community project, or sometimes it's [changed] because we need to meet a standard.

Ultimately, the teacher and student lists were integrated into a unified curriculum with content goals and explanations from professional readings, all of which were aligned with students' expectations, state standards, suggested teaching processes, assessments, observation logs, and instructional materials (primary sources, literature, etc). Naturally, this curriculum development process and product brought out conflicts over teaching philosophies and preferences. As one veteran first-grade teacher explained,

> We really had some difficult conversations as we wrote our curricula. With our last principal, when site-based management first came into play, we just sort of picked out new textbooks and then wrote our curricula from there. Then we aligned our curricula with the state standards. That was it. Now we had to agree on what we thought should be taught to our kids. Some teachers really did not think our students could attain some of the recommended curriculum. At the same time, there was a concern about the new teachers and how they would be able to use this curriculum that really required them to know what they were doing.

In response to the concern about "new teachers," Mr. Grant hired someone to take digital videos of exemplary classroom lessons to accompany the new curriculum, which were then uploaded into the curriculum web site. Teachers could enter reflection logs or notes about their observations of students and various authentic assessments, then click on expectations to monitor student progress. The software also allowed teachers to record notes about classroom experiences that shaped their thinking about particular expectations. These were then pasted into a chat space and became a subject of conversation at weekly faculty meetings. Further, teachers could click on any teaching strategy, watch a short video clip of an exemplary lesson, then download the lesson plan or teacher notes. As part of the process, Mr. Grant also granted teachers release time for common planning and peer observations. Mr. Grant reflected, "Initially, we developed the videos for new teachers, but I think the veteran teachers also needed the support as they were making philosophical and pedagogical shifts in their practices." Teachers met regularly in grade-level teams to talk about how they were implementing the curriculum and to make revisions as needed. Mr. Grant met with each group on a regular basis as well.

Over time, Principal Grant and other school members changed the curriculum development norms dramatically in order to ensure consistent "coverage" of state standards and tested items. As the following quotations make clear, Grant's curriculum development process also changed in relation to school members' perceptions about the need for externally developed, standardized programs.

*October 2003*

*Mary (sixth-grade teacher):* We spent a lot of time last year and through the summer really aligning our curriculum with the standards. We collapsed our old curriculum down so that all of the objectives fit under the state standards.

*October 2004*

*Mary:* This year we've been mapping our curriculum for each grade level.

*RY:* Are you still working on the curriculum process you used in the last couple years?

*Mary:* Well, I have to say we really don't write curriculum anymore. We're taking from outside experts to make sure that what we're teaching each day and each month aligns with the standards and the state tests.

*October 2005*

*Mary:* This year, we've been looking at textbooks that will help students learn and help them prepare better for the state tests. We're improving performance on the state tests, but we need a program to make sure all of the teachers are teaching the standards appropriately.... Overall, I think our curriculum is more focused on tested academics. We used to incorporate students' perspectives and interests, but now there's little time for that after we finish preparing for the tests.

Mary's comments were typical of many Elmhurst teachers' perspectives and indicated how the curriculum had narrowed to focus explicitly on officially sanctioned knowledge contained in state standards and textbooks, all aimed at passing the tests. By 2005, there was no discussion of students' needs or interests outside of tested standards and outcomes. As Mary put it, "We don't write curriculum anymore as teachers, and we certainly don't look at our children's knowledge sources when we think about what we teach." In other words, grassroots curriculum development processes and reliance on teacher decision making had given way to reliance on state standards, pacing guides, and packaged programs. Likewise, the curriculum committee had also narrowed to include only those teachers who were vocal proponents of standardized teaching and testing programs.

### Curriculum Shifts

Other scholars (e.g., Au, 2007) have also illustrated how popular, externally developed curriculum designs, such as maps and pacing guides, reinforce dominant views about the need to teach "the right knowledge" in academic subjects. Although some of these designs are intended to help students attain deeper understandings and critical thinking skills, the pressure of high-stakes testing and efficiency in student outcome improvement has resulted in forms and practices that narrow the curriculum and leave little emphasis on children, their interests, or the broader changes necessary to promote a more just and caring community and society.

It is also important to note the ways that the teachers' and principals' curriculum language and practices shifted in relation to dominant discourses regarding standardized tests, state standards, instructional consistency, pacing guides, and so forth. These shifts were closely connected to the ways in which the principals and teachers viewed curriculum leadership in these schools. As a further example, notice the discursive shifts between 2002 and 2006 in Greenway and Elmhurst teachers' and principals' responses to the question of what they meant by "good" curriculum. Responses are compiled in order to show similarities in discursive shifts among Greenway and Elmhurst School members. In 2002, "good curriculum" was described as:

- innovative
- engaging
- supporting the teacher as decision maker
- research-based
- aligned with instruction and assessment (formative and summative)
- integrated across content areas, arts, and humanities
- teaching the whole child

When I asked the same question in the fall of 2006, the same interviewees had different views of "good" curriculum. It should:

- be aligned with standards
- be efficient and easy to use
- be competitive with other district and area schools
- ensure instructional consistency
- ensure student learning and achievement
- be data-driven
- be research-based

- be aligned with state [standardized] tests
- be supportive of critical thinking and skills development

The driving forces behind these shifts in beliefs about curriculum at Greenway and Elmhurst were concerns about low test scores and the need to compete with charter schools, as well as the historically political nature of these schools and communities. Although Johnson and Johnson (2005) report similar discursive shifts in their ethnography of teachers' accountability practices, the reasons for the conservative politics and discursive shifts appeared to be quite different. Johnson and Johnson suggested that the school district deliberately aligned curriculum with items on standardized state tests in order to preserve the school's reputation for supporting community ideals.

In the Treelane and Hillside communities where Greenway and Elmhurst schools are located, however, the politicization of the curriculum is not so much about preserving "community ideals" as that productivity in the form of test scores functions as a commodity used to compete with charter schools and market their schools to excellent students who are interested in technology. Although test scores may function to preserve community ideals, in the final analysis, they are not the true driving force for political decision making in these schools. Many teachers talked to me privately about the district propensity for marketing high test scores at Greenway, and many noted that teachers receive overt payoffs (in the forms of attractive classroom assignments and merit pay) for securing high student performance on tests. It is clear why such a high proportion of teachers reported the emphasis on high academic performance and an accompanying loss of morale.

### Effects on Teacher Morale

In the recent era of accountability reforms, many principals and teachers reluctantly see a large part of their jobs and their roles as being to boost test scores. Greenway and Elmhurst teachers recognize that they must be "highly productive workers," and they articulate the positives of teaching mainly in terms of having a pleasant work environment compared to menial laborers. This does not mean that teachers are entirely satisfied with their schools. As I pointed out in chapter 4, rituals of control and conflicts over pedagogical philosophies remain points of contention for many teachers. Nonetheless, on balance, teachers tend to equate teaching with a professional career and opportunities to help children. The following quotations reflect the positives of teaching at Greenway and Elmhurst.

*Greenway School, 2002–2005*
*Mitch:*    I went into the teaching profession because I like children and I
             wanted a more professional job instead of working in the car factory

like my dad and my grandpa. I get my summers off, and there's no
such thing as a double shift. I like the job, but I do get tired of all the
pacing guides and turning in the plans and looking at data all the
time.

Myla:     I like teaching because I really like working with kids. We don't
have as much opportunity for creativity in designing our curricula
now. We have to use the pacing guides and do all the test prep stuff,
but the kids are great.

Allison:  I like teaching children, especially children from urban communities. I don't entirely like all of the emphasis on data, but I think
it's important that we're aligning our teaching with the standards.
Sometimes I feel like we're just supposed to act like monkeys implementing the pacing guides and scripts, but the kids are great.

*Elmhurst School*

Betty:    I like to have fun when I teach. I have to say it's a challenge sometimes when we have to do all of the test preparation stuff. I still like
teaching overall because I get to connect with children and other
teachers every day. It's funny because I have so many connections
with the students. I teach my neighbor's kids. I teach my niece in
one class…. I remember when we used to write thematic units and
have more of a say in curriculum, and I miss that creativity. The
kids are great, though.

Marianne: I like teaching the children. They really want to learn, and they
work very hard. Many of them struggle and they have a lot to overcome at home, but I love working with them. Sometimes I'd like to
use different approaches from what the school and district mandate, but we're not in that kind of environment as teachers now.

Troy:     I enjoy the kids every day. They are really appreciative of everything
we do, and I truly feel like I'm making a difference with the kids.

Sharon:   I like teaching because I really enjoy working with the kids. In some
ways, we have to be more technical now because we have to align
everything we do to standards and tests, but I have to say it's a good
profession for me. I don't know what else I would do. I know I don't
want to work in the steel plant or do anything like that. The benefits
for teaching are as good or better than factory work, too.

The positives of teaching at Greenway and Elmhurst Schools revolve around
working with students and the perception that teachers' working environment
is superior to factory work, which is the main alternative in these communities.
As the comments indicate, many teachers cite the benefits of teaching as having
good working hours, having summers off, and receiving health and retirement
benefits. In other words, teaching is viewed as easier and somewhat less alien-

ating than menial labor. At the same time, teachers also recognize that they are increasingly deprived of the ability to make professional decisions in their work, especially in terms of developing their own lessons and teaching units. In fact, many Greenway and Elmhurst teachers do not totally adhere to the prevailing ideology that teachers must use externally developed materials in order to ensure instructional consistency and good test performance, but these teachers are often silent in faculty meetings. As Rachel put it, "I don't agree with all this standardization, but I don't think the administrators feel like they can do anything because they have to implement these policies."

### Effects on Student Morale

Teachers' concerns with regards to diminished creativity are not lost on students, as the following quotations convey:

*Greenway School*
Student 1: I do well in school, but sometimes I feel like we're doing the same thing over and over day after day.
Student 2: A couple years ago, we used to have a say in what we were learning, but now we just have to work through the books.
Student 3: Sometimes all the workbooks are boring, but they're not hard.

*Elmhurst School*
Student 1: We don't get a lot of chance to make choices on projects, but the workbooks are not hard.
Student 2: It makes it easier to know what to expect from one grade to the next. All the teachers do the same thing.
Student 3: If they would ask us again, I think a lot of students would tell the teachers we already know what they're teaching.

Clearly students recognize the curriculum changes that have occurred in their schools, yet they feel powerless to raise any objections or change the situation. These students recognize the value of academic performance, but at the same time, unconsciously recognize that there is much more to learning.

### The Nature of Curriculum under Critical Curriculum Leadership

In this section of the chapter, I argue that curriculum leaders' influence, combined with school and community commitments to democratic principles and progressive education, create an environment where teachers, students, and parents or community members are able to question the underlying assumptions of circulating discourses and the new (conservative) common sense about curriculum and develop progressive educational content, instruction, and projects.

Thereby, they lay the groundwork for a new consciousness about inequities that arise from relationships among curriculum practices and broader social institutions as well as a proactive role in the politics of these broader movements. As school and community members develop this critical consciousness about curriculum and mobilize their own agency and growth, they foster meaningful community-based curricula and revitalization. They become coleaders of new progressive educational and social movements. The following examples illustrate how, *over time,* principals, lead teachers, students, and community leaders affirm their own capabilities to develop curriculum that is grounded in students' lives and in social justice. They begin to take action.

In 2002, the principals at Babcock and Pinehurst Schools were committed to democratic curriculum development processes as a way to support and work with teachers and influence what is important in students' lives. Principals Juidici and Hughes engaged teachers in developing curriculum "from the ground up," using their experiences and ongoing professional study to craft curriculum content, instructional strategies, and assessments that were appropriate for their particular school context. Their curriculum processes were also collaborative and open to ongoing improvements based upon research as well as empirical classroom feedback from teachers.

As accountability pressures increased, principals and curriculum committees at both schools naturally gave more attention to state standards and test scores. As Principal Hughes described in the fall of 2003, "We have had to set aside some of our curriculum-writing norms to spend time aligning our curriculum with the standards and state tests." And Principal Juidici commented, "We have had to pull back on some teacher creativity in order to ensure that we were implementing the federal and state policies effectively and also making adequate yearly progress on the state tests." Other scholars have recently documented the same phenomenon, including, particularly, Johnson and Johnson (2005) in their study of Louisiana schoolteachers and Wohlstetter and colleagues (2008) in their study of the effects of standardized testing on pedagogical practices.

Whereas all schools in my study attained adequate yearly progress on state tests and significantly improved their literacy and math outcomes, the principals and several lead teachers at Babcock and Pinehurst became increasingly concerned about the narrowing of curriculum and overt differentiation of knowledge according to race and class. As Angela, a veteran teacher, explained, "In the last couple of years, we have been focusing more and more on academic subjects to the detriment of the arts, multicultural education, and the community needs overall." Principal Hughes added his concern: "As our population became more diverse, we were making curriculum more uniform to align with state tests. At the same time that the industrial base of the community was eroding, we were teaching basic skills to working-class students. It was hard to imagine a better future for these kids beyond the test scores."

Principal Hughes, Angela, and a few other teachers were also active in community organizations and began to dialogue about various economic injustices afflicting the region and local communities, and how these injustices were connected to broader educational policies and reform movements. These dialogues ultimately led to major curriculum changes and social movements in both communities. These new, more critically oriented curriculum development processes are described next.

### Critical Curriculum Development Processes

In the spring of 2004, Babcock and Elmhurst educators, community members, and students initiated progressive curriculum processes, modifying Freire's work with peasants in Brazil. Freire's (1970/1993) *Pedagogy of the Oppressed* is not only pedagogical, but also presents his political and philosophical motivations. Freire's fundamental concern is with the liberation of poor and powerless people who have been dominated by and made to serve wealthy people. The social reality that maintains this class-based oppression is impressed upon the minds of the oppressed through words, images, customs, myths, popular culture, and in countless obvious and subtle ways that pervade public life. According to Freire, the oppressed accept this construct as truth and are psychologically devastated by it. In accepting the dominant view, oppressed individuals come to think of themselves as worthless, helpless, and inferior. They accept the personality traits of oppressed people: fatalism, self-deprecation, and emotional dependence.

In both the Treelane and Hillside communities, there are clear separations between high-poverty, minority areas and middle- or upper-class White areas. In both communities, a 30-minute drive takes you from the green space, country clubs, million-dollar new homes with swimming pools, and vast restaurants and entertainment complexes in outlying subdivisions to an inner city of vacant homes, boarded-up businesses, crack houses, and homeless people pushing their lives in shopping carts.

Both Babcock and Elmhurst school and community members used Freire's problem-posing method for developing curriculum to stimulate and sustain *critical consciousness*. In these schools and communities, the primary intent of curriculum was to replace fatalism about accountability and the potentially unjust effects of standardization with freedom, interdependence, and mutual responsibility for responding to social concerns.

Recall from chapter 2 that principals Juidici and Hughes experienced moments of critical consciousness in which they recognized how circulating conservative discourses affected their school curriculum practices and the students. As these two principals analyzed policy discourse, they held dialogue sessions in parents' homes and community centers, developing relationships with community organizers, business leaders, and parent groups in the process. I further explore the community relationships and projects that inspired these neoprogressive social movements. These dialogue sessions led to significant changes in the school curriculum development processes and practices. Early dialogue sessions are quoted below. As the principals and members of the school and community expressed concerns about cultural political shifts and discursive practices, they purposefully became colearners of curriculum accountability problems as they relate to broader economic and social institutions, and ultimately coworkers for educational and social change.

### Pinehurst School–Community Dialogue, January 2004

Diverse stakeholders are meeting at a community center near Babcock School. Mitch is an African American community organizer with a background in urban issues. He is articulate and passionate, and everyone pauses to listen when he speaks.

*Mitch (community organizer):* So many of our inner-city kids do not have computers at home, and [even if they do] they're so slow to load, they can't keep up in preparing for these tests.

*Steve (White teacher):* We've been keeping the schools open so kids can use computers after school. We really can't change the policy.

*Marianne (African American teacher):* We're caught in this, too. We have to teach for these tests or we get in trouble with the district. Some of the requirements are too high or they're not right, but we can't change it.

*Sarah (African American parent):* It's hard to say this in front of everyone, but I really don't think schools work for many poor, inner-city kids, kids like mine. It works for children who have parents with good jobs and nice homes and all the advantages. I know we have policies and tests now, but I don't feel like I have any more control to help my kids than I did before. We still live in a rental apartment and struggle to put food on the table, and I work two jobs.

*Principal Hughes:* I don't have any more authority to change the policy either, but I would like your help to take actions with our curriculum practices. It seems like some of the problem is connected to changes in income level within the city. A few years ago, a lot more kids had resources at home, but many of them have moved to higher priced homes in the far suburbs.

*Mitch:* That's right. I've been taking classes in urban planning and that's what happens. Housing here is like a commodity. We need to think about how the community is designed and organized to help get resources where they are needed.

*Steve:*     That's interesting. I'd like to read more about that. Well, we control what happens in our classrooms in terms of instruction, and we control our partnerships with the community groups. What can we focus on to make a difference?

Open-ended questions dominated the meeting, primarily as a function of community organizer Mitch's tutelage and the principal's support. As I observed these sessions, I was struck by the gradual increase in participant diversity and openness to discuss social problems connected to current policies. Perhaps the community center location helped parents feel more comfortable. The center had a freshly painted multicultural mural on one wall; well-used, comfortable couches and armchairs; and computers along one wall. The kitchen was well stocked, with a coffee pot in constant use and the smell of freshly baked cookies wafting through the meeting room. As Principal Hughes later commented, "We have tried for years to develop community partnerships, but we always started with the school. I think having a base at the community center and having the expertise of the organizers have helped our efforts to get parents more interested in education in an activist kind of way." Stone's (1998) study of community organizing supports the notion that educational changes are most effective when they develop from the outside in, initiated in communities and supported by schools. When curriculum conversations take place in this neighborhood, which shows dramatic, overt evidence of the economic downturn and social inequities, participants have content for problem-posing conversations as well as evidence of needs for curricular changes. Similar dialogues and activities took place in Babcock School and the surrounding community, although in a very different setting from the Pinehurst meetings.

### *Babcock School–Community Dialogue, February 2004*

The Babcock dialogue sessions occurred in a business council meeting room. Unlike the community center described above, the building and furnishings are relatively new. Business leaders are present, and they are wearing suits. Parents and teachers in attendance are also well dressed, but less formally. Yet the passion and concerns about testing and social inequities are just as authentic as in the dialogue held at Pinehurst Community Center.

*Sheila (African American teacher):*  We can't stop these tests from coming. It's getting so it's hard to remember what we did before we had to do all this data analysis.
*Dawn (White teacher):*  I know. We can't do anything about these tests. We have less and less control over curriculum now.

*Principal Juidici:* I've been concerned about the students who have to take intervention courses year after year. Now the state is mandating scripted programs in those interventions.

*Mike (White business council leader):* We have to have accountability. We can't change that, and I don't think we should. All of our kids have to perform well on tests in order to have opportunities later on in life.

*Sam (African American parent):* I want our kids to perform well, but we need to make sure they are getting the right instruction and learning the knowledge and skills they need to have the best chances. What can we do?

*Margo (White parent):* Who decides what goes in the standards? Why can't we decide what else we want our kids to know? We need more information.

Notice the largely fatalistic perspective and somewhat tacit acceptance of accountability policies in these early dialogue sessions. Here, the formal leader (principal) does not offer answers, but enters the dialogue as a student ready to follow the course of the dialogue and learn about curriculum content needs from parents and other community members. Educators and community members were fully involved in this and other dialogues, examining problems together. At these early sessions, participants (including the principal) confronted the reality of testing policies on their working conditions and on their students/citizens. At subsequent dialogue sessions, participants coexamined accountability in relation to broader social, cultural, and economic institutions and took joint responsibility for change.

From the outset, Principals Juidici and Hughes resolved the leader–follower and teacher–student contradictions. Via dialogue, the "leader-of-the-followers" and the "followers-of-the leader" ceased to exist and new terms emerged: leader-follower and follower-leader. By the fall of 2005, the formal leader (principal) was no longer merely the one who leads but was one who was taught and followed in the dialogue about curriculum and policies with teachers, students, and community members, who in turn led while also being led.

More specifically, educators, students, and community members gathered information about accountability and its effects on curriculum content and students. They all took joint, ongoing responsibility for curriculum development. In this process, arguments based on curriculum leadership authority were no longer valid. As Freire (1970/1993) argued, authority must be on the side of freedom, not against it. In such a context no one leads another, nor is anyone self-led. People teach each other and lead together, mediated by broader cultural politics and by knowledge, which in the current accountability systems, are "owned" by teachers and various authorities. In fact, the Babcock and Pinehurst school members often talked at length about the value of what they learned about various ethnic groups and cultural knowledge from parents and community members for teaching and learning in their schools.

In these new curriculum development processes, the task of educators/community leaders was "posing of the problems of men in relation to their world" (Freire, 1970/1993, p. 62). The leaders/teachers and their followers/students became collaborators and coinvestigators, developing together their critical consciousness of reality and their images of a possible, better reality. By critical consciousness, Freire (1970/1993) means the ability to step back from an unconscious, fatalistic acceptance of the way things are and to perceive the world critically, even in the midst of pervasive, powerful, subtle forces tending to distort and oppress.

In order to develop a curriculum that fosters critical consciousness among the masses, Freire proposes that a team of educators work with the people of a given locality to develop generative themes that reflect their view of reality, based on and taken from the local way of life. To accomplish this, representatives from the Treelane and Hillside community dialogue groups (teachers, students, and parents/community members from Babcock and Pinehurst neighborhood areas) met with more community members, educators, and students to discuss their plans and to secure the latter's permission and cooperation. In both cases, local community organizers and university faculty members provided training and support in how to observe and document field notes. Members of this team visited neighborhood organizations, businesses, homes, churches, and other local venues to observe and document how the people lived, worked, and played in these settings. Observers looked for anything and everything that would indicate how the people construed reality and their situations (e.g., abandoned homes, vacant lots full of trash and drug needles, drug dealers who provide employment, boarded-up grocery stores and pharmacies in their neighborhoods, and economic growth, expensive homes, and businesses located in areas that involved long bus rides from their homes and schools) in order to present broader community and school members with full documentation of the current reality. These field notes later helped raise broad community and school consciousness about current inequities.

In Freire's (1970/1993) model, preliminary findings of these local investigations are presented in a series of evaluation meetings held in the locality and involving members of the team and volunteers from the community. As the observers report the incidents they observed and their feelings and perceptions about them, the group discusses various ways these incidents might be interpreted to reveal other aspects of the people's lives. From these discussions emerge the contradictions that, if clearly perceived, reveal to the people their oppressed state. These, then, become the initial themes for use in discussion and in the designation of the curriculum content targets necessary to end social and cultural reproduction in schools. Example themes include African-centered curriculum, urban decline, housing problems, effects of abandoned lots, lack of viable businesses. Curriculum targets within these themes featured neighborhood and cultural knowledge about how to solve these urban issues as well as state standards related to problem solving, critical thinking, process writing, data collection, and research skills as well as language conventions and other basic skills.

In both school cases, the teams presented their data at a series of meetings held at local community centers and school gymnasiums. Team members presented excerpts from interviews, notes, photos, videos, and sample artifacts (e.g., teacher's editions, curriculum guides, and test items) from their various observations, asking audience members to interpret the data. Naturally, several different interpretations were provided, as the following quotations make clear:

*Tara (parent):* We've seen information about the testing policies before, but seeing how the community has been economically divided and how dividing our kids by groups to pass the tests can make that worse was really powerful.

*Sheila (teacher):* I think we have made some gains by being more focused on achievement, and I think focusing on achievement over time can actually help the inequities.

*Tim (student):* If we're supposed to learn to think and learn how to be good citizens, then we need to do more than prepare for the tests with these worksheets.

The investigative teams later reviewed the range of contradictory views and perspectives, and then used them to develop themes for interdisciplinary curriculum study and community development. Findings were always presented as problems, not as answers. For example, Mitch, (the Pinehurst community organizer) synthesized the contradictory views about the relationships among testing and community development as follows:

We have a number of perspectives about the testing here. Some of us see it as a way to improve children's lives, and others see it as a detriment to equality. Many people talked about how surprised they were by the parallel urban decline and progress in the suburbs. As Angela noted, these urban declines also correspond to children who are less prepared to think critically in schools. Our children remind us that if we want them to think critically, we have to give them more than worksheets. We need to make sure that they all have opportunities for good instruction, and that they all have good materials. Some parents and, actually, teachers are not sure everyone can be prepared the same way and that the challenge is too big for us to take on with economic decline happening so quickly. Is preparation for school an issue we should focus on? Is it preparing our children to construct the community change that is best for everyone regardless of race, gender, and class background?

In this excerpt, as Freire (1970/1993) proposed, the people's own lives are reflected back to them, but in a way that encourages critical awareness of their situation, not passive acceptance of an oppressive interpretation. The Babcock and Pinehurst school members and surrounding community members spent over a year (fall, 2003–spring, 2005) in dialogue sessions about what should be taught in schools. Rather than taking the state standards and rewriting these in curriculum documents, these curriculum leaders debated choices about curriculum content and rules over selection of that content. In particular, they recognized the politics surrounding their curriculum content and access decisions as well as the social and cultural implications of their curriculum choices for growth of their children and communities. A compilation of curriculum-related questions considered in these dialogue sessions appears below.

As educators, students, and community members talked about their perspectives and the data in front of them, they were encouraged to question their community life situations. The resulting shifts in curriculum development work are reflected in the following teacher comments.

*Marianne (Elmhurst teacher):* We are really taking more of our curriculum into the community with these forums informing how we make changes. I've also seen a shift in making the curriculum more authentic with kids doing projects in the community that have also been infused with critical thinking as well as more basic skills in the state standards.

*Sheila (Babcock teacher):* Our curriculum has definitely been taken into the community based on responses from these forums.

It is also important to note that students were included in these problem-posing and curriculum-development groups and the resulting documents. As Linda, a sixth-grade student, described, "We need to be in charge of our learning, because the future of the community depends on us. We need to be part of making our community better for ourselves now and for future generations."

**Table 5.1** Curriculum Questions

1. Why should we teach this content objective, idea, or strategy rather than others?
2. Why should this content get more emphasis than others?
3. Who benefits from emphasis on this particular content? Who loses?
4. Who gets access to this curriculum content? Who does not?
5. How can our school curricula relate to community and cultural needs?
6. How have we connected curriculum content choices (beyond the state standards), instruction, and assessment (beyond the state tests)?

Likewise, Tim, another sixth grade student noted, "We have to take responsibility for what we learn and for how well we learn it. It really helps to be involved in discussions with important businesspeople and others who help us decide what we need to learn to have a good life in the future."

The contrast between this student and the students at Greenway and Elmhurst Schools is striking, particularly in terms of agency and growth. As Dewey (1916/2008) posited, growth is not simply a personal matter but is of concern for the whole society. The concept of growth brings forth deep intuitions regarding the distinctiveness and humanity of each student (adult as well as child). As Noddings (2002) clarified, the growth strategy is to make [learners] see the process." According to Babcock and Pinehurst Principals Juidici and Hughes, it is important for learners (adults and children) to have their eyes opened and become aware of the process, to take part in it fully, and to become conscious of the steps that take them there. As their eyes open, learners of all ages come to understand their uniqueness and gain a better control of the process. When students find the strengths within themselves, however small they initially may be, these strengths then become the source of their agency.

Unlike Principals Grant and Draper, Juidici and Hughes did not place a high priority on supervision to ensure instructional effectiveness and consistency of these curriculum targets. Only when I probed about support for pedagogical excellence in classrooms did the principals mention their direct classroom supervision roles at all. This is not to say that these principals ignored their instructional supervision responsibilities; in fact, I directly observed them providing pedagogical coaching for teachers and conducting formal evaluations on several occasions. Rather, as Hughes put it,

> My primary roles now are to be a community advocate and political mediator, working to ensure excellence and equity in our communities, of which schools play a major part. I expect excellent teaching in classrooms, and a major part of excellence is teachers' commitment to accessing and building upon children's background knowledge and treating all children as capable of being lifelong learners and excellent citizens, regardless of social class, race, or gender.

This comment is in striking contrast to the new professional curriculum leaders I interviewed and those described by Wohlstetter and colleagues (2008), for whom the establishment of standards and data-driven classroom supervision instruments were their foremost priorities. The Babcock and Pinehurst principals' attitudes reflects an interesting inversion of past instructional leadership models that focus first on the microlevel of building school culture, setting high expectations, and supervising classroom instruction, as these two critical curriculum leaders focus first on broader sociocultural and political influences.

## Curriculum, Meaning, and Development Processes

As I stated at the beginning of this chapter, curriculum is the content of education—what is taught and to whom—the meanings of which are inextricably linked to broader social, political, and economic institutions. With some progressive exceptions, the meanings of curriculum at Greenway and Elmhurst Schools revolved around state standards and the particular set of ideologies circulating through the schools and communities. While some teachers personally advocated for the former district whole language philosophy, the more vocal and dominant teachers and community members silenced them, imposing their personal concerns for scripted, skills-based pacing guides. Curriculum development processes in these schools are in many ways symbols of shifts toward professional work norms, beliefs, and ultimately, leadership. Each Greenway and Elmhurst educator and student is engaged in an ongoing process of constructing new beliefs and values about curriculum as standardized materials aligned with state requirements and tests. Further, many of these individuals see standardization as a necessary means to improve students' academic performance and enable them to attain better jobs in a 21st century work environment.

It is important to note that these teachers are embedded within the same class structures as their students, and that they believe education is what enabled them to attain professional jobs instead of the factory jobs that were available to their parents and grandparents. The faculties at both schools are primarily local, yet they are not totally oblivious to the politics that influence academic and nonacademic decisions in their schools. In fact, many teachers use political connections to attain more favorable schedules and classroom assignments. Even as many of these teachers take advantage of the political system and support the use of standardized curriculum, they also resent administrative mandates and control over their working conditions. I do not mean to say that teachers from middle-class backgrounds would be more likely to resent and challenge these political conceptions of curriculum and working conditions and adopt an oppositional attitude toward curriculum and schooling. There is evidence that some teachers do both.

In the Greenway and Elmhurst cases, these constructed curriculum meanings and practices must be seen in light of the broader (conservative) movement. Here the emphasis on conservative discourses and pedagogy contributes to the dominant curriculum meanings and practices in the schools. The school leaders and overall school norms actively (though not necessarily consciously) encourage aspects of new professional curriculum leadership identity. In this sense, then, the school environment acts to encourage a potential relationship among curriculum meanings, development processes, leadership identity, broader cultural politics generally, and the new public management in particular. These schools do not, however, encourage a link between progressive leader-activists and movements in the same way. I will return to these points in chapter 7.

While the Babcock and Pinehurst curriculum leaders were realistic about and cognizant of current policy requirements, they also firmly echoed Dewey's (1916/2008) argument that the finest outcomes of education are not test scores but human beings willing and able to engage intelligently and ethically with a changing world. In the problem-posing curriculum development processes that took place in these communities, all learners (adults and children) cultivated their own sense of agency and purpose as they explored neoprogressive curriculum meanings, practices, and social movements. In short, these curriculum leaders envisioned that curriculum development would ultimately lead to a better community and society. These critical curriculum development processes were not without challenges and difficulties, as the following problem-posing case conveys. In the next chapter, I further explore curriculum development processes and effects on social movements from parent and community vantage points.

---

**PROBLEM-POSING CASE**
**Democratic Philosophies meet School Realities**

Babcock School's basic operating philosophy is based on the principles of democracy, freedom, and participatory leadership. At the beginning of each academic year, the school community members—teachers, students, and concerned parents—meet to review and revise the curriculum as needed and to seek collaborative agreement on the themes.

Zach Minor, who had taught language arts and social studies at a nearby school for 18 years, was pleased that his request for transfer to Babcock had been approved. He firmly believed that an atmosphere of freedom and human development was conducive to genuine and meaningful learning. However, he soon had reason to doubt his basic beliefs.

During the first week of school, the curriculum dialogue sessions went well. A balance of standard academic curricula and elective courses was approved. Zach felt that school members had laid a strong foundation for meaningful learning and that he and his students would have a good year. Two months into the academic year, however, the curriculum was not working out as well as Zach had envisioned. Students often surfed the Web and texted their friends instead of attending to their studies. Many had chosen only the elective courses. In the regular courses Zach taught, few students prepared for class and they basically crammed before tests to attain a passing grade. Consequently, classes were hard to teach because students had not done their homework. Serious students and most teachers, including Zach, became frustrated. Parents who expected their children to be admitted to strong secondary schools complained. Zach wondered if he had made a mistake in transferring to Babcock. The curriculum decision-making processes—and unintended outcomes— seemed beyond anyone's control.

Another community curriculum meeting was called to address what was recognized as a serious problem. Many of the veteran teachers spoke about the value of freedom for individual growth and of learning to take responsibility for one's own choices and decisions. They argued that this year's experience would be a good lesson for next year's classes. On the other side, many parents objected that if things were allowed to continue as they were, their children would lose a year of education and do poorly on upcoming state tests. To the surprise of many, a number of students complained about the lack of discipline structure in the classes. Others wanted things to remain as they were because they were enjoying the freedom and choices.

A new teacher stood up and offered a solution. She argued that it was time to be rational about freedom and self-determination. "When these principles do harm, they are not good," she said. She suggested ways to restrict the realm of free choice for students and to set up more demanding curriculum maps, a more standardized instructional program, and stricter standards of behavior. Zach was one of several teachers who were vocally opposed to these kinds of actions that would undermine the democratic school philosophy. It seemed that no agreement would be reached at this meeting.

Make up your own ending to this case.

### Questions

1. Should the community try to maintain its basic democratic philosophy or establish restrictions to ensure optimal learning?
2. Can freedom be made a basis for learning without also being a potential basis for anarchy?
3. How would you characterize Babcock School's philosophy? What might you want to change as a curriculum leader in the school?

## Summary

In the current political context, schools must maintain official written curricula aligned with state standards and assessments. Over time, curriculum leaders have been pressured to use restrictive pacing calendars and to adopt standardized, externally developed programs that promise rapid improvements in student outcomes. In so doing, curriculum leaders begin to see themselves as professional curriculum leaders capable of efficient curriculum management and achievement. Like many U.S. schools, Greenway and Elmhurst members make curriculum content decisions largely based upon test items and state standards—a major change from the grassroots, teacher led committee decisions of the past. While these districts and communities have a history of patronage and political decisions with regards to curriculum committees, teachers believed that they had more voice in educational decisions before the intensification of accountability pressures. Curriculum meanings and constructed practices must be seen in light of the broader conservative modernization and related movements (e.g., new public management).

In the other two cases, critical curriculum leaders initiated progressive curricula and community-based decision-making processes. Here curriculum development processes were reminiscent of Freire's curriculum work in *Pedagogy of the Oppressed* (1970/1993) and various community organizing models. Community members and educators worked together on the designation of curriculum targets aimed at academic achievement and community revitalization. While the Babcock and Pinehurst curriculum leaders were realistic about and cognizant of current policy requirements, they also firmly echoed Dewey's (1916/2008) argument that the finest outcomes of education are not test scores but human beings willing and able to engage ethically with a changing world. In the problem-posing curriculum processes that took place in these community areas, members cultivated agency and purpose as they constructed and attained curriculum targets grounded in community needs and cultures.

# 6

# The Influences of Curriculum Leadership on Community Relationships, Revitalization, and Progressive Education

Scholars have suggested that effective principals and other curriculum leaders should build relationships with parents and leaders of external organizations in order to gain support and resources for various reforms aimed at educational improvements (e.g., Deal & Peterson, 1999; Hoy & Miskel, 2007). For the most part, these scholars advise leaders to develop relationships and manage numerous external environmental groups in order to improve the core technology of schools, namely, teaching and learning. In other words, schools are embedded within society, and effective curriculum leaders must reach *outward* to develop positive working relationships with external social groups. In particular, curriculum leaders must develop involvement strategies that provide parents and guardians with the knowledge and skills to help children master the curriculum objectives at home.

Recent studies (e.g., Leithwood & Mascall, 2008) further suggest that effective district and school leaders should cultivate and sustain school–community relationships that create a cohesive direction for curriculum implementation and academic improvement. According to Leithwood and colleagues, districts must develop a cohesive leadership system that includes defining (a) quality leadership, (b) a basis for holding leaders accountable, (c) leadership preparation, and (d) a range of external conditions aligned with the goal of improving learning for all students. Although this cohesive leadership system is more inclusive than earlier definitions of community involvement, the basic premise that school leaders must reach outward to cultivate relationships with external social factions remains unchanged. In other words, across mainstream literature, the aim of school–community relationships is to enhance rather than radically change school curriculum efforts—aims that are fundamental to critical and progressive education. Further, there is little mention of the potential for transformation of individuals or revitalization of communities as a whole. The critical and progressive perspective on the interrelationships among school–community relationships, leadership, and curriculum reform has been most fully articulated by Stone (1998) in his study of school–community relationships in 11 diverse school settings. As Stone argues,

> A currently touted reform strategy is to put forward a coherent set of [state or federal] directives around academic achievement for schools to follow. An assumption underlying this strategy is that schools can be responsive [and build community support] but only if the signals are clear.... Baltimore posits a different scenario. The proximate barrier to action [in that case] was not a set of contradictory directives. It was the unresponsiveness of school district employees. That unresponsiveness, the anxieties that feed it, and the capacity to deflect efforts to heighten accountability are best understood in community context. Perhaps, then, the best advised strategy is one that calls for change in the larger context in which schools are embedded. What may be most promising is not a continuation of sponsorship of pilot reform projects, which are unlikely ever to be scaled up. Instead, it may be more productive to search for leverage points for democratic, social change through which the school–community relationship can be altered. (p. 271)

Stone's approach to democratic school–community relationships reinforces Freire's (1970) curriculum development approach and echoes Alinsky's (1971) work on community relationships, which proposed community organizing as a leverage point for neighborhood and educational empowerment. In the late 1930s in Chicago, Saul Alinsky and Joe Meegan organized a coalition of Catholic churches, volunteer organizations, and formerly feuding neighborhood groups in an effort to address the poverty of the Great Depression. According to Alinsky (1971), community organizing begins with these premises: (1) The problems facing inner-city communities do not result from a lack of effective solutions, but from a lack of power to implement these solutions. (2) The only way for communities to build long-term power is by organizing people and the money they raise around a common vision. (3) A viable organization can be achieved only if a broadly based, indigenous leadership can knit together the diverse interests of their local institutions and grassroots members.

Further, according to Alinsky, the major dimensions that distinguish community organizing from other collaborative, school–community approaches to educational reforms are its focus on power relationships, large-scale and continued involvement of people *from the base,* leadership development, and the strategic role played by the professional organizer. Organizing begins with the assumption that educational and social injustices, whether minor or great, are typically the result of power imbalances. Those most hurt by the system are those who are most powerless to act on it. The problem is not the absence of good ideas and strong relationships among actors in the system, but rather, institutional resistance from people in positions of power to the full inclusion and consideration of marginalized parent and community voices. From the perspective of community organizing, school–community power imbalances must be eliminated in order for school and community members to enter authentic dialogue about the curriculum and other aspects of education. In other words, community organizing may be a powerful strategy for school and curriculum improvements. It is also important to remember that many of these parents and community members have learned to equate schooling with oppression and failure, and therefore fear to enter schools. In this instance, school outreach to the community may need to begin in community settings rather than on the school campus. As we shall see, the community-based curriculum development projects described in the last chapter also influenced reciprocal school–community relationships and inspired neoprogressive social movements.

The key point I want to make in this chapter is that effective school–community relationships can have a transformative effect on communities as well as schools. One could ask what role parents and community members play in shaping curriculum leadership identity. It is not my intention to pursue this issue here, but I will point out that a number of scholars have discussed, from a variety of perspectives, the role of community–school relationships in curriculum work. This literature does not, however, specifically consider the relationships among parents and community members' perceptions of school curricula, community transformation, and curriculum leadership.

It is for this reason that I discuss community members and parents in this volume. I did not gather nearly as much data from parents and community members as I did from principals, teachers, and students. I did, however, interview half of the parents of the students I interviewed, as well as community members from various backgrounds who were involved in the curriculum development processes described earlier. The data I present here are admittedly incomplete but do indicate certain premises regarding the role of parents and community members in curriculum leadership development processes. They provide an indication of how parents and community members contribute to forming a principal's curriculum leadership identity and to shaping curriculum content over time. I hope that future studies will probe these issues in more depth than I do here.

It is not clear from the data that parents fully recognize the dialectical relationships among curriculum, leadership, and broader cultural political movements. At the same time, they do overwhelmingly recognize the importance of curriculum leadership to quality schools characterized by small class sizes, individualized support for children, cultural relevance, values, and the kind of academic rigor that prepares children for higher education. What stands out most from my interviews with parents and community members is their desire for their children to experience a higher quality of education and community life than they themselves have had and than their children have received in the recent past. Parents' and community members' sense of agency and commitment to changing their school and community differ considerably in the four case-study schools.

In the two new professional curriculum leaders' schools, Elmhurst and Greenway, parents and community members feel powerless to act against economic declines and the schools' failure to address issues of large class sizes, poor teachers, safety, and lack of a rigorous academic education. Their position is not aligned with any political movement in education: they concur with neoconservative agendas in certain areas and yet simultaneously argue for progressive educational reforms. On the other side, many school members blame the parents for their lack of involvement, unconsciously promote conservative discourses within their policy explanations, and consciously focus on improving academic achievement by focusing on "what they can control within the school," often through the use of (conservative) comprehensive reforms. Consciously or unconsciously, school members turn away from social needs in their communities and erect barriers that discourage parent involvement. In contrast, in the latter two (critical curriculum leadership) cases, Babcock and Pinehurst schools, parents, community leaders, and school leaders all express a clear and collective sense of agency and commitment to educational and social change. By making common cause with outside forces, school leaders take advantage of parents' and other community members' desires for quality education, opportunities for higher education, and community revitalization, and, in so doing, inspire neoprogressive movements.

To highlight these contrasts, I have organized this chapter into two main sections, addressing school relationships with parents and community leaders in, respectively, the two new professional case studies and the two critical ones. In the first section, I highlight how parents' desires to give their children a better future and community leaders' perceptions about poor curriculum in the local schools are motivating them to encourage their children to leave the Treelane and Hillside communities. The second section elaborates on how community organizing and community dialogues initiated and supported the schools' curriculum changes and critical curriculum leadership identity formation. The chapter concludes with a problem-posing case.

### Professional Curriculum Leaders' Relationships with Parents and Community Members

Principals Draper and Grant know that they need to build parent relationships and otherwise compete for students in an open community market with growing numbers of charter schools, and yet they consider parent and community involvement in their school to be a bonus, not something they can expect. In common with their staffs, these principals believed that they could not rely on parent involvement or community support in their high-poverty, culturally diverse communities. Both principals and many teachers I interviewed talked at length about their perception that parents wanted traditional instruction in basic academics and American values rather than student-centered instruction, promotion of higher-order thinking, and rigorous, advanced coursework aimed at college preparation. Yet I found the opposite in my interviews. The overwhelming majority of parents and community members expressed the desire that children be prepared for higher education, primarily due to the declining local job opportunities and their belief that a college education would enable children to attain stable, high-paying employment elsewhere. In this section, I explore the following themes: (1) attitudes of parents' toward higher education; (b) parents' desires to "escape" their neighborhoods; and (3) parent cultural conflicts with the school. Within each subsection, I probe possible reasons for the disconnect between parents and educators in my study and other similar schools.

### Desire for Higher Education

Across all four schools in my study, parents overwhelmingly expressed a desire for their children to complete some form of postsecondary education. These perspectives echo Weis's (1990) findings that working-class parents want their children to go to college as a way to escape a future of low-paying jobs in declining urban communities. In my study, the parents I interviewed talked at length about how difficult it is to make a living without a college education, and they have strong wishes for their children's futures even if they are not very hopeful that their children will be sufficiently educated to accomplish more. They recognize that their children need a high-quality education in order to break out of their poor, working-class neighborhoods and lives. Interestingly, Greenway and Elmhurst parents frequently punctuated their wishes for their children's future with expressions of concern about the schools' curricula, as the following comments illustrate:

RY:        What do you think your child will do when she leaves high school?
Mrs. Lake (African American parent):  She's planning to go to an area college. We're not sure which college yet. There are quite a few right here. She wants to take up something in the medical field, maybe even be a doctor. She's very smart...much smarter than I was at her age. I just hope the schools get better so she'll have the best chance. It seems like they've been going downhill lately...keeping bad teachers in the classroom and letting discipline get out of hand and falling down on reading and math.

*RY:*      What kind of career is your son, Jeff, looking for?

*Mr. Gwinn (White parent):* Oh, I don't know…anything he wants.

*RY:*      What would you like him to do?

*Mr. Gwinn:* Well, I never went to college so I don't know what the best fields are now. I keep asking the teachers at the school, but I haven't really gotten any great information. I tell him he's got to pick something he can stay with for 40 years and make good money and a good retirement, but something where he won't have to work double shifts and scrape by paycheck to paycheck.

*RY:*      What do you expect your daughter will do when she leaves school?

*Mrs. LaCombe (African American parent):* I want her to go to college. I never had a chance to go. I got married very young, and my family never had the money anyway. But I've always said, "Whatever you want to do in life is fine, but one thing is for sure. You're going to college." There's no choice about that. That's the only way to get ahead in this world. Whatever field she goes into is fine with me, as long as she goes to college. That's why I keep on the schools to make sure they're teaching the skills our kids need so that they have a better future than we had in this area.

*RY:*      So you would like Raymond to go to college?

*Mr. Sawyer (African American parent):* Yes, that's for sure. But I don't think Ray will be ready for college unless he catches up a lot. There are so many kids in each class, and it's hard for the kids to get individual attention. At least I want him to go to the community college or some kind of trade school so he can be an electrician or a plumber or something where he can make good money without having to break his back like I did.

The parents I quote universally express strong sentiments about wanting their children to receive a quality education that prepares them for some form of higher education. Interestingly, from these parents' perspectives, a *quality education* means smaller class sizes, individualized attention, and rigorous instruction in reading and math. In fact, the strength of their convictions and language is striking. These parents clearly recognize that postsecondary education is their children's only option to improve their economic future, earn enough money for a secure retirement, and break out of scraping by from paycheck to paycheck. In other words, these parents have high aspirations for their children to gain access to higher education and employment with economic stability. Mrs. LaCombe, for example, states outright that her daughter does not have a choice about attending college, her only choice is in the field of study. Even parents who realized their children were not prepared for college wanted them to learn some trade or profession. For example, Mr. Sawyer wanted his son "to be a plumber or something where he can make good money without having to break his back like I did." Other parents encouraged their children to enter the armed forces, typically as a means to earn money for college or to develop maturity:

RY: What would you like your child to do after leaving school at Hillside?

Mrs. Reynolds (White parent): Well, Carl's not ready for college. He's smart enough, but his academic skill levels are not quite there, for one thing. He just doesn't have the study habit either. The curriculum just was not relevant [enough] for him to really get interested and apply himself. If he develops that more in high school, great.... Otherwise, I think he should go into the Air Force. At least that way, he can grow up a bit more and make some money.

RY: Would you like to see him go to college?

Mrs. Reynolds: Oh, definitely. But I have an idea he won't be ready right away. When he gets out of the Air Force, he can go to college and do anything he wants.

The parents I spoke with all value education highly and hope their children will develop the maturity and skills necessary to improve their life chances through postsecondary education, if not college, then through the armed forces or various trade schools. They want their children to receive the kind of K-12 education that would prepare them for higher education and social mobility, and express support for progressive education practices, such as small class size, personal attention, critical thinking, and authentic pedagogy. At the same time, it is noteworthy that parents encourage certain neoconservative curriculum practices, particularly in relation to the importance of instruction in basic skills like spelling. In part, these parents echo the Treelane Education Foundation chairman's arguments that "states need to raise standards and hold educators accountable for basic skill instruction in reading and math." It may be that many parents equate basic skills instruction with a quality education, or at least one in which they can easily measure progress. For example, parents can easily recognize successful progress when their children spell 20 words correctly on a spelling test, but they may not be able to recognize flexible thinking and creativity in actual writing. It may also be that their fears and frustrations over their children's futures have led them to articulate conservative agendas. This ambivalence presents opportunities for curriculum leaders to engage these parents and community members in progressive social movements, but school leaders did not fully realize or take advantage of these opportunities at Greenway or Elmhurst Schools.

It is also significant that no parents expressed a desire to preserve the current working-class lifestyle in the Hillside and Treelane communities, nor did they feel much sense of attachment to their community. They want their children to achieve social mobility in order to "get out of this place." Given the parents' diverse demographics and largely working-class backgrounds, however, many of them do not know what steps their children need to take to prepare for college, nor how to support them in the process. These parents feel that they can provide little concrete support to their children other than to emphasize the importance of higher education and encourage their children to work hard in school. Many parents expressed frustration over the schools' failure to provide a quality education for their children and over their perception that school district officials viewed them either as complainers or as uninvolved with their children's education.

In their investigation of a textbook controversy in a small community in the U.S. West, Apple and Oliver (2003) found similar dynamics of identity formation and subject positions. Parents in their study were concerned about what they perceived as culturally unfamiliar and disturbing materials in their children's textbooks. But those who complained encountered a defensively postured state (represented by school and district leaders) resisting further challenges from what it impatiently branded as organized forces of right-wing censorship. This response from the local school district bureaucracy polarized what was in fact a relatively heterogeneous group of parents without a strong ideological bent by slotting them into only two subject positions through which they might be seen, heard, and understood: either the responsible parent who supported the "professional decision making" of school district officials and teachers regarding curriculum, or the irresponsible right-wing censor. Forced into the latter subject position as a result of their unmet and persistent concerns, many politically unaligned parents became quite ideological as they turned to right-wing national organizations for help in overcoming the intransigence of the school bureaucracy. In this process of "accidental and highly mediated subject positioning and identity formation,... the agency of the concerned parents became articulated to the agency of the broader Right, [and] the Right grew" (Apple & Oliver, 2003, p. 64).

Greenway and Elmhurst parents found themselves in a similar situation as their counterparts in the Apple and Oliver (2003) example. Many parents found that district officials ignored them when they complained or expressed their concerns about their children's values, education, academic achievement, and economic futures. In various subtle ways, school officials told parents that efficiency and productivity matter more than parent involvement in curriculum decisions. Their feelings that their concerns were being ignored led some parents to look to the right's neoconservative agendas for traditional curriculum and accountability measures. Yet this turn to the right was driven not by ideology but by a desperate desire for their children to have the kind of public education that would give them opportunities for social mobility. Ironically, this turn to the right was, in some ways, motivated by parents' desires for what some have termed progressive education with relevant pedagogy and materials.

### Escaping Treelane and Hillside

For the most part, the parents I interviewed live in Treelane or Hillside either because they or their parents or spouses are from the community. These areas have a feeling of community in the sense that many people live there to be near family. Yet the parents largely advise their own children to leave the area because of its depressed economy and lack of employment opportunities. There is, in fact, a sense that their children will have to "escape" while they are young and able to get the kind of education necessary for professional jobs elsewhere.

RY: What kind of future do you envision for your child in Treelane?

*Mrs. Lake:* Not much of a quality future. She'll probably have to go to the West Coast, where we have family, or somewhere else where she can find a good job after college.

RY: Do you envision your children staying in Hillside?

*Mrs. Gwinn:* Not really. I would personally like to see my girls stay close to home, but I can see the job situation is not what it used to be. The city is declining economically. It's not just Hillside, it's the whole state really. If young people have a chance to get a good education and move, I am in full support.

RY: So you believe your son will have to leave Hillside and the area?

*Mrs. LaCombe:* Yes, I do. All of his classmates will have to do the same thing to get a better life. This place is really difficult to get a good job in now. The other thing is that so many stores and businesses have also closed down in this area. You have to take the bus for 20 minutes to get to a large grocery store with reasonable prices. Even if you want your kids to work in a grocery store bagging groceries, we don't have those kinds of jobs either.

RY: So the opportunities are limited in terms of services as well as jobs?

*Mrs. LaCombe:* That's right. I want better for my kids.

RY: Do you see a future for Carl in Treelane?

*Mrs. Reynolds:* No. He has to leave. There really is no future for anyone in Treelane now. If the kids happen to get a job at the new technology plant, that's great, but you can't count on it. Those jobs are few and far between. People stay when they get those. My older son went into the army right out of high school, and when he got out he went to a local community college and got training for an electrician. He makes good money and will be able to retire at a younger age than my husband.

In point of fact, most parents appreciate the sense of family life and community in Treelane and Hillside, but believe that their children will have to leave because of the job situation. The few parents who do hope that their children will be able to find a good job in the area feel this is contingent on their mastering sufficient literacy and math skills. Basic literacy skills are important, in their view, because those job applicants who complete error-free application forms will be more likely to get one of the few good jobs available locally. The father quoted next passionately expresses this sentiment:

*Mr. Nibbelink:* If he wants to find a job in Hillside, then he'll be able to find one. His brother did. It took a while, but he kept at it, and eventually he was successful. He's doing well. I can see John doing the same thing. Sure, the job situation is not what it used to be. When I graduated, all I had to do is fill out an application down at the plant and I got called. My father and grandfather both worked there, and did very well. That was right out of high school. I didn't need college. There are a lot of jobs even if you can't get into the plant. As long as the schools do a good job teaching the skills our kids need for future jobs, they'll be fine.

The high percentage of parents who expect their children will leave the area in order to find jobs represents a major change in attitude from previous generations in Hillside and Treelane. As Mr. Nibbelink pointed out, all he had to do was fill out a job application at the factory where his father and grandfather worked, and he was offered a secure job. And as Weis (1990) pointed out in her ethnography of working-class parents in a Rust-Belt city facing a declining industrial economy, this shift has important implications for the sense of community:

The fact that Freeway parents are strongly encouraging their children to *leave* town reflects a fracturing of the collective, as parents know it. They are encouraging their children to obtain a college education, move out of the community, and secure stable employment elsewhere, often far from home. The degree to which these sentiments represent a major cultural shift cannot be underestimated. (p. 169)

The fact that these Treelane and Hillside parents are strongly encouraging their children to leave the area constitutes a loss of the family and community life these parents experienced when they were children. The degree to which these perceptions represent a major cultural shift for this community is significant. In other words, these parents have little belief that there is anything left for future generations in Hillside and Treelane, and they have made a conscious decision that their children's economic stability is more important than family ties.

Importantly, the educational bureaucracy and local advocacy groups seem largely unaware of parents' sentiments, as the following quotation from the Hillside Education Foundation's web site illustrates:

Many Hillside neighborhoods are experiencing economic revival as businesses return to the area and create new job opportunities. As the city approaches its 100-year anniversary, there is much to celebrate. Still our schools are not keeping up with the demands for a new, quality workforce. We need top-quality schools for a future in this city and so far test scores are not as high as they should be. We need to make sure our schools are teaching basic facts.

This statement contradicts Greenway and Elmhurst parents' interview comments in certain respects, but in fact the Foundation's remarks are beginning to be realized in the areas around Babcock and Pinehurst Schools. Although there is considerable agreement about the poor quality of local school curricula, there is a considerable disconnect in terms of local opportunities and what the curriculum should look like. Parents, of course, are trying to survive in these communities as the economy declines, whereas the Education Foundation manager is not. He lives in an affluent suburb and sends his children to private schools. When asked why he does not send his children to public schools, he remarked, "I will when they improve sufficiently. They still are not hiring the best teachers. They have so many teachers that are not teaching up to high standards, and they're not teaching the rigorous kind of curriculum our children need to be successful in college and in future employment. The other thing is they do not have the technology to prepare our kids for a global world." Here, the desire for technological education in a global world appears contradictory to the web site's call for basic skills instruction, but school curriculum leaders (and critical education scholars) have not helped the community foundation leaders realize the need for progressive and critical education processes (e.g., multicultural education, authentic pedagogy) that prepare children for a global world.

### *"Us vs. Them": Contradictions in Parents' and Teachers' Attitudes*

There are, as I noted earlier, tensions between parents and many Greenway and Elmhurst school personnel in relation to the schools' success in teaching basic skills and preparing children for college and 21st-century employment opportunities. Although parents talk quite positively about individual teachers and believe in the importance of education, they complain that the school does not, in their estimation, prepare their children adequately for college and future middle-class employment. In other words, parents believe that the school should prepare their children in a way that the parents themselves are unable to do because of their working-class background. Specific complaints center on what parents perceive to be lack of adequate attention to both basic and higher level academic skills as well as guidance about how to get into college. Parents feel that the schools should take responsibility for preparing their students to hold good, stable jobs in a declining industrial economy. As noted earlier, the principals and school members frequently articulate goals to develop children for 21st century employment. Although parents often level their criticism at the principal, they also reflect on teachers and the Greenway school as a whole:

*RY:* Do you think your children are being prepared for college or a career?

*Mr. Gwinn:* No.

*RY:* Why do you think that's the case?

*Mr. Gwinn:* Because I don't think they are doing much. They've had this whole language program for years, and they really didn't teach spelling and reading skills adequately. They've changed at Greenway in recent years. I can see more skills worksheets coming home, and the spelling looks better, but they still aren't testing the kids enough. I don't think they know what skills they have and what they need. There are almost no new computers, and other technology is old and often doesn't work. They still have a long way to catch up to what our kids need to learn to get new jobs. The old ones aren't going to be around much longer.

*Mrs. Sawyer:* I think the school district is very good overall for what our kids need right now. As far as having a vision for the future and knowing what our kids need to be taught so that they can go to college and do well, I don't see them doing much in that regard. The computers sure aren't up-to-date. I don't think the principal has done enough, although that's changing with more emphasis on skills and tests from the state.

*RY:* Do you think the high school guidance counselor encourages children in their career goals?

*Mrs. Nyman:* They are okay in getting kids in a track and telling them what classes to take and what they have to do to pass the tests. Most of the time, the kids need to ask for an appointment and know what questions to ask. My older daughter has had a lot of state test preparation and things like that.

*RY:* So the kids have to ask for help in order to get it?

*Mrs. Nyman:* It seems that way. The counselors really don't tell them much, especially when it comes to how to get into advanced placement classes and other classes they need to pass the SATs. Unless kids go down to guidance or ask their teachers, they don't really get enough help.

*RY:* How much encouragement do you think kids get about going to college?

*Mrs. Nyman:* I think some teachers encourage the kids. They are spending a lot more time worrying about the state tests, but it takes the kids asking the questions. Some kids don't know what questions to ask until it's too late.

Without a doubt, parents believe their children should receive more guidance and support in learning what they need to know to be successful in a technological economy, not only in terms of academic skills, but also in how to make the transition into a college-educated, middle-class life. Parents, in a sense, blame the schools for the poorly educated, jobless future they fear for their children—a future that is unchanged from their present struggles. Parents may feel powerless to change the economic situation for their children or to teach their children what they need to know to attain a more prosperous life, but they are far from silent with regard to their concerns about the poor quality of education offered by the public schools.

Greenway and Elmhurst principals and teachers view these issues quite differently. They hold parents responsible for what they see as students' lack of involvement, commitment, and discipline. As the following excerpts suggest, teachers and principals are often frustrated that parents lack knowledge about how to communicate with teachers, help their kids at home, work with the school to improve their child's performance, and so forth. The professionals in the school spend time strategizing about how to educate children without adequate parent involvement. Their comments also reveal that the principals are making numerous efforts to cultivate stronger relationships with parents and the community, but these efforts are somewhat conventional and not as successful as they could be. It is important to remember while reading the following comments that the teachers are primarily local, have strong ties to the community, and come from similar working-class backgrounds as their students' families.

*Melanie (White Greenway teacher):* [talking about parents] There's just a lack of interest in the schools and education. We send out so many newsletters and we have umpteen parent meetings to try to educate them about the new standards and tests, and we still hardly get anyone at parent conferences, and parent meetings are not well attended. If we have entertainment or food, parents will show up for that, but that's about it. Still the parents expect you to do everything for their kids with little or no support from home.

*RY:* Why don't they come to conferences and other education activities that are not focused on entertainment?

*Melanie:* I don't really know for sure. I expect it's because many of them are working two jobs and it's hard to find time to come to school. Some of them have had negative experiences in school when they were growing up, too. It might just be a low priority for education overall.

*John (White Elmhurst teacher):* I don't know why parents are not involved. They complain enough about us at the local coffee shop my cousins run, but they don't come in to school when we ask them to come hear about education for the future and what their kids will need. They're just not concerned. If they were, we would have more parents coming to school meetings, parent conferences, and the like.

*John:* I don't think parents care the way they used to. I'm not saying they don't care about their kids, but they need education themselves. I hate to generalize, so here's an example. When we have PTA meetings, there are so few parents [in attendance]. Teachers come to the meetings, but there are so few parents it should hardly have a "p" in the title. The few parents that show up really don't need education about what we're doing with the curriculum standards or anything like that.

*Sarah (African American Greenway teacher):* It's gotten to a point where parent involvement is a bonus. We have to get kids prepared for the jobs of the future. If parents help, that's great, but we *have not been able to count on it.*

Sarah's comment echoes almost exactly what the principal said when I asked her the same question, as well as echoing wording on the Hillside Education Foundation web site, an important source for the perspectives of influential *business* leaders.

Teachers clearly think parents do not do enough to support their children's education, and many perceive the parents as disinterested. One might speculate that the teachers' perceptions are fueled by the fact that for many years, parents were uncomfortable about coming to the school, and they did not feel that their children's education was a priority when local factory jobs were readily available. That is, many teachers assume that parents' attitudes today are the same as they were a generation ago when the teachers were children in these communities. While the parents' attitudes have clearly shifted overall, their behaviors with regards to school involvement have not.

Another important point to note is that parents, principals, and teachers all express contradictory attitudes toward curriculum—they recognize the importance of emphasizing critical thinking skills and creativity but utilize skill-and-drill test preparation exercises and teacher-centered pedagogies that stifle critical thinking and creativity. Parents clearly echo and fuel these contradictory attitudes as they, on the one hand, advocate for critical thinking skills, and on the other, complain about teachers' failure to teach their children "basic skills necessary in a new economy." Parents also blame educators for the fact that they are struggling financially in the midst of an economic downturn. In certain respects, both groups are right, but neither group clearly recognizes the broader cultural political shifts and related movement toward globalization that have moved industrial jobs outside of their area, and indeed, outside of the United States.

At this point, readers may recall that teachers in both schools overwhelmingly focused on curriculum forms like maps to document deeper understandings, but largely used worksheets and other standardized practices to ensure that students would pass standardized tests. In other words, the teachers, under the principals' leadership, have largely narrowed the curriculum to the tests and lost sight of the authentic, substantive classroom practices that have been shown to prepare students to take college entrance exams and succeed in higher education. Parents want their children to take school seriously and learn the kinds of skills that will prepare them for higher education and future employment. Yet because they do not know what such an education would look like, they demand evidence that their children are mastering basic skills and expect children to complete worksheets that reinforce the kind of low-level knowledge and passive learning that does not produce top students able to compete for scholarships at prestigious universities. Further, few parents show up at school meetings where the curriculum is discussed.

We might understand these tensions and contradictions in light of historic working-class attitudes that did not take a serious interest in schooling (e.g., Sennett & Cobb, 1972; Weis, 1990). The tensions between parents and educators reflect a tension that exists within the working class of these communities and centers largely related to the purpose and meaning of education in a changing economy. Another tension arises because school curricula have historically been geared to promote social and cultural reproduction, yet these parents are seeking to disrupt the current social situation and expect the school to aid their children in making this transition. Greenway and Elmhurst teachers have made personal strides by getting an education that moved them from the working class into the new middle class (Apple, 2004). We might expect that the similarity between the teachers' and parents' backgrounds would lead to more congruence in their attitudes toward education, but that clearly is not the case here. As noted in chapter 2 and earlier in this chapter, Greenway and Elmhurst faculty members frequently expressed tensions between their desire to involve parents and the prevailing view that they could not rely on support from parents and community members. We might also understand these tensions as demonstrating that traditional school–community relations and practices that "reach outward" to "educate" parents and community members about the school's agenda without taking into account broader social and economic needs in the community are doomed to fail. In the next section, I present a different approach to community relationships, one that resonates with critical and progressive education but is also cognizant of current accountability realities and other professional demands.

## Critical Curriculum Leaders' Relationships with Parents and Community Members

At Babcock and Pinehurst, the other two case study schools, parents, community members, and school leaders expressed many of the same aspirations for the students to go on to higher education, as well as similar concerns about curriculum, but they also demonstrated agency and belief that they could make a difference in their schools and communities. This shared sense of agency and community efficacy did not result from two charismatic principals convincing the masses of the value of a particular vision. Rather, individual and some collective agency emerged from community organizing focused on community-based service learning that not only increased academic achievement but also increased commitment to community revitalization. In this section, I explore themes related to desires for community revitalization; attitudes toward lifelong education; and emerging progressive educational and social movements.

### Desires for Community Revitalization

Parents and community members are working to revitalize the economically depressed areas of Hillside and Treelane where Babcock and Pinehurst Schools are situated. Many of these people cited education as a key factor in community improvement and social mobility. Because they recognized the important role of education, they sought to engage in cooperative efforts with school leaders, seeking common ground and strategies to revitalize education and the overall quality of life in their diverse communities. Such practices are reminiscent of Dewey's philosophy about the link between democracy and diversity in community life (1916/2008). "Dewey's transformative ideal can be reconstructed as the deeply democratic community, a not-yet-real possibility within experience that can guide the ongoing cooperative development of a comprehensive and practical democratic philosophy" (Greene, 1988, p. 55). Greene applies Dewey's democratic ideal to contemporary transformative praxis, in which educational experiences are key tools and components of the ongoing growth of individuals, cultures, and societies. Further, Greene explores how to build diverse transformative coalitions and self-educating communities through democratic communication, action, goals, and effective coordination. The following comments from Babcock and Pinehurst parents describe the emergence of deeply democratic practices that have inspired parents and children to work toward a better future in their respective communities:

RY:  What would you like to see as a future for your child?
*Mrs. Manelli (White parent):*  She's going to college, definitely.
RY:  What kind of career is she looking for?

*Mrs. Manelli:* Something in design, like architecture. I'd be glad to see her in any career that makes her happy. The most interesting thing is she wants to come back to Hillside and redesign neighborhoods so they have more green space, and the buildings that are abandoned, she wants to fix those up.

*RY:* That's an interesting career. Where do you suppose she got that idea?

*Mrs. Manelli:* She's been helping the community organization work on creating the park where that strip of absentee landlord houses used to be. It makes me so happy to work on this project with her. I can't tell you how much it means to see this place start to get cleaned up. And to think my daughter wants that kind of career—oh, it's called urban planning, I think—that's even better.

*RY:* What would you like to see as a future for your child?

*Mr. Hedrick (African American parent):* I want him to go to college. It would be nice if it were the local college, but I'm okay with him moving away if he has to do that to get a good job and be happy. That's what I wish for him.... I would love to see him become a doctor and come back to work in our neighborhood. We need services so badly here. So many medical offices and businesses have moved out. The community group has plans to fix that, though.

*RY:* How is the community group planning to fix the loss of services?

*Mr. Hedrick:* We're fixing up the office buildings and [influential business leaders] are putting up seed money to get doctors to start a medical practice there. The buildings are beautiful, and the rent is cheaper than in most city office buildings. It's actually just a few blocks off the freeway, not that far from the theater district and some nice restaurants, so there's some incentive as long as the facilities are nice. I'd love to see my son as one of the first doctors in that park, but I'm really hoping the changes will come sooner than that. He can come there later and make it better!

*RY:* What would you like to see as a future for your child?

*Mrs. Ellis (White parent):* I want her to do anything she wants. That means she needs to be able to go to college, and that means we need to have good schools in our area. We need small class sizes, individual attention for kids, the best teachers, and interesting materials. That means we need to clean up and really change the course of this community. It's been going downhill, but we're going to stop that. If we have businesses that can make it in this economy, and if we have schools that have good reputations, people will move here. The taxes are lower than some places, and with the new neighborhood police and fire center, it's getting to be safer, too. When I think of how this place looked 20 years ago, when trees lined the streets and people would take walks in the evening and not be afraid and when people could get good, high-paying jobs, that's what we need.

*RY:* So you want to see the community back like the good old days so that your child can have a better future?

*Mrs. Ellis:* No, I mean we want the community to be better than ever, and I want my child to go to college. That means the schools need to teach with the latest equipment and teaching practices. Our homes and businesses need to look good, and the streets need to be cleaner. So we want a better future, and we're working on it. I think we're making some little changes that will pay off in the end. That way, if our kids want to stay and raise their families, they will have that chance to be part of a better city. If she wants to live somewhere else, that's fine, too. I just want this community to have a chance.

*RY:* Has your daughter, Sheryl, discussed her future plans?

*Mr. Taylor (African American parent):* She wants to go into art. I have been worried that the sort of jobs you get in art may not be secure, but I want her to do something she loves. She and some of her friends were involved in painting a mural on the wall of the school. It's multicultural and represents our dreams for the future of our kids and for the community. I was so proud that she did that. It's beautiful, and I can see how talented she is. I told her she still has to work hard to get into college and get a back-up career that's more secure. I can see where she'll be able to have art in a career that gives her security. Many of us in the neighborhood used to say this place was done…our kids would have to get out. But I see now that we need to be a part of making it better. We have strikes against us with the economy the way it is, but we don't have to stay down. We can make a difference, but we have to recognize all the problems from the economy and the way they developed this city so that the Black people would be stuck in the urban area and the White people could get the nicer houses out in the country. We have to fight to make our own country in the city, and we're going to do it, too.

These parents clearly express strong, passionate feelings that their children and their community will have a better future. They have hope in the future and a glimmering sense of agency and internal accountability that they can make a difference. This nascent sense of agency is a far cry from the attitudes of Greenway and Elmhurst parents and community members, who have lost hope in their schools and communities. The differences in perspectives about the future of their communities are striking, especially when we recall that Greenway and Elmhurst Schools are located in other parts of the same cities as Pinehurst and Babcock. Further, as I drive through Treelane and Hillside, I am increasingly struck by the differences in the neighborhood communities surrounding these four schools. As I drive to Babcock School, I pass through the Greenway neighborhood area, which has exhibited little change from 2002 to 2006 except for an increase in closed and boarded up businesses and two or three new vacant lots where homes have been demolished. There is a noticeable difference as I near Babcock School with its new community park, nearby medical complex, pharmacy, and grocery store along with evidence of remodeling in three homes across the street.

Babcock and Pinehurst principals and teachers also note the community changes described above, and their views about curriculum issues parallel those of the parents quoted above. They see parents and community members as coleaders of education and growth in schools and communities, and their parent/community-school relationships are much less adversarial than the other two schools. As the following excerpts suggest, teachers and principals are often struck by what they learn from parents' cultural background knowledge about how to work collaboratively in ways that help improve children's academic performance and community revitalization. The curriculum leaders in the school spend time strategizing with and through parents and community leaders about what to teach and how this curriculum content may or may not be relevant to children. In other words, the community–school relationships stem from community-based curriculum projects; however, the Babcock and Pinehurst principals also used traditional parent involvement strategies like newsletters and parent meetings within their schools, strategies that yielded a much better parent response rate than their counterparts described above and many similar U.S. schools today. Their comments also reveal that the principals are making numerous efforts to cultivate stronger relationships with parents and the community, and these efforts are part of a broader community revitalization strategy.

*Seth (White Babcock teacher):* [talking about parents] There's been such a dramatic increase in parent and community interest in the schools and education. If the principal sends out a notice that parents and community members are needed, we get a flood of people in our school the next day. That was not the case before we started these community dialogue groups and working so much on curriculum projects in the community.

*RY:* Why do you think you've been so much more successful with community involvement in recent years?

*Seth:* It's hard to know for sure, but I think it's because the principal and teachers have been learners in the curriculum development process. We ask the parents and community members what they need and

what kinds of cultural knowledge we should build on in the curriculum. They feel like they are part of school improvement, I think.
They are.

*Marianne (White Pinehurst teacher):* I think we have made a priority of getting
parents really involved in the curriculum in meaningful ways...not
just having them come in so we can "educate" them on what their
kids need to know. We ask them and really want to know what they
say. I think that's helped build mutual respect and trust.

*Marianne:* I think parents really care about the community and their children's growth as citizens in the community. They see the economy
declining and they know their kids will be the future.

Parents in all four schools want a high-quality education for their children, but among the Pinehurst and Babcock parents, this desire is embedded
in their plans for community revitalization, quality education, and authentic accountability for both outcomes. Dewey's writings on experience and
education (1916/2008), Gonzalez, Moll, and Amantinds's (2005) research on
community funds of knowledge, and Alinsky's (1971) accounts of community organizing, all promote the notion that education should be experiential,
authentic, and community-based. The idea that education should engage students through connections to their lived experiences is central to the notion
of critical curriculum leadership and progressive education. In these cases,
progressive (authentic, culturally relevant, community-based) learning by
doing helped children identify their talents, such as art and architecture that
eventually became the basis of careers. The parents of Greenway and Elmhurst
children could not identify such explicit future goals for their children outside
of finding stable employment outside of their communities. Further, these
community-based learning projects created a forum through which the school
and community members dialogued and articulated common understandings and goals. This is very different, and in many respects, more successful
than the traditional school–community relationships developed at Greenway
and Elmhurst in their attempts to reach out to their communities.

### Coleading Educational and Community Improvements

Previous studies of working-class parents in urban, culturally diverse school
settings report that parents frequently express a contradictory attitude toward
education, simultaneously expressing respect for schooling and a disparaging
attitude about educational authorities and their own educational experiences.
Ultimately, it has been argued, this contradictory attitude toward schooling
leads to the same "us versus them" ideology evidenced in the historic struggle between capital and labor (Willis & Aronowitz, 1982) as well as among
Greenway and Elmhurst parents and educators. Babcock and Pinehurst par-

ents are more likely to express a joint responsibility with other community members and school members to prepare their children to become educated, democratic citizens in a better community that they helped create. Although these parents did complain about schools and education generally, they overwhelmingly expressed a belief that they were coleaders of school-community improvement efforts. The following comments are typical of Babcock and Pinehurst parents I interviewed:

RY: Do you think your children are being prepared for college or a career?

*Mr. Taylor:* Yes, and I think this is getting better all the time.

RY: Why do you think that's the case?

*Mr. Taylor:* Because I work alongside the Babcock principal and teachers to decide what we should teach and how it should be taught. They do not act like they are superior to parents, but they help us access information about what our children need to be successful. We have a say in how things will be done, which has not always been the case.

*Mr. Taylor:* The state has been using a lot of testing to improve the schools. In some ways, that's been good, but we also know our children need to be healthy and caring citizens who want to make this community a better place to live. The principal has worked at the state level, and we've had a chance to really look at these policies and figure out what they're saying and what sort of hidden effects there are on our kids. There are a number of them. These policies sort of divide kids by where they live when they test the way they do, and of course, our schools do not have as many resources as the suburbs. So we've had to decide that we want our kids to do well on the tests so that they can get into college, but that we have to be careful to not just drill the kids on these tests so they don't know how to think for themselves. Kids need to learn that by doing the community projects we have, and they need to learn to care about their neighbors who are less fortunate. That's what we're about here.

RY: Do you think your children are being prepared for college or a career?

*Mrs. Manelli:* I think they are being prepared for that, but they're prepared for more than that. I think the curriculum we've worked on over the last couple of years also prepares the kids for life, whether that life is in this community or not. I think the school is very good overall for our kids, both now and for the future. I've been much more involved since we started the community dialogue groups, so I know what people are saying when we hear advertisements about how this program competes with that program. We've been able to get a lot more resources, too. The [local business] gave us computers for the learning center so our kids have a place to go and work on new equipment. It feels like we're all in this together.

RY: Do you think the high school she's going to encourages children in their career goals?

Mr. Hedrick: Most of the high schools are not as good as our school right now, but that's okay. I plan to stay involved and make sure my child gets the best possible education and advice so that she can get into college. I've learned from the dialogue groups that our kids need to do well on SAT tests and be prepared for those, so I'll know enough when the time comes that I need to make sure she has every chance to do well.

Up until last year, I think there were a lot of guidance counselors in the high schools, but I think the budget cuts have eliminated some of those positions. That's unfortunate: kids need advice, or they can get caught in a track and not be able to get into the right courses that prepare them for college.

RY: Do you think your children are being prepared for college or a career?

Mrs. Ellis: Yes, I do. A few years ago, I would not have been as confident about the schools, but they really are working to help kids do well in academic subjects and want to learn. That's important. If kids want to learn and they are interested in what they are learning, it's much easier to teach them and have them make good progress

Mr. Taylor: It seems like the schools are better. I have not been actively involved in the dialogue groups, but we get the notes and information from other parents. You don't hear about the safety problems of a few years ago. The test scores seem good, and I've seen good teaching in the classrooms. It used to be we had the worst teachers, but that's not true anymore. There seems to be a whole community effort to improve the school and the neighborhood around it, fix up the houses and the park. There's been a couple of new businesses that have moved into our area in the last few months. All of those things help improve the school from the outside in.

RY: How much encouragement do you think kids get about going to college?

Mr. Hedrick: There's a lot of encouragement from all angles, from parents to teachers and even the pastor at the church where a lot of kids go. That makes a difference when we're all working toward the same goals for our kids.

Although the majority of parents agree that the schools are helping their children prepare for college and future employment, a few parents believe that their children are underprepared for the future. Like their counterparts at Greenway and Elmhurst, these parents believe that their children struggle to master basic academic skills and that the teachers are not teaching the kind of skills necessary for the 21st century workplace. Mr. Hedrick expresses these sentiments well:

*Mr. Hedrick:* I don't think the schools are really up to the task of preparing the kids for the future. If my kid wants to find jobs in this area, he will need to be competitive with students from the charter schools and private schools. It's not enough to know someone down at one of the plants and be able to get a job. Young people have to compete for fewer jobs. It helps if he can go to college. We're not sure about that yet, but anyway he needs to have good grades and skills with technology, good writing, and math skills.

Many community organizers and business leaders were involved in Babcock and Pinehurst school–community dialogues and community-based service-learning projects. I was able to interview about half of the community members who attended the sessions on a regular basis. What is most striking from these interviews is community members' advocacy for teaching the whole child and fostering growth beyond "the tests." Several excerpts from the interviews expand on these points:

*RY:* What would you like to see as a future for children in Treelane?

*Mrs. Bajarajas (Latina):* I want our children to attend schools where they will have all opportunities and doors open to them. The state has imposed all of these tests that seem like they make schools improve what they are teaching. The problem is that's been the ceiling. We've had a lot of conversations about how to go beyond the bottom line of the tests so kids have activities with real-world practice.

*RY:* How is the community group planning to support this kind of curriculum?

*Mrs. Bajarajas:* We're getting kids involved in urban planning activities so they have to study the soil and water quality, and they have to solve problems that arise as they plan for a community garden. They have to study the history of this area and how the economy declined in the city. We're starting to see some changes, and the kids have been writing about what they see and how they feel about changes in the community. They're writing well, from the examples that I have seen. They care about the community and their neighbors, and so they write with conviction, but they also have to practice the writing skills from the state tests.

*RY:* What would you like to see as a future for the children and the community?

*Mr. Ryan (White):* I want to see the community thrive again. That means new jobs, but more than that, it means residents who care about this community and about each other. We're getting more businesses into this area, and we've been having community events down here. A lot of kids show up, and they have a belief that there's a collective sense of hope about the future. I feel good about my involvement in that. I have a good business, but I want to give back to this community. That kind of civic involvement is important to me, and I'm thrilled that the school is teaching kids to be involved and take care of their community.... At one community meeting, someone brought pictures that showed a tree-lined, peaceful, and beautiful street, and it actually looked like the scene from *It's a Wonderful Life*. We all decided that it would be a wonderful life in our community, and we would make it happen.

*RY:* What are the plans to make that happen?

*Mr. Ryan:* We've been revitalizing the neighborhoods, one at a time. The absentee landlord situation has been problematic, and we've be able to get the city council to crack down on that, make them provide funds to fix up the places. We've also bought a couple of vacant lots and developed new housing units that are affordable and subsidized but high quality. At the same time, the school principal and teachers are doing an amazing job teaching and getting kids to perform at a high level. All of these things add up to economic and cultural revitalization in the area. It's a long-range plan, but there's a lot of commitment.

*RY:* How is the community organization working with the school to make improvements?

*Mrs. Marris (African American):* The neighborhoods around Pinehurst have been in decline for years. Many of us who grew up in the city used to think this neighborhood was a lost cause. Kids had to leave the area. There was a steady flight into the suburbs. Abandoned homes were all over the place. The worst thing is that when the city tore down some of these houses to keep them from being safe houses for drug dealers and so forth, all of the lead paint got into the soil. We have a great group of parents and business leaders and educators working together to tackle these kinds of issues. A few of us have been involved from the beginning. The most interesting thing is that as the schools improve, more business leaders have become interested in the revitalization project. They realize that if schools are excellent, people will want to move into the area. That's beginning to happen.

A brief glance at home prices in the community shows a clear upward trend in home values in the area immediately surrounding Pinehurst School, and to a lesser degree, in the area surrounding Babcock School.

Capacity for regional curriculum revitalization is also evident in both of these cases. More specifically, school personnel have developed themes and lesson plans for wider regional distribution beyond their own schools. The aim of these lessons is to "cultivate guardians for public, democratic education for the masses." These units involve students, educators, and community leaders in working together as coleaders to accomplish two interrelated subgoals: (1) *developing appreciation for diversity* in education and society, whereby each individual is recognized for his or her own abilities, interests, ideas, needs, and cultural identities; and (2) *developing socially engaged intellectuals who have a critical consciousness about the relationships among broader cultural politics and curriculum* and participate effectively in the affairs of their community to achieve a common benefit. Both schools emphasized similar progressive educational practices, including particularly student-centered curricula grounded in students' academic needs, cultural backgrounds, and consciousness about social inequities in particular communities. As principals and teachers immerse themselves in community needs and students' cultural backgrounds, they can develop socially engaged and critically compassionate intellectuals inspired to lead movements that make their communities better places to live.

### Effects of Community Transformation Process on Curriculum Leadership Identity

The Babcock and Pinehurst principals talked at length about the effects of the community transformation process on their views about what it means to be a good curriculum leader. Consider, for example, the following comments from the Babcock principal, Angela Juicidi:

*Angela Juidici:* Because we have been so active in the communities, I have come to see myself as a guardian for democracy and public education in a multicultural society. I know that sounds bold, but I am not alone. I am a leader with many leaders in the community. Schools are only a part of the effort.

*Ken Hughes (Pinehurst principal):* I have had a lot of leadership classes and I know many theories. I'm supposed to be an instructional leader and a transformational leader and a distributive leader, but I really see myself as an advocate for public education that includes academic performance on culturally relevant curriculum targets. Schools are part of communities; they are not a separate entity so we need to work together for the greater good. This is only getting more challenging when we keep hearing that we're supposed to teach someone's version of knowledge and test everyone and compete with everyone. That's not what public education should be about.

In these comments, we get a glimpse of a new curriculum leadership, one that has a heightened awareness of the needs in culturally diverse communities, broader cultural political movements, and the relationships of these to student-centered and community-based curriculum work. These critical curriculum leaders see themselves as guardians for public education and democratic societies as well as students' academic performance; they inspire emerging progressive educational and social movements. They give us hope for the future. The following problem-posing case explores the challenges and possibilities involved in a curriculum leader's efforts to balance local community and student needs against larger social mandates.

---

**PROBLEM-POSING CASE**
**Balancing Local Community and Student Needs against Larger Social Mandates**

In the spring of 2004, Pinehurst School members were in the midst of developing test-preparation activities aligned with standards, textbooks, and assessments. Over the past decade, this culturally diverse school had been widely recognized for its use of holistic educational practices, including the use of literature, the arts, and portfolio assessments. Following the passage of state testing mandates, the No Child Left Behind Act, Put Reading First, and other curriculum reforms, school personnel decided to increase academic rigor and achievement through the use of packaged instructional materials and other standardized practices. Over time, several teachers and Principal Hughes became concerned that these changes were narrowing the curriculum, and argued that a truly rigorous education required exposure to a variety of learning experiences.

During the same time frame, the community's economic base declined when a major factory and several key businesses closed. The concerns of a more activist generation of students that expected the school to prepare them for economic success in uncertain economic times placed further demands on the school and its leaders. These students also wanted an education that was more relevant to their present experiences and concerns. Meanwhile, a local community organization and the parent–teacher group contended that Pinehurst School ought to continue to mirror the needs and interests of its students. Principal Hughes took steps to alter the school's curriculum in response to the students' and community members' feedback. He approached a local community organizer and several other key business leaders to help develop plans for learning projects that worked to improve the community. As a result, community-based service-learning projects were added to the curriculum, along with thematic units on such subjects as ecology, financial planning, business development, and computer sciences.

These curriculum changes and their implications for school identity and curriculum integrity have triggered a crisis at Pinehurst School. Some veteran teachers charged that the principal's acquiescence to community and student curriculum proposals was proof that the school had lost sight of its mission and abandoned its authority for directing education in the community. They were extremely concerned that these new curriculum projects would result in declining assessment scores. They asked Mr. Hughes to exert his leadership in this matter.

Mr. Hughes is concerned about his curriculum leadership role in this situation. He is reflecting upon his role as a leader and upon the curriculum meanings and mission of the school.

### Questions

1. What would you do if you were Mr. Hughes?
2. Whose curriculum perspectives should be most influential in shaping school policy? Those of the students? Of the parents? Of the community and the broader society? Of the principal and veteran teachers?
3. How can a curriculum leader balance local community and student needs against larger social mandates?
4. How can curriculum developers reconcile these perspectives? Should a curriculum necessarily seek to reconcile such conflicts? Why or why not?

### Summary

There is a great deal of congruence among parents at all four schools in terms of their desire for their children to gain a quality education. Many parents' expectations may be becoming progressively closer to the conservative modernization view, but other parents' descriptions of ideal education are aligned with the progressive and critical ideal of education. More specifically, parents overwhelmingly want their children to attend schools with small class sizes; excellent teachers; rigorous, authentic pedagogy; and individual attention—approaches that align with progressive and critical education advocated by principals like those at Babcock and Pinehurst. In the same interviews, parents also expressed concerns that the public schools were not teaching basic skills. Yet many Greenway and Elmhurst parents are not committed to school curriculum initiatives, and in fact, feel disconnected from the schools. These parents frequently told me that they expected their children to "escape" their neighborhoods and surrounding communities in order to gain economic security. As I have indicated throughout, however, these ways often embody the complex identities of today's curriculum leadership.

In the other two cases (Babcock and Pinehurst), parents, community members, teachers, and principals all demonstrated a joint commitment to improved school curriculum and community revitalization. Almost to a person, Babcock and Pinehurst educators and community members articulated similar beliefs that they could make a difference in their schools and communities. This shared sense of agency and efficacy resulted from relationships and coactive leadership focused on raising community consciousness about economic and social injustices, empowerment, and ultimately, community transformation.

In the next chapter, I return to a cultural political perspective on curriculum leadership identity. As outlined in the Introduction, the broader conservative modernization and progressive movements both shape and are forged within curriculum leadership as constituted in a particular school–community context. In chapters 2 through 6, I explored new professional and critical curriculum leadership identities, school culture, curriculum development processes, community relationships, and focused on the relational aspects of curriculum leadership. I suggested that curriculum leadership is constructed in relation to broader political movements and local community values, and that this set of ideological constructions is fueled directly by some school cultures. I also touched briefly upon community members and explored the ways in which they contribute to curriculum priorities in schools. Yet, curriculum leaders clearly have opportunities to interrupt and change these ideological constructions. In the next chapter, I move to the ways in which curriculum leadership identity, meaning, and practices may articulate with broader social movements in the future as well as implications for curriculum leadership preparation, policy, practice, and research.

# 7

# Toward a New Field
# of Curriculum Leadership

## Implications for Research, Policy, Preparation, and Practice

> Implicit in the learning of inclusive instructional leadership is the growth of a personal and collective praxis and the valuing of a professional ethic grounded in the notion of the professional learning community. (Rayner, 2010, p. 439)

While there are many reasons to propose new curriculum or instructional leadership approaches, Rayner's (2010) references to inclusion and growth as well as personal and collective praxis suggest that it cannot be studied and conceptualized with educational administration theories alone. The need to create a new curriculum leadership field comes upon realizing that the well-meaning instructional leadership rhetoric is betrayed not only by its emphasis on professional (data-driven) procedures but also by its failure to link leadership with broader cultural political movements and critical theories required to make inclusion and democratic education a reality.

At this point, you may wonder why I call for a new field of curriculum leadership. After all, various instructional leadership theories and training models have long been part of an educational administration field. The most recent "shared, inclusive instructional leadership for learning" theory is, at least in part, a response to accountability demands, such as the No Child Left Behind Act and already well established in educational leadership. In fact, educational leadership programs across the United States have modified courses to teach skills related to accountability. Yet, Anderson (2009) and others have suggested that accountability reforms may be losing legitimacy, in which case a new curriculum leadership identity may be possible, one that moves away from viewing leadership as a series of professional qualities and practices that indirectly influence student outcomes. Unless this new curriculum leadership theory is accompanied by theoretical understandings and proactive approaches to curriculum and cultural politics—understandings and theories that currently reside in fields outside of educational leadership—things will change little in schools, particularly in low-income communities.

Although cultural political shifts toward neoliberalism, neoconservativism, Authoritarian populism, the new middle class/new public management, and accompanying ideological shifts toward market-based, back-to-basics curriculum targets, and high-stakes accountability policies began in the 1980s, these trends have played little role in even the most recent instructional leadership literature used for preparation, certification, and degree programs in the educational administration field. Rather, many educational leadership certification programs increasingly emphasize efficient data analysis processes, capacity building in professional learning communities, curriculum pacing calendars, and expanded supervision techniques, such as classroom walk throughs, designed to increase teacher quality as defined by student outcomes. While all of these techniques may be considered essential for educational administrators to survive in the current accountability environment, these leadership program strategies may actually enhance administrators' tendencies to articulate with new public management and related neoliberal and neoconservative discourses. Such is the case in many contemporary U.S. schools, including the Greenway and Elmhurst school principals and others in my study.

It is, therefore, striking that some curriculum leaders, primarily at Babcock and Pinehurst Schools differ so markedly in terms of critical consciousness and community-based activism with regard to curriculum. The Babcock and Pinehurst principals are not only exhibiting the typical functions of curriculum leadership (e.g., data analysis, classroom supervision, and learning communities) but also mediating state policy requirements and advocating for student growth, democratic education, and community transformation. These principals exhibit an emerging critical curriculum leadership identity grounded in deep understandings of progressive curriculum theories, critical perspectives, and politics. Critical curriculum leaders have the background and analytical tools to actions in the face of regressive policies and inspire neoprogressive educational and social movements in their communities.

As critical curriculum leaders like those at Babcock and Pinehurst exhibit moments of critique about conservative curriculum discourses and ideologies, they seek new ways of understanding and developing curricula that inspire new progressive educational and social movements in their communities. At this time, however, the Babcock and Pinehurst principals as critical curriculum leaders do not unite with their administrative peers in a collective struggle. For many other study participants (particularly teacher leaders), individually wish to avoid overt confrontations in their schools and instead look for private solutions in their classrooms to the dominance of conservative discourse and practices. At present the Babcock and Pinehurst principals and teacher leaders do not, therefore, see their curriculum leadership identities as a collective effort. The Babcock and Pinehurst principals exhibit more overt critical curriculum leadership perspectives and tendencies in their own schools and neighborhood communities, yet neither of them overtly encourages critical leadership in their peers, including the principals at Greenway and Elmhurst. Furthermore, the Babcock and Pinehurst principals live in nearby communities and know each other professionally, but they do not coalesce around their critical views and activist activities.

I will propose in this chapter a new field of curriculum leadership at the intersection of educational leadership, critical education studies, and curriculum studies. Curriculum leadership studies and preparation may provide a space for curriculum leaders of all kinds to coalesce as well as an opportunity for research and practices to change schools, communities, and beyond. Many schools, as I noted in chapter 4, do not provide a cultural context in which members can explore critical perspectives as curriculum leaders or social justice educators. In fact, the schools serve to promote, rather directly, the assumed "right knowledge" or curriculum content on tests, and back-to-basics teacher-centered pedagogical practices promoted by current policies. Schools thus fracture, in many ways (although some contradictions and challenges exist as I noted in chapter 4) the emergence of a critical curriculum leadership consciousness about broader cultural political shifts, particularly among teachers and students. Here I will discuss critical curriculum leadership consciousness in relationship to broader cultural political shifts and neoprogressive movements as well as changes in the economy that may impact the development of critical curriculum leadership identity in the future. In so doing, I argue that these principals/curriculum leaders and their future peers of all kinds need the research and preparation support of a new field of curriculum leadership.

I will also, in this chapter, further discuss the new professional management movement of the new middle class and speculate as to the possible relationship with what may appear to be an emerging new professional curriculum leadership identity among many educational leaders. Given the press for standardized curricula with the simultaneous pressures for accountability, I raise the possibility that many school leaders may be in the process of articulation with the conservative modernization, including particularly professional identities of new public management, in ways that promote an emerging conservative identity and related practices. As such, this chapter is a projection as these curriculum leadership identities and movements are dynamic and constantly in the process of formation. All of these possible relationships among curriculum leadership and broader cultural political movements require critical perspectives, analytical tools, and curriculum theories that are not emphasized at present in policy, curriculum leadership preparation, and practice. Finally, I will attempt to provide some idea of what a new field of curriculum leadership might look like, provide implications for policy, arguing that we need leaders who can inspire and cultivate progressive education with and through a broader community of educators and organized citizens.

The questions are: (1) Under what conditions will curriculum leadership identities, whether largely conservative or critical, be seen as shared or collective? (2) How will curriculum leadership identities be articulated in relation to broader educational and social movements? (3) What is needed for the study and practice of curriculum leadership? (4) What are the implications for policy and leadership preparation? The next two large sections of this chapter describe relationships among new professional curriculum leaders, critical curriculum leaders, and broader movements.

## New Professional Curriculum Leadership Identities and Broader Movements

A movement within which curriculum leaders like the Greenway and Elmhurst principals have begun to articulate is the continually renewing conservative modernization. There are several issues to be explored here: (1) the importance of technical knowledge and professional skills which today's curriculum leaders must exhibit; (2) the recent history of accountability and reform policies; and (3) the way in which the conservative modernization may potentially give shape and form to curriculum leadership identity as new professionals and public managers of the new middle class. I will explore each area in turn below. Each is related to commonsensical perspectives about the need for technical, rational curriculum forms, efficiency, and productivity expressed by principals and other curriculum leaders at Greenway and Elmhurst Schools as well as some Babcock and Pinehurst school members.

Pollett (1991) examined educational reforms across the United States and United Kingdom, noting growing trends toward neo-Taylorism curriculum forms and managerial ideology grounded in five core beliefs of new public management (NPM). The five core beliefs of NPM are: (a) progress defined according to and pursued through economic productivity; (b) faith in information and organizational technology to enhance productivity; (c) dependence on a disciplined workforce pursuing a productivity ideal; (d) the promise of professional management to improve productivity through effective planning, implementation, and monitoring; and (e) a crucial need for managerial discretion to pursue productivity improvement. More recently, Maxey (2009) examined NPM in an urban Texas school and argued that legitimacy and power are the keys to understanding the establishment of "good" educational leadership identity generally and curriculum leadership in particular. Examining school leadership and community relations in a Texas Independent School District, Maxey documents the ways in which district leaders use organizational and information technologies to manage instruction, including classroom Learning Walks, scripted instructional programs, benchmark assessments, and curriculum pacing calendars. All of these activities were designed, in part, to provide legitimacy for the district in the midst of concerns over the inadequacy of public education to meet current accountability mandates. Further, the Texas Independent School District used Learning Walks in conjunction with scripted curriculum and pacing calendars, as a disciplinary system enforced by a performance pay system. More, not less, power (over others)—is actually consolidated within administrative structure, [such as Learning Walks, scripted curricula, and performance pay systems]. More time and energy is spent on maintaining a public image of a "good school" and less time and energy is spent curriculum content decisions. At the same time, teachers seem to be experiencing not increased autonomy and professionalism but intensification (Apple, 2000, p. 34). In other words, the disciplinary practices and accountability pressures subsume the espoused professional intentions of current practices like Learning Walks. Wohlstetter and colleagues (2008) likewise suggest that a current sense of being a curriculum leader is attached to analyzing and being able to use data and evidence to reflect and make informed curriculum decisions. "This is, in part," they state, "because curriculum leaders must maintain an image of 'a good school' at all costs, and good schools have high student achievement. Their professional identities are then dependent upon those leadership activities that are explicitly linked to improvements in student outcomes" (p. 255).

Zipin and Brennan (2003) further examine the sense of professional identity attached to school leaders and suggest that a crisis in professional identity is ensuing for contemporary curriculum leaders. Using an illustrative "morality tale" with regards to accountability politics and curriculum decisions, Zipin and Brennan use Bourdieu's concepts and take a critically reflexive perspective to explore the significance of recent policy shifts. They explore policy shifts as they are lived and experienced at an intersubjective level of what Bourdieu calls habitus. Zipin and Brennan argue that the "new rules of the accountability game" (i.e., data-driven decisions, school and student labeling from test scores, free market competition) are creating severe conflict within the dispositional constitution of professional identity, especially in the suppression of dispositions to be ethical, social justice agents in the everyday life of the leadership field of work. While this may be true, and Zipin and Brennan offer some empathy for accountability pressures on contemporary school leaders, it must be pointed out that these "new rules of the accountability game" and related professional, managerial images of a "good curriculum leader" have almost totally suppressed leaders' beliefs in the value of teacher and student creativity, growth, and democracy. It is this point that serves partially to explain the formation of the growing conservative curriculum leadership identity, meanings, and practices of the Greenway and Elmhurst principals. As Zipin and Brennan explain:

> "In crisis" is a strong claim to make about the whole K-12 public school sector or *field* in the language of the late French sociologist, Pierre

Bourdieu. After all, the institutions of public schools are (most of them) fiscally afloat, if hard put. None as of yet have gone under. Crisis surely is a value-loaded description, a strongly interpretive adjective, never a simple attribution of fact. If we consider the inter-subjective level of working life among school leaders who inhabit the field, we can make the case that professional identity crisis—with deeply ethical implications—are brewing, perhaps aboil.... We discuss, under such conditions, a certain kind of "professional managerialism" [which] has emerged, altering the functions and nature of curriculum leadership positions, and the practical relations between principals and teachers, including pay-for-performance kinds of supervision, accountability pressures to improve test scores, and a singular focus on objective, data-driven decisions. (p. 361)

On some level, at Greenway and Elmhurst, the principals have aligned with professional, managerial images and identities popularized in "professional learning communities" that focus most teacher dialogue on improvement of test scores. Principal–teacher interactions frequently revolve around curriculum forms, such as pacing calendars and supervision linked to merit pay. Over time, the curriculum leadership focus on professional, managerial functions overwhelms principals and other school members' work lives at Greenway, Elmhurst, and many U.S. schools. Many school leaders are concerned about the singular focus on tests at the expense of cultural relevance.

Although I am unwilling to speculate at this moment as to these professional, managerial aspects of curriculum leadership in relation to future movements, it can be argued that the Greenway and Elmhurst school members' tendencies to deemphasize teacher and student empowerment as well as broader community needs reflect the sentiments that Zipin and Brennan and others express. Now that principals cannot envision their work beyond implementation of state content standards and accountability mandates, what is it that they have? It is clear from the Greenway and Elmhurst data that principals are not contemplating new forms of curriculum leadership identity but are rearticulating old forms of directive, *instructional* leadership but with visions and pedagogical practices shaped by neoliberal and neoconservative discourses and recent accountability politics. In other words, here I agree with Zipin and Brennan. It does appear as if the principals are affirming directive leadership approaches to curriculum, but unlike early 1970s directive models, the Greenway and Elmhurst principals rely on externally developed curriculum design forms, state standards, tests, instructional programs, and supervisory systems tied to performance pay. These curriculum aims and supervisory practices are not without contradictions, however. Although the Greenway and Elmhurst principals frequently touched upon neoliberal and neoconservative educational and social themes, I want to suggest that the critical thinking skills and process writing programs that the principals endorsed align more with the critical and progressive educational agenda than they do with neoliberal, new public management, and neoconservative curricular forms.

Overall, the Greenway and Elmhurst school members criticized lecture modes of instruction for failure to engage students' critical thinking skills and to deepen students' understandings of curriculum standards. A few teachers also pointed out the harmful effects of narrowing the curriculum to exclude culturally relevant curricula and emphasize normative frames from middle-class and White contexts in school contexts of high urban poverty. It is also significant that the Greenway and Elmhurst curriculum leaders are affirming, on one level, the idea of teaching for deep understandings and critical thinking skills that characterize progressive education, and on the other level, they are affirming a neoconservative emphasis on basic skill instruction.

The lack of rejection of deep curriculum understandings and critical thinking skills, however, should not be confused with practices aimed at deep democracy and authentic curriculum practices embedded centrally within the progressive notion of growth (Dewey, 1916/2008). A cursory review of many standardized curriculum pacing calendars and other applications of popularized curriculum design programs reveals little depth beyond critical thinking skills required on state tests. What Greenway and Elmhurst leaders have embraced is the *form* of curriculum and a seemingly positive valuation of it, but this should not be confused with educational content decisions aimed at human freedom and democracy. At the same time, these principals and other school members' intentions to develop students' abilities to critique have the potential to rearticulate with more progressive educational movements in the future.

The apparent acceptance of standardized curriculum forms among many principals and other educational leaders also needs to be seen in light of administrator licensure requirements and circulating policy discourses that have affected school and community members' common sense about education. The professional leadership identity of the Greenway and Elmhurst principals and the increasingly standardized curriculum development process—from organic, grassroots processes to standards alignment and application—have to be understood in light of the history of the American curriculum. As Kliebard (1992) and others have suggested, the history of the American curriculum must be seen in relation to broader cultural and political movements. Specifically, as Kliebard describes, "...successful reforms are not simply someone's good idea; they are supported by or at least consistent with broad social and political forces in which schools are situated" (p. 102). Clearly, recent curriculum trends and policies have supported standardization and consistency over grassroots teacher-led curriculum development, creativity, and progressive education.

Today's principals have not had a broader progressive educational movement with which they might link, whether consciously or not. The movements that exist currently with which many principals may link are neo-Tylerism and new public management as part of a conservative modernization. What is key here is that since the dawn of the 21st century and the conservative modernization, including new public management, coherence in schools has been realized largely in terms of curriculum leaders' increased valuation of accountability mandates that label schools as "excelling," rigorous, capable of closing achievement gaps, and competitive in the marketplace, which may be the main link to the Greenway and Elmhurst principals and other curriculum leaders in the future. The new public management aspect of the conservative modernization thus holds out some possibility for many of today's curriculum leaders in the sense that it may give shape and form to much of today's curriculum work. More specifically, the new public management of the conservative modernization offers a possible movement for curriculum leaders in light of the current emphasis on technical rational practices, standardization, consistency, efficiency, and productivity.

The fact that many principals and teacher leaders gain reputations as "exemplary curriculum leaders" by establishing order and "happy consensus" about the content on curriculum pacing calendars and other popularized design programs and textbook series—all of which are marketed to minimize conflict, maintain instructional consistency in all classrooms, and help schools attain "exemplary" labels rather than "failing" labels—also thrust many contemporary curriculum leaders into legitimate professional identities that consciously or unconsciously reinforce neoliberalism, neoconservativism, and new public management discourse (i.e., technical rational practices, standardization, consistency, efficiency, productivity). Although many curriculum leaders were involved in ongoing professional development through state and regional curriculum leadership organizations in order to develop and maintain current backgrounds in progressive curriculum and critical pedagogy before cultural political shifts legitimized standardized curricula and assessments, their professional development experiences failed to alter the current tendency toward a technical, rational implementation of state standards in maps and pacing guides, current accountability policy requirements, and a nearly singular focus on student outcomes. Anderson (2001), on the basis of an extensive discourse analysis of professional leadership standards and other related accountability policies, concluded:

> The increasing reliance on accountability through standards and testing has been linked by some researchers to a neo-liberal global policy agenda (e.g. Meyer et al. 1992; Gordon & Whitty, 1997). Neo-liberal systems of government present themselves as anti-intervention and anti-regulation, arguing that the free market should be allowed to operate within the policy arena. However, in reality, they have merely changed the modalities of regulation, shifting their emphasis from

controlling policy inputs at the planning and implementation stages to controlling policy outputs within a decentralized system. In this way, evaluation and accountability in the context of school autonomy become the technologies of control that allow the neo-liberal state to steer the system from a distance. (pp. 202–203)

With the demise of progressivism in the United States, and the rise of accountability politics and new public management, it is possible to argue that if conservative curriculum leaders see their identity as collective and articulate with a broader movement, it *may* be that of the new public management (conservative modernization), which has the potential to further narrow children's curriculum experiences in schools. While this new professional curriculum leadership is currently expressed largely via individuals, the new right may well encourage these sentiments to become shared or felt as a collective. It is, therefore, arguably the case that as these curriculum leaders move forward, the new right will be able, as a cultural political movement, to offer shape and form to conservative curriculum leadership identity and work, as described here, thus further changing the direction of the American curriculum (and leadership thereof) to that of new right politics.

By suggesting in this and earlier chapters that curriculum leadership has been absorbed into accountability and professional (new public management) discourses within our educational institutions, I am not arguing that this co-optation of curriculum leadership is done with malicious intentions. In many cases, including Greenway and Elmhurst, accountability measures are used to leverage much-needed improvements in challenging school settings. Professional learning communities, while overwhelmingly focused on data-driven decisions, are often constructed with intentions to improve student outcomes and close minority achievement gaps. Over time, the narrowed focus on academic form rather than substantive content, teacher creativity, and the humanities became the norm for today's professional curriculum leaders.

There is a sense in which many schools encourage the identity formation of professional curriculum leadership, and if I am correct, expansions of the conservative modernization in the future. These schools encourage, as I argued in earlier chapters, separatist forms and conservative dominance. Again, however, this is not total, since there are countervailing tendencies within many schools themselves, reflective of the fact that the school is a state institution and, therefore, embodies certain contradictions. Thus, there are countervailing critical tendencies in the schools due to the fact that they reflect the gains of the very cultural political movements that some students and teachers are embedded within or oppose. At the moment, however, many school members and school cultures appear largely to further the identity of conservative curriculum leadership and constrain the moments of critique among many critical and progressive educators.

## *Critical Curriculum Leadership Identities and Broader Movements*

It is in the context of the above arguments that the Babcock and Pinehurst principals'/critical curriculum leadership responses become so interesting. Given the recent context of accountability and policies designed to close racial achievement gaps, which enabled critical curriculum leadership identity to be at least an envisioned possibility (not necessarily a reality, of course) for some educational leaders and the very real fact that few school districts now value grassroots, teacher-led, or community-based curriculum development processes, authentic participation, and critique, critical professional identity as even a possible reality for curriculum leaders is undermined.

Nonetheless, there has been a growing concern for social justice among many educators, generally expressed in terms of what it means to be an educational leader in schools (e.g., Frattura & Capper, 2007; Marshall & Oliva, 2009; Theoharris, 2009). The principals and teacher leaders at Babcock and Pinehurst reflect, in differing degrees, this emerging consciousness about social justice and advocacy as part of their critical curriculum leadership identities. While it is not my intention to unpack the "causes" for this consciousness in the same communities that support more conservative ideologies and practices in the other two schools in my study, the very fact of such consciousness is important. As data from my study point out, leaders can have influence on neoliberal and neoconservative discourses, politics, and policies in their schools and communities, both in positive and negative terms.

Politics operates at three interrelated levels, each of which influences and is influenced by critical curriculum leadership: microschool level, community and regional level, and macrolevel (federal, state, cultural-political movements, such as neoliberalism). The Babcock and Pinehurst principals' glimmerings of critique and changing consciousness about curriculum (and leadership thereof) must be seen in relation to each of these points, which I will expand on below.

One of the most striking micropolitical changes to take place within the last 2 decades (in addition to accountability mandates on school) is the movement of schools, and consequently principals, into decentralized school governance. Decentralized governance structures have affected and changed school cultures and micropolitics or negotiations over resources, professional status, and ideological commitments (Ball, 1987). Whereas it was previously common for school districts to develop and require the same curricula and resources district-wide, it is now the case that many school councils composed of teachers, the principal, and sometimes students and parents) develop their own curricula and select their own textbooks/materials.

Site-based management significantly alters principals' curriculum leadership roles and how they spend their time. However, it is important to look not only at principals' roles in site-based curriculum decision making but also at the content, underlying ideologies, and the relationships to broader cultural political movements behind these curriculum decisions. While the Greenway and Elmhurst school members enacted decentralization through professional learning communities (i.e., largely data-analysis and curriculum mapping structures), critical curriculum leaders like those at Babcock and Pinehurst developed community-based curriculum projects with content focused on empowerment and compassion as well as academic subjects.

With decentralization policies and practices, principals are increasingly responsible for their school's performance label with regards to student progress on standardized tests, and regardless of federal and state policy revisions, principals are not likely to escape these pressures in the near future. The Babcock and Pinehurst principals' solutions now are to minimize the threat of accountability sanctions and engage in individualistic solutions aimed at minimizing the potentially negative effects of accountability on particular students. It is possible, however, that these curriculum leaders may be postponing the moment of open conflict over curriculum content in their communities. At that point, the contradictory intentions of curriculum ideology outlined in the Introduction through chapter 4 may become more apparent, especially in light of the economic downturn and resulting pressures to compete for students and adequate funding.

The Babcock and Pinehurst school leaders, nevertheless, use decentralization as a vehicle to challenge conservative discourses circulating through their schools and communities. Working with and through school and community members, they challenge the notion that their primary role is to supervise teachers' consistent implementation of curriculum pacing guides that ensure coverage of "the right knowledge" in all classrooms. These principals also challenge the notion that they must account to district, state, and federal policymakers telling them what to do for children while at the same time, they reaffirm the need for a broader notion of accountability in their schools, communities, and regions. Such challenges can also be seen as a critical awareness of broader cultural political shifts, offering the potential to cultivate critical curriculum leadership identities. Critical curriculum leadership identities cannot be understood only in relation to cultural politics. These must also be seen as reflective, at least partially, of the identity-formation process of educators in general and in particular individuals.

In particular, the curriculum leadership identity formation process of Babcock and Pinehurst principals and some study participants from Greenway and Elmhurst, then, largely reflect the beginnings of a conscious critique of conservative discourses, particularly with regards to new public management. It is also possible that these beginnings could, at some point, be woven into the collective interests of educational leaders of all kinds for human freedom and community. In certain respects, race and gender play a role in how principals and other curriculum leaders identify with the need to revitalize communities and close achievement gaps. At the same time, Dr. Draper and others clearly illustrate the powerful influences of conservative discourses on their back-to-basics curricula and differentiated instructional practices that unintentionally provide poor and minority students with test preparation activities and more affluent students with enrichment activities.

What the Babcock and Pinehurst principals exhibit are individualistic solutions in the form of critical discourse analysis and community-based curriculum development and community revitalization. Their curriculum leadership identities do not represent at the moment, a collective challenge to conservative dominance of high-stakes accountability policies and data-focused curriculum activities. They do represent a challenge to "traditional" or new professional versions of instructional leadership as envisioned and validated in current administrator tests and standards. The challenge is limited in some ways, however. It will take research and study in a new field of curriculum leadership with implications for a different kind of preparation that supports and enhances leaders in this challenge.

The role of the schools, as I have suggested in chapter 4, is largely to constrain these moments of critique, although there are aspects of schools (primarily Babcock and Pinehurst) that promote it: for example, conscious attempts to present debates within academic subjects, the inclusion in the curriculum of minority and women's struggles, and community service/curriculum development projects. In other words, many schools do not provide a space in which teachers and students can explore their emerging identities and allow a critical consciousness to take hold. There are contradictory tendencies within the schools, but at this moment, they are too weak and unarticulated to challenge the dominance of accountability and standardized curriculum dominance. As the Babcock and Pinehurst leaders developed and implemented curriculum in the heart of their communities, they cultivated students and citizens as curriculum leaders interested in social justice and equity as well as academic performance.

### Understanding and Using Curriculum Theories

Many principals use curriculum mapping and pacing calendars with development processes reminiscent of Tyler's rationale. While the Tyler model assumes a certain level of teacher discretion with regard to curriculum target selection, today's curriculum maps often rely on state standards and other sources of broad goals (big ideas), specific benchmark objectives, and so forth. Like many principals today, the Greenway and Elmhurst principals and teachers rely heavily on state standards in their curriculum maps. Although teachers in both schools are expected to map curricula based upon actual classroom practices, they often copy from each other and the teachers' guides. The Greenway and Elmhurst principals identify with a host of curriculum reforms and gradually see their curriculum leadership in relation to their expertise in these reforms and in relation to "other" progressive (or what they call laissez-faire) leaders. Like many of their peers, the Greenway and Elmhurst principals recognize the need for curriculum expertise, but neither has a background in curriculum theory or development processes.

The Babcock and Pinehurst principals' understandings and enactments of critical curriculum theories may explain the differences in their curriculum development processes, emerging consciousness of cultural political shifts and discourses, and community-based curriculum work. Yet these curriculum development processes as solutions to narrow, standardized curricula also tend to be articulated in a highly individualized manner. In order to press for critical curriculum leadership in their schools, districts, and beyond, individual curriculum leadership problems must be seen as shared and needing collective action. In other words, these principals and other curriculum leaders are not conscious of their shared political identity even though the glimmerings of such consciousness are there.

Shifting our notions of curriculum leadership to more critical perspectives may require not only a heightened awareness of broader cultural political shifts and contradictions in conservative ideological agendas surrounding current policies but also creating new discursive practices grounded in deep understandings of curriculum theory and critical education studies. Such discourses will address local community needs as well as broader issues of social justice that help students, educators, parents/community members overcome barriers to growth and freedom in a democratic society.

## Toward a New Field of Curriculum Leadership

There is growing interest in curriculum leadership in the fields of teacher education, curriculum studies, and educational administration. For instance, there have been recent debates over curriculum theory, practices, and politics in teacher education and curriculum studies; however, there have been no scholarly attempts to clearly define curriculum leadership. In the field of educational administration, curriculum theory and politics have received little attention. Instead, educational administration books focus on technical, rational approaches of instructional leadership that influence improvements in classroom instruction and student outcomes. In my view, we need to create a new field of curriculum leadership grounded in curriculum theory and politics and dealing with those engaged in struggles around curriculum, pedagogy, and assessments in schools.

To begin, additional research is needed to confirm and expand findings from this study in regions of the United States beyond the Northeast where it took place. Going forward, it will be important to follow these and other curriculum leaders as they grow and articulate with new and expanded movements. In particular, it will be important to examine what happens to the emerging moments of critique about the conservative modernization exhibited by critical curriculum leaders of all kinds. Further, research is needed to explore curriculum leadership identities and struggles through a range of critical perspectives, including feminist and critical race theories. At the same time, it will be important for scholars, practitioners, and community leaders to develop and share lesson plans, reflections, and other practical ideas to support new progressive educational and social movements across the United States and the world. Research and study in a new field may also support scholars and practitioners to coalesce and advocate for policy changes.

### Policy Implications

Policymakers also need to be more critical and consider more fully the ways in which policies may unwittingly support a particular (e.g., conservative) set of ideologies. When federal and state governments sign laws that support vouchers and other strategies for marketization, mandate standardized tests, support curriculum alignment forms more than substance, and fund only programs that demonstrate an overreliance on basic academic skill instruction for all children regardless of language proficiency and cultural background knowledge, they help circulate neoliberal and neoconservative discourses. Further, by supporting a cottage industry of basic skill programs and curriculum design formats, policymakers enable the growth of the new middle class and new public management discourses that promote technical rational practices, efficiency, and productivity at the expense of authentic, community-based, and culturally relevant curricula, democratic education, and lifelong growth.

With a growing student population of second language and culturally diverse students, policymakers can no longer assume that it is enough to hold schools accountable for excellence on standardized tests that privilege the right knowledge for middle class, White, native English speaking students. It is time for policies to hold schools accountable for meeting community (cultural) needs, preparing children to be intellectually curious, analytical, and compassionate future citizens. Accountability is not the problem; the problem is holding schools accountable for narrowing the curriculum primarily to official knowledge of literacy and math as tested on state exams. Obama's administration has taken steps to reduce the singular emphasis on high-stakes tests with Race to the Top and yet it remains to be seen whether this policy is just old wine (No Child Left Behind) in a new bottle. Educational policies would do well to consider the Babcock and Pinehurst School examples in which community members, parents, administrators, teachers, and students assumed collective responsibility for making their culturally diverse neighborhood communities better places to live. What might happen if a federal policy held schools accountable for students' academic and democratic human performance on community-based service projects? What kinds of tests would states develop and mandate? Answers to these questions would require more than standardized test measures as well as scholars and practitioners prepared in a new curriculum leadership field.

### Preparation

In the remaining sections of this chapter, I will revisit the conceptual frame from the Introduction and use it as an aid for considering how administrative and teacher leadership preparation programs may create spaces for curriculum leaders of all kinds to coalesce around issues of politics, policy, curriculum content dilemmas, and pedagogical debates. Regardless of personal philosophies and identities, present and future curriculum leaders must be prepared to mediate broader cultural political shifts, discourses, and policies in their schools and communities. They must learn to cultivate a heightened awareness of political discourses and effects on their schools and communities. They will be prepared to use leadership influence and new analytical tools, such as discourse, to counter potentially negative effects of cultural political shifts, curriculum reform trends, and accountability policies—tools that require background in critical curriculum studies as well as educational leadership.

Critical curriculum leaders will learn how to move beyond an almost singular reliance on state standards and tests and how to draw on community needs and cultural sources of knowledge as bases for curriculum content decisions and projects. They will be able to build reciprocal community–school relationships that not only serve as the basis for community project-based curricula but also support growth in democratic education and community revitalization. Such practices are reminiscent of progressive education from Dewey and others who advocate authentic and culturally relevant educational practices, but critical curriculum leaders are realistic about the role of state tests and standards as gateways for historically marginalized populations to succeed in higher education. Current and future citizens of our communities (parents, community organizers/leaders, and students, and educational administrators) will be inspired to work together and make our communities, and indeed, our world a more compassionate and intellectually satisfying place to live.

Curriculum leadership preparation must provide a space for educational leaders to deal with current struggles over curriculum, pedagogy, and assessment. Today more than ever, curriculum leaders need deeper theoretical understandings of educational content and the role of politics in decision-making processes. Educational leadership preparation programs often include one course on "curriculum and instructional leadership" that emphasizes classroom supervision techniques and strategies. Courses in curriculum studies and critical education studies provide educators with understandings of curriculum theories and cultural politics that are essential for contemporary curriculum leadership and yet these programs primarily serve a teacher education audience. Leadership receives little attention in these fields. Educational leadership students need curriculum and critical education courses as well as underlying social foundations in order to develop the perspectives and analytical tools to deal with the struggles and challenges of an accountability era and beyond.

It is a challenge to prepare curriculum leaders with typical university divisions among leadership, teacher education, and curriculum studies. The barriers to substantive curriculum leadership development are real, and the likelihood of a licensure policy paradigm shift in the near future is slim. Further, because schools are implicated within broader cultural political shifts and related power relations, there will always be some risk involved in using critical perspectives in school environments that have long established norms of collegiality, harmony, and limited critical analysis. Critical perspectives are largely repressed by the day-to-day workings of the school. Aspects of new public management and the conservative modernization, on the one hand, are not. The costs of technical–rational curriculum practices that focus all attention on test scores are high indeed. However, the future of curriculum in public education is worth the risk.

It has been my task in this book to chronicle cultural political changes through a look at curriculum leadership identity formation through critical perspectives, understandings of curriculum theory, and the role of politics. I have captured aspects of the identity formation process among principals and other school/community participants. Identities, however, are always in flux, and it is important for others to follow such curriculum leaders as policies, curriculum trends, and broader cultural political shifts occur, and to test carefully my notions and speculations regarding the future. This needs to be looked at both in terms of the individual/personal level as well as the movement level and relationships among them. I encourage others to look carefully at curriculum leadership identities and analytical tools as we move into a new phase of policies and reforms beyond the No Child Left Behind Act (2001). Our children and the future of public education depend on us, and they are both worth the challenge and effort.

# Research Methods

## Approach to Inquiry

Surprisingly few studies of instructional leadership examine curriculum leaders' identities and lived experience in the determination of the content of education (curriculum), what schools teach explicitly, and to whom. Instead, even the most recent educational administration studies focus on the effects of leadership tasks that are presumed to be more important, such as supervision of teaching practice, or they infer the importance of indirect leadership processes, such as culture building and organizational redesign, on student learning and outcomes. My research on curriculum leadership is grounded in the educational leadership and curriculum fields and explores the lived experiences and perspectives of principals, teachers, parents, and students actively engaged in neoprogressive educational and social movements.

Some theorists seek to understand people's lived experiences in the social world, assuming that the social world is distinctly different from the natural world because human behavior is mediated by the meanings people give to situations (Burrell & Morgan, 2003). Clearly, real differences exist: principals/curriculum leaders differ in terms of prior teaching experience, personal beliefs about curriculum and pedagogy and their role in guiding these, political savvy, specific training, race, gender, and numerous other characteristics. However, the meaning of any difference emerges as the principal and teachers interpret and act on it. In other words, none of these characteristics is universally or automatically important. They become important as school members make (or do not make) them significant in particular ways. Consequently, the principal's, teachers', and students' specific understandings of differences are not extraneous to inputs (curriculum leadership functions) and outputs (student achievement), as more traditional studies would suggest. Rather, meanings are the inputs and outputs, and principals', teachers', and students' understandings of differences are intrinsic to curriculum leadership.

Several ideas emerge from an emphasis on human meaning-making. First, meaning is both common and individualistic. Individuals express their own unique understandings of the world; however, predominant social principles, such as those concerning social class and cultural difference, also shape those understandings. Thus, rather than assuming that humans either follow common, predictable social scripts, or exercise complete freedom and agency in their decision making, interpretive studies acknowledge and seek to explain a structured sociocultural world within which variation in human agency (choice) exists (Erickson, 1986).

From this perspective, the meaning of curriculum leadership is also a social construction. Regardless of how effective or ineffective the leadership is, it cannot be attributed to individual administrators or groups (i.e., curriculum governance councils), because individuals assign meanings in response to other people with whom they interact. Neither can leadership qualities be attributed to a grand social order because their reach is neither absolute nor unmediated; nor can they be attributed to a senseless randomness, because human practices impose patterns on events.

Within the phrase "social construction," "social" has two connotations. First, meaning is mutually produced and constructed. Each individual's identities, perspectives, and understandings are constantly being shaped by the perspectives and understandings of others. People construct their understandings of a learning situation during face-to-face interactions. For example, teachers and administrators construct their understandings of what the No Child Left Behind Act (NCLB; 2001) means to them as they talk about policy requirements and implications together. Moreover, such social (modifications) are also hierarchical within the school culture: the principal has more formal power than do teachers, students, or parents to insist upon his or her point of view. "Social" also implies the impingement of wider contexts on the meanings individuals construct during face-to-face interactions. The principal and other members of the school community are not completely free to designate their school curriculum in accordance with current federal and state requirements. For example, they do not reinvent categories such as "test," "proficient," or "remedial." Rather, they "live" within those categories. Into their local school and classroom interactions and negotiations, they bring institutionalized, cultural, historical, and normative precepts of membership, as well as differences arising from their past experiences in other schools, the school district, their families, and their communities.

Specifically, I posit that familiar curriculum leadership processes, such as teacher supervision and textbook selection, are difficult to examine because they are inherently commonsensical and contextual. That is, all principals observe their teachers, do some work on curriculum, and oversee choices of the primary instructional materials used in their buildings. Likewise, all exemplary teachers exercise leadership that influences the curriculum decisions and practices of their peers and their principals. Thus, I cast curriculum leadership as no less "strange" than the exotic customs that anthropologists record in foreign lands. I treat members of the school community as complex meaning-makers rather than scripted actors; I treat their words as reminiscent rather than as scripted responses in a supervision handbook or teachers' manual; and I treat curriculum not as a neutral artifact but as a powerful resource that faculty and staff use in establishing social, cultural, and academic relationships in their school.

The longitudinal study that forms the basis of this volume shares with other interpretive accounts of curriculum leadership a general theoretical emphasis on meaning, process, and context, but it adds a critical orientation toward curriculum work and an explicit analysis of politics. As noted earlier, since the 1990s, there have been radical changes in curriculum policy, which have rendered inadequate some of the traditional assumptions and claims about curriculum leadership and have opened the door to a critical orientation on curriculum leadership.

A critical perspective also maintains that structures are socially constructed, serve material interests, and privilege some groups over others (Burrell & Morgan, 2003). Because of the subjective nature of radical humanism, theorists argue that oppression occurs at the level of *consciousness* when individuals (often poor women and minorities) lose the belief that they have any ability to change social circumstances that, for example, keep them living in high-poverty communities with few jobs, dilapidated housing, and failing schools. Gramsci (1971) referred to this hegemony as "the process by which the dominant classes or class factions propagate their values through their privileged access to social institutions (such as the media)" (p. 81). Apple (1990) drew on Gramsci when he argued, "Hegemony acts to saturate our consciousness so that the educational, economic, and social world we see and interact with, and the commonsense interpretations we put on it, becomes the world tout court, the only world" (p. 5). Although critical theorists suggest that the individual is subsumed in larger social groups, Gramsci (1971) argues that the individual "creates his [or her] own source of consciousness, and is, therefore, most able to resist the forces of hegemony" (p. 407).

Accordingly, the cases featured in this book attempt both a "thick description" (Geertz, 1973) and a critique of the strangely familiar curriculum leadership world in four different schools in two different communities, thereby conveying the subtle yet enduring processes by which some principals and teachers gain clarity about the current politics of curriculum decisions and learn to change their consciousness as they change their curricula.

In sum, it is time to reconsider the assumption that the experiences of curriculum leaders and other school members can be separated from deep understandings of curriculum theories and the larger cultural and political context of the United States. As Apple (2004) pointed out, curriculum work is inherently political, and curriculum decisions about the content of education are political acts. Essentially, the menu of individual or collective leadership strategies that figures prominently in traditional studies of "instructional" leadership must be replaced by robust theories of "curriculum" leadership that consider the complex relationships among leadership, curriculum theory, the role of politics, and the influences of these on curriculum leadership identities and practices in schools and communities.

My primary data are the words of principals, other school participants (teachers and students), parents, and community members. In particular, I consider how principals, teachers, and students use words to construct explicit and implicit meanings and to perform different leadership and social roles and relationships. From this perspective, the meaning and significance of leadership to the designation of official school knowledge(s), social problems, and cultural reproduction (or transformation) is public and constantly evolving, not established in labels on an administrative roles-and-responsibilities chart or curriculum improvement plan.

## An Ethnographic Study: Research Methods and Design

This study used an ethnographic case study design to examine principals and curriculum leaders in the Northeastern region of the United States. Using the voices of these particular principals and other study participants, I consider what curriculum leadership means in the current political context. That is, I seek to reveal the ways in which these principals reinterpret their own particular curriculum leadership meanings and practices as examples for others to interpret their own. I was particularly interested in challenging urban contexts and those contexts with changing demographics. In the remainder of this section, the ethnographic case study methods and design, including sampling of the participants, school site contexts, data collection, and data analysis procedures.

### *Sampling and Access*

This study featured four principals selected through purposeful sampling (Glaser & Strauss, 1967). More specifically, I used a snowball network method and examination of local newspapers, looking for excellent principals with an awareness of current politics related to curriculum decisions. I wanted to study principals who had excellent reputations in the district and surrounding areas. To discern this quality, I consulted the state web site, area university faculty members, district superintendents, and numerous newspaper articles. In other words, I wanted a broad movement perspective and state academic evidence as well as internal perceptions about principals as excellent curriculum leaders in the current political environment. In the end, I decided that the identified schools and principals were considered excellent in the region and state. The principals included two men (both White) and two women (one White and one African American), ranging in age from the late 30s to early 50s. Two principals held doctoral degrees.

I gained access to the schools through an adjunct faculty member at the State University at Buffalo and a doctoral student. Because these two individuals were familiar with my work and course readings, they knew I was likely to have mixed views about current accountability policies and that I was opposed to the high-stakes testing emphasis of the No Child Left Behind Act but supportive of the goals for closing minority achievement gaps. For this main reason, they were willing to help me gain access to schools wherein I could chronicle the lived experiences and perceptions about the impact of policies on children and communities. My acquaintance with respected colleagues within the district and in a neighboring district helped me gain access and build relationships and trust with my participants. The adjunct faculty member and doctoral student introduced me to the principals and school members during initial fieldwork. This was especially important given my positionality as an Anglo, middle class, female academic. One school principal refused to participate because I wanted to interview parents, and he was concerned about parent anxieties that the school might be merged with a neighboring school. Over time, my relationships and trust with participants helped me engage in authentic, meaningful data collection and analysis.

### Ethnography: Data Collection and Analysis

The fieldwork, interviews, document reviews, and overall data analysis conducted for this study were designed to provide contextualized understandings about the ways in which broader social-cultural-political influences and movements (e.g., conservative modernization) affect perceptions of "good" curriculum leaders, "good sense" about curriculum practice in schools, and how curriculum leaders may or may not align themselves with broader influences. Discerning subtle shifts in beliefs and ways of thinking about curriculum and leadership thereof may uncover possibilities for progressive counter movements.

Carspecken (1995) offers a five-stage scheme or framework for data collection and analysis in critical qualitative research. These are the five stages: (1) compiling the primary record through qualitative collection of data; (2) preliminary reconstructive analysis; (3) discovering dialogical data generation; (4) describing system relations; and (5) using system relationships to explain the findings. I utilized this five-step method as I undertook the project.

During stage 1, Carspecken (1995) recommends the "method of priority observation, taking the record of everything the subject says or does in the field observations as thickly as possible. During observation sessions, I shifted focus roughly every 5 minutes in order to observe a new individual as "the priority person," making myself as unobtrusive as possible. Carspecken argues that the primary record is a "sort of massive claim to represent what took place in a manner any observer or participant would report under ideal conditions"

(p. 88). In order to validate the claim, I used a number of research procedures. For example, I used a recording device, a flexible observation schedule, wrote with a lower inference vocabulary, used peer debriefing, and used member checks. The point of this is to ensure that I was able to claim that events occur frequently or infrequently as indicated by the observations.

Numerous nonparticipant observations were conducted during meetings related to curriculum (Spradley, 1979). Intensive naturalistic observations in classrooms and meeting rooms for curriculum development or assessment analysis provided categories of data that arose from the context and the school participants rather than strictly from the researcher. This action is important for an inquiry into the bases for curriculum leadership that people actually use at this point in time rather than precepts from theories of curriculum (instructional) leadership selected a priori. Following the observations, I met with participants to share, clarify, and discuss my field notes. I also analyzed curriculum documents (i.e., meeting minutes, curriculum maps, community meetings dealing with curriculum, newspaper articles quoting the principal and curriculum leaders' interpretations of state accountability and curriculum politics) in order to triangulate practitioners' perspectives on how circulating conservative discourses have affected curriculum leadership meanings and practices.

During the second stage of research, I began the coding process to speculate as to the meanings of the observations. In so doing, I began to discover normative and subjective references, as well as concretely articulate themes in the data gathered over time. I also began to observe formation of curriculum leadership roles as well as the ways in which broader cultural politics mediate curriculum leadership formation. This stage is coned "reconstructive analysis" because it reconstructs into "explicit discourse, cultural and subjective factors that are largely tacit in nature" (Carspecken, 1995, p. 93). Validity requirements for stage 2 included conducting member checks and using peer debriefing.

Stage 3 included gathering data through interviews. My primary data are the words of principals and other school participants (i.e., teachers and students) and community participants (i.e., parents and community leaders). In particular, I consider how study participants use words to construct explicit and implicit meaning and to perform different leadership and social roles and relationships. From this perspective, the meaning and significance of leadership to the designation of official school knowedge(s) and cultural reproduction (or transformation) in public and in process, is not established in labels on an administrative roles and responsibilities chart or curriculum improvement plan. Principals, teachers, and students make curriculum leadership visible and consequential in their daily lives of school and beyond.

Qualitative interview questions and protocols were developed in a manner that allowed for maximum flexibility. As Carspecken (1995) suggests, I used five lead-off interview questions and from these questions used other, more probing questions as the interviews progressed. The 314 interviews probed the relationship between the principals' constructed meanings of curriculum and leadership, their experiences and interactions with teachers and policymaking at state and local levels, and evolving effects of both on their work. All interviews were audiotaped and transcribed. Validity checks included recording the interview, matching observations to interview questions, using nonleading questions, peer debriefers and member checks, and finally, encouraging subjects to use and explain terms in a naturalistic manner.

Stages 4 and 5 seek to explain the meaning of the study. Theoretical concepts make it possible to link the analysis to cultural politics, related systems of power and subordination, and meanings of curriculum. At this point, I was able to suggest reasons for the experiences and structures the subjects encountered. Carspecken (1995) suggests that it is the fifth stage that truly gives the study its force and contributes to real social change.

In conclusion, I want to suggest that the politically charged nature of issues like racial inequities and access to quality education, curriculum political debates, and the potentially punitive ways in which states report test results inevitably impacted the conversations and interactions in this research. While I routinely consulted with participants regarding my interpretations of their perceptions and work, the final analysis is my own. I hope that the research examples and analyses provided in this volume are helpful for aspiring and seated curriculum leaders as they reflect on their own work within particular contexts and in relation to current and future movements.

# Challenging the Rhetorical Identity
# of Curriculum Leadership

**Sample Course Activity**

*Challenging Rhetorical Identity of Curriculum Leadership*

1. Provide students with a reading list from curriculum studies and critical education studies (e.g., Michael Apple's *Cultural Politics* [1992]; Herbert Kliebard's *Forging the American Curriculum* [1992]). Tell students they have to show up smart to an online chat room.

2. Task: Students (aspiring and seated administrators) talk about curriculum leadership work without using the vocabulary commonly used in their work life (e.g., standards, testing data, curriculum maps, alignment, etc.) and without using traditional educational administration vocabulary (e.g., capacity building, professional learning community, strategic planning).

3. Students must use terms from curriculum theory and critical education studies (e.g., *discourse, knowledge, power, ideology*) to talk about their work during the chat.

4. Students begin with a finite point system (20) and lose a point every time they use a taboo (traditional educational administration) word.

5. Students then write a paper about this experience, using transcripts from the chat room and reflective questions as a guide.

# References

Alinsky, S. (1971). *Rules for radicals.* New York, NY: Vintage.

Allington, R. (2002). *Big brother and the national reading curriculum: How ideology trumped evidence.* Portsmouth, NH: Heinemann.

Anderson, G. (2001). Disciplining leaders: A critical discourse analysis of the ISLLC examination and performance standards in educational administration. *International Journal of Leadership in Educational Administration, 4*(3), 199–216.

Anderson, G. (2009). *Advocacy leadership: Toward a post-reform agenda in education.* New York, NY: Routledge.

Apple, M. (1990).Restoring the voice of curriculum specialists, *Education Digest, 56*(2),48–52.

Apple, M. (1992). The text and cultural politics. *Educational Researcher, 21*(7), 4–19.

Apple, M. (1996). *Cultural politics and education.* New York: Teachers College Press.

Apple, M. (2000). *Official knowledge: Democratic education in a conservative age.* New York, NY: Routledge.

Apple, M. (2001). *Educating the "right" way: Markets, standards, God, and inequality.* New York, NY: Routledge.

Apple, M. (2004). *Ideology and curriculum.* New York, NY: Routledge.

Apple, M. (2006). *Educating the "right" way: Markets, standards, God, and inequality.* New York, NY: Routledge.

Apple, M., & Jungck, S. (1990). You don't have to be a teacher to teach this unit: Teaching, technology, and gender in the classroom. *American Educational Research Journal, 27*(2), 227–251.

Apple, M., & Oliver, A. (2003). Becoming right: Education and the formation of conservative movements. In M. W. Apple, P. Aasen, M. K. Cho, L. A. Gandin, A. Oliver, Y. K-Sung, et al. (Eds.), *The state and the politics of knowledge* (pp. 156–175). New York, NY: Routledge.

Au, W. (2007). High-stakes testing and curricular control: A qualitative metasynthesis. *Educational Researcher, 36*(5), 258–267.

Au, W. (2008). *Unequal by design: High stakes testing and school organizations.* London: Methuen.

Ball, S. (1987). *Micro-politics of the school: Towards a theory of school organization.* New York, NY: Routledge.

Ball, S. (1994). *Education reform: A critical and poststructural approach.* Buckingham, UK: Open University Press.

Berman, P., & McLaughlin, M. (1976). Implementation of educational innovation. *The Educational Forum, 40*(3), 345–370.

Blasé, J., & Blasé, J. (1999). *Handbook of instructional leadership: How successful principals promote teaching and learning.* Thousand Oaks, CA: Corwin Press.

Bohlman, L., & Deal, T. (2008). *Reframing organizations: Artistry, choice and leadership.* San Francisco, CA: Jossey-Bass.

Bossert, B., Dwyer, S. T., Rowan, D. C., & Lee, G. V. (1982). The instructional management role of the principal. *Educational Administration Quarterly, 18*(3), 34–64.

Bourdieu, P. (2001). The forms of capital. In S. Gronoviter & M. Swedberg (Eds.), *The sociology of economic life* (pp. 96–111). Boulder, CO: Westview Press.

Bourdieu, P. (1996). *Theory, culture, and society.* London, England: Sage.

Brunner, C. C. (1998). Can power support an ethic of care? An examination of the professional practices of women superintendents. *Journal for a Just and Caring Education, 4*(2), 142–175.

Burrell, G., & Morgan, G. (2003). *Sociological paradigms of organizational analysis: Elements of the sociology of corporate life.* Brookfield, VT: Ashgate.

Capper, C. (1993). *Educational administration in a pluralistic society.* Albany, NY: SUNY Press.

Carspecken, P. (1995). *Critical ethnography in educational research: A theoretical and practical guide.* New York, NY: Routledge.

Clegg, S. R. (1989). *Frameworks of power.* Thousand Oaks, CA: Sage.

Coleman, J. (1966). *Equality of educational opportunity.* Washington, DC: U.S. Government Printing Office.

Cornbleth, C. (2008). *Diversity and the new teacher: Learning from experience in urban schools.* New York, NY: Teachers College Press.

Daly, A. (2009). Education and productivity: A comparison of Great Britain and the United States. *British Journal of Industrial Relations, 24*(2), 251–266.

Dantley, M. (2005). African American spirituality and Cornel West's notions of prophetic pragmatism: Restructuring educational leadership in American urban schools. *Educational Administration Quarterly, 41*(4), 651–674.

Deal, T., & Peterson, K. (1994). *The leadership paradox: Balancing logic and artistry in schools.* San Francisco, CA: Jossey-Bass.

Deal, T., & Peterson, K. (1999). *Shaping school culture: The heart of leadership.* San Francisco, CA: Jossey-Bass.

Dewey, J. (2008). *Democracy and education.* Chicago, IL: Seven Treasures. (Original work published 1916)

Edmonds, R. (1979).Effective schools for the urban poor. *Educational Leadership, 37,* 15–24.

Erickson, F. (1986). Qualitative methods in research on teaching. In M. Whittrock (Ed.), *Handbook of research on teaching* (pp. 119–161). Washington, DC: American Educational Research Association.

Fenstermacher, G. (2006). *Rediscovering the student in democracy and education.* Albany, NY: SUNY Press.

Foster, W. (1986). *Paradigms and promises: New approaches to educational administration.* Amherst, NY: Prometheus Books.

Foucault, M. (1977). *Power and knowledge: Selected interviews and other readings, 1972–1977.* New York: Pantheon.

Foucault, M. (1980). *Power/knowledge* (C. Gordon, Ed.). New York: Pantheon Book.

Frattura, E., & Capper, C. (2007). *Leading for social justice: Transforming schools for all learners.* Thousand Oaks, CA: Corwin Press.

Freire, P. (1993). *Pedagogy of the oppressed.* New York, NY: Continuum. (Original work published 1970)

Freire, P. (2001). *Pedagogy of freedom: Ethics, democracy, and civic courage.* Lanham, MD: Rowan & Littlefield. (Original work published 1998)

Fullan, M. (2007). *Leading in a culture of change.* San Francisco, CA: Jossey-Bass. (Original work published 1999)

Geertz, C. (1973). *The interpretation of cultures: Selected essays.* New York: Basic Books.

Giroux, H. (2001). *Theory and resistance in education.* New York, NY: Praeger.

Glaser, B., & Strauss, A. (1967). *The discovery of grounded theory: Strategies of qualitative research.* Piscataway, NJ: Aldine Transaction.

Glatthorn, A., Boshee, F., & Whithead, B. (2004). *Curriculum leadership: Strategies for development and implementation.* Thousand Oaks, CA: Sage.

Glickman,C. (2006). Educational leadership: Failure to use our imagination. *Phi Delta Kappan, 87*(9), 689–690.

Glickman, C., Gordon, S., & Ross-Gordon, J. (2009). *SuperVision and instructional leadership: A developmental approach* (8th ed.). Upper Saddle River, NJ: Prentice-Hall.

Educate America Act Title III (1998). *Goals 2000: Reforming education to improve student achievement.* Washington, DC: U.S. Government Printing Office.

Gonzalez, N., Moll, L., & Amandind, C. (2005). *Funds of knowledge: Theorizing practices in households, communities, and classrooms.* New York: Erlbaum

Gramsci, A. (1971). *Selections from the prison notebook of Antonio Gramsci* (Q. Hoaren & A. Smith, Trans.). New York, NY: International.

Greene, M. (1988). *The dialectic of freedom.* New York, NY: Teachers College Press.

Grogan, M., & Andrews, R. (2002). Defining preparation and professional development for the future. *Educational Administration Quarterly, 38*(2), 233–256.

Hallinger, P., & Murphy, J. (1985). The social context of effective schools. *American Journal of Education, 94*(3), 328–355.

Hallinger, P. (2003). Leading educational change: Reflections on the practice of instructional and transformational leadership. *Cambridge Journal of Education, 33*(3), 329–352.

Hallinger, P. (2004). Meeting the challenges of cultural leadership: The changing role of principals in Thailand. *Discourse: Studies in the Cultural Politics of Education, 25*(1), 61–73.

Hallinger, P. (2005). *Developing instructional leadership.* Dordrecht, The Netherlands: Springer-Kluwer.

Hansen, D. (2007). *John Dewey and our educational prospect: A critical engagement with Dewey's democracy and education.* Albany, NY: SUNY Press.

Hayes-Jacob, H.(2005). *Mapping the big picture: Integrating curriculum and instruction K-12.* Arlington, VA: ASCD.

Heck, R., Larsen, T., & Marcoulides, G. (1990). Instructional leadership and school achievement: Validation of a causal model. *Educational Administration Quarterly, 26*(2), 94–125.

Henderson, J., & Gornik, R. (2006). *Transformative curriculum leadership* (3rd ed.). Upper Saddle River, NJ: Prentice-Hall.

Henderson, J. (2001). Deepening democratic curriculum work. *Educational Researcher, 30*(9), 18–21.

Henderson, J., & Kesson, K. (1999). *Understanding democratic curriculum leadership.* New York, NY: Teachers College Press.

Hirsch, E. D., Jr. (1996). *The schools we need and why we don't have them.* New York, NY: Anchor Books.

Hood, C. (1991). A public management for all seasons? *Public Administration, 69,* 3–19.

hooks, b. (1991). *Essentialism and experience.* New York, NY: Oxford University Press.

Houle, J. C. (2006). Professional development for urban principals in underperforming schools. *Education And Urban Society, 38,* 142–159.

Hoy, W., & Miskel, C. (2007). *Educational administration: Theory, research, and practice.* New York, NY: McGraw-Hill.

Ingersoll, R. (2006). *Who controls teachers' work? Power and accountability in America's schools.* Cambridge, MA: Harvard University Press.

Jackson, D. (2000). The school improvement journal: Perspectives on leadership. *School Leadership and Management,, 20*(1), 61–78.

Johnson, B., & Johnson (2005). *High stakes: Poverty, testing, and failure in America's schools.* Lanham, MD: Rowan & Littlefield.

Kliebard, H. (1992). *Forging the American curriculum.* New York, NY: Routledge.

Kumashiro, K. (2008). *The seduction of common sense: How the right has framed the debate on America's schools.* New York, NY: Teachers College Press.

Lakoff, G. (2002). *Moral politics: How liberals and conservatives think.* Chicago, IL: University of Chicago Press.

Leithwood, K. (1994). Leadership for school restructuring. *Educational Administration Quarterly, 30*(4), 498–518.

Leithwood, K., Louis, K., Anderson, S., & Wahlstrom, K. (2004). *How leadership influences student learning: Learning from leading project.* New York, NY: Wallace Foundation.

Leithwood, K., & Riehl, C. (2005). *What do we already know about successful school leadership?*

Paper prepared for the American Educational Research Association (AERA) Division, A Task Force on Developing Research in Educational Leadership.

Leithwood, K., & Mascall, B. (2008). Collective leadership efficacy effects on student achievement. *Educational Administration Quarterly, 44*(4), 529–561.

Louis, K., & Kruse, S. (1995). *Professionalism and community*. Thousand Oaks, CA: Corwin Press.

Madaus, G., & Clark, M. (2002). The adverse impact of high-stakes testing on minority students: Evidence from one hundred years of test data. In G. Orfield & M. Kornhaber (Eds.), *Raising standards or raising Barriers: Inequality and high-stakes testing in public education* (pp. 85–106). New York, NY: Routledge.

Marks, H., & Printy, S. (2003). Principal leadership and school performance: An integration of transformation and instructional leadership. *Educational Administration Quarterly, 4*(3), 293–331.

Marzano, W., Waters, T., & McNulty, B. (2005). *School leadership that works: From research to practice*. Arlington, VA: ASCD.

Maxcy, B. (2009). New public management and district reform: Managerialism and deflection of local leadership in a Texas school district. *Urban Education, 44*(5), 489–521.

McNeil, L (1998). *Contradictions of control: School structure and school knowledge*. New York, NY: Routledge.

McNeil, A., & Valenzuela, A. (2000). *The harmful impact of the TAAS System of Testing in Texas: Beneath the accountability rhetoric*. ERIC ED 443-872.

McNeil, L. (2005). *Contradictions of school reform: Educational costs of standardized testing*. New York, NY: Routledge.

Mintrop, H. (2003). *Schools on probation: How accountability works (and doesn't work)*. New York, NY: Teachers College Press.

Mintrop, H., & Trajillo, T. (2005). Corrective action in low-performing schools: Lessons for NCLB implementation from state and district strategies in first-generation accountability systems. *Educational Policy Analysis, 21*(3), 173–200.

Mitchell, C., & Sackney, L. (2009). *Sustainable improvement*. Boston, MA: Sense.

Murphy, J. (1984). Instructional leadership in effective schools. *Educational Evaluation and Policy Analysis, 6*, 5–13.

Murphy, J., & Hallinger, P. (1985). The social context of effective schools. *American Journal of Education, 94*(3), 328–355.

Murphy, J., Peterson, K. D., & Hallinger, P. (1986). The administrative control of principals in effective school districts: The supervision and evaluation functions. *The Urban Review, 18*(3), 149–175.

The National Commission on Excellence in Education. (1983). *A nation at risk: The imperative for educational reform*. Washington, DC: U.S. Government Printing Office.

No Child Left Behind Act. (2001). *Stronger accountability for stronger results*. Retrieved from www.ed.gov/nclb/landing.jhtml

Noddings, N. (2002). Educating *moral people: A caring alternative to caring education*. New York, NY: Teachers College Press.

Office of Elementary and Secondary Education (2002). Reading first. Retrieved from http://www2.ed.gov/programs/readingfirst/index.html

Page, R. (2006). Curriculum matters. In D. Hansen (Ed.), *John Dewey and our educational prospect: A critical engagement with Dewey's democracy and education*. Albany, NY: SUNY Press.

Parsons, T. (1963). On the concept of political power. *Proceedings of the American Philosophical Society, 107*, 232–262.

Pedroni, T. (2007). *Market movements: African American involvement in school voucher reform*. New York, NY: Routledge.

Pedulla, J., Abrams, L., Madaus, G., Russell, M., Ramos, M., Miao, J. (2003). *Perceived effects of state-mandated testing programs on teaching and learning: Findings from a national survey of teachers.* ERIC Ed. 481836.

Pinar, W. (2003). *What is curriculum theory?* New York, NY: Routledge.

Pollitt, C. (1991). *Managerialism and the public services: The Anglo-American experience.* Oxford, UK: Basil Blackwell.

Pollitt, C. (2003). *The essential public manager.* Philadelphia, PA: Open University Press.

Purkey, S., & Smith, M. (1983). Effective schools: A review. *The Elementary School Journal, 83*(4), 427–452.

Skrla, L., Scheurich, J. J., Garcia, J., & Nolly, G. (2004). Equity audits: A leadership tool for developing equitable and excellent schools. *Educational Administration Quarterly, 40*(1), 135–163.

Schwaub, J. (1978). *Science, curriculum, and liberal education.* Chicago, IL: University of Chicago Press.

Sennett, R., & Cobb, J. (1972). *The hidden injuries of class.* New York, NY: Vintage Books.

Shannon, P. (2001). *Becoming political, too.* Portsmouth, NH: Heinemann.

Sheppard, B. (1996). Exploring the transformational nature of instructional leadership, *Alberta Journal of Educational Research, 18*(4), 325–344.

Silver, H., Strong, R., & Perini, M. (2008). *The strategic teacher: Selecting the right research-based strategy for every lessson* (Thoughtful Education Network). Upper Saddle River, NJ: Prentice-Hall.

Spillane, J., Diamond, J. Walker, L., Halverson, R., & Jita, L. (2001). Urban school leadership for elementary science instruction: Identifying and activating resources in an undervalued school subject. *Journal of Research in Science Teaching, 38*(8), 918–940.

Spillane, J., Hallett, T., & Diamond, J. (2003). Forms of capital and the construction of leadership: Instructional leadership in urban elementary schools. *Sociology of Education, 78*, 1–17.

Spradley, J. 1979). *The ethnographic interview.* San Diego, CA: Harcourt Brace Janovich.

Stone, C. (1998). *Changing urban education.* Kansas City, KS: University Press of Kansas.

Stryker, S., & Burke, P. (2000). The past, present, and future of identity theory. *Social Psychology Quarterly, 63*, 284–297.

Theoharris, G. (2009). *The school leaders our children deserve: Seven keys to equity, social justice, and school reform.* New York, NY: Teachers College Press.

Tierney, W. G., & Foster, W. (1991). Educational leadership and the struggle for the mind. *Peabody Journal of Education, 66*(4), 273–302.

Tucker, P., & Heineche, W. (2003). The principalship: Renewed call for instructional leadership. In C. Duke, M. Grogan, P. Tucker, & W. Heineche (Eds.), *Educational leadership in an age of accountability: The Virginia experience* (pp. 61–79). Albany, NY: SUNY Press.

Tyler, R. (1949). *Basic principles of curriculum and instruction.* Chicago, IL: University of Chicago Press.

Walker, D., & Soltis, J. (2004). *Curriculum and aims.* New York, NY: Teachers College Press.

Weis, L. (1990). *Working class without work: High school students in a de-industrializing economy.* New York, NY: Routledge.

Whitty, G. (1997). Social theory and education policy: The legacy of Karl Mannheim. *British Journal of the Sociology of the Education, 18*(2), 149–163. DOI 10.1080/0142569970180201

Whitty, G., Power, S., & Halpin, D. (1998). *Devolution and choice in education: The school, the state, and the market.* Buckingham, UK: Open University.

Wiggins, G., & McTighe, T. (1998). *Understanding by design.* Upper Saddle River, NJ: Prentice-Hall.

Williams, R. (1977). *Marxism and literature.* Oxford: Oxford University Press.

Willis, P., & Aronowitz, S. (1982). *Learning to labor: How working class kids get working class jobs.* New York, NY: Columbia University Press.

Wohlstetter, P., Datnow, A., & Park, V. (2008). Creating a system for data-driven decision-making: Applying the principal agent framework. *School effectiveness and school improvement, 19*(3), 239–259.

Woods, P. (2005). *Democratic leadership in education*. London: Sage.

Ylimaki, R., & McClain, L. (2006). Instructional leadership and US accountability policies. In R. Openshaw & J. Soler (Eds.), *Reading across international boundaries: History, policy, and politics*. Greenwich, CT: Information Age.

Ylimaki, R. (2007). Instructional leadership in challenging US schools. *International Studies in Educational Administration, 35*(3), 11–19.

Ylimaki, R., & McClain, M. (2009). Wisdom-centered educational leadership. *International journal of leadership in education, 12*(1), 1–21.

Zipin, L., & Brennan, M. (2003). The suppression of ethical dispositions through managerial accountability: A habitus crisis in Australian higher education. *International Journal of Leadership in Education, 6*(4), 351–370.

# Index